PHILIPP MAINLÄNDER

The Philosophy of Redemption

Translated by
Christian Romuss

IRUKANDJI
PRESS

Published by Irukandji Press
Irukandji Press is a trade name of Irukandji Media Pty Ltd

Irukandji Media Pty Ltd
Unit 9 204 Alice St
Brisbane City Qld 4000
AUSTRALIA

ISBN 978-0-6454980-7-3

This is a translation of a work in the public domain.

Translation copyright © C. Romuss, 2024

Cover design and typesetting by Arthur Arek

Typeset in Crimson Pro

Cover Image:
Night, from *On Death Part I*, 1888–9
by Max Klinger (1857–1920)
The Art Institute of Chicago

All rights reserved. No part of this publication may be reproduced, stored in a retrieval system, or transmitted in any form by any means without the prior permission in writing of the publisher.

CONTENTS

Acknowledgments   iv
A Note on the Text   v
A Note on the Translation   vi
List of Works Consulted   vii

Foreword   3
Analytics   7
Physics   45
Aesthetics   99
Ethics   145
Politics   193
Metaphysics   267

ACKNOWLEDGMENTS

I am grateful to Stephan Atzert and Geoff Wilkes for their input on various chapters at various stages in both substantive and linguistic regard, and to Daryl Morini for his advice on scriptural and religious matters. Naturally, as the formula goes, any shortcomings of this translation are my responsibility alone.

C. R.

A NOTE ON THE TEXT

This translation is based on the 1876 edition of the first volume of Philipp Mainländer's *Die Philosophie der Erlösung*. It does not include the appendix but only the main text, in which Mainländer—in his own words—sought to present his work "as if cast from a single mould: pure and simple."

Translations of quoted texts, where not directly made, are taken, with occasional modification, from existing translations in the public domain or are made from original works also in the public domain. Bible quotations are from the King James Version. Any similarities to works under copyright are coincidental.

Italics are used for emphasis and correspond to S p e r r s c h r i f t (spaced type) in the German edition, except in quotations from languages other than English, where italics serve merely to distinguish the text from the surrounding English. Latin words and quotations, however, appear in SMALL CAPS not italics, except those terms or phrases which either have established themselves as expressions in English (e.g., "de facto") or appear so frequently in the text that the use of small caps would be distracting (e.g., "à priori" and "à posteriori"). Such terms are handled in the same way as standard English; consequently, when terms of this sort appear in italics, this indicates emphasis.

The diacritic on "à priori" and "à posteriori" serves to differentiate the initial "a" from the English indefinite article and thereby facilitate reading.

Each page of this translation has two numbers (or sets of numbers) in the footer. On the outer margin is the page number of this translation, on the inner margin is the corresponding page number of the German edition. Where these page numbers are preceded by a single | or double ‖ vertical bar, a corresponding mark in the text indicates approximately where that page begins in the German edition.

A NOTE ON THE TRANSLATION

Two German terms occasionally have the same English translation. To preserve the distinction in English and assist the reader's understanding, I have in several instances used a capital letter to differentiate one translation from the other. Thus, English "object" translates the German *Gegenstand*, which denotes an object in the most generic sense, while "Object" translates *Objekt*, which denotes "the thing-in-itself that has passed through the subjective forms" (p. 68). (Given the interdependency of Subject and Object in Mainländer's epistemology, I have also translated *Subjekt* with upper case "S".) Likewise, the English noun "state" translates the German *Zustand*, which denotes a state in the sense of a condition (e.g., *Naturzustand*, state of nature), while "State" translates *Staat*, which refers to a state in the sense of a polity.

The terms "Analytics", "Physics", "Aesthetics", "Ethics", "Politics", and "Metaphysics" refer to the corresponding chapters of this work; "analytics", "physics", "aesthetics", "ethics", "politics", and "metaphysics" refer to the discipline or subject domain. I use "Nature" where Mainländer personifies nature, otherwise I write the term in lower case. The orthography of the corresponding German terms does not vary with the sense, since German nouns are always written with a capital letter, i.e., *Analytik, Physik, Aesthetik, Ethik, Politik, Metaphysik, Natur*. The foregoing distinctions therefore reflect my contextual reading rather than any explicit cues in the text itself.

I translate *Vorstellung* in most instances as "presentation" (consistent with Pluhar's translation of Kant and Aquila's and Carus's translation of Schopenhauer), occasionally as "notion", and as "idea" only in the context of Mainländer's discussion of wit (p. 119f.). With this sole exception, "idea" translates German *Idee*.

Erkenntniß is translated as "cognition" or "recognition", never as "knowledge", which translates *Wissen*. Accordingly, the verb *erkennen* is translated as "to cognise" or "to recognise", while *wissen* is translated as "to know".

Finally, the German modal verb *wollen* can be translated as "to want" but also as "to will". In German, the shared etymology of the verb *wollen* and the noun *Wille* ("will") is obvious when one considers the verb's conjugated forms: *ich will, du willst, er-sie-es will*. This etymological relationship is absent in English. I have therefore sometimes translated *wollen* as "to want", sometimes as "to will", and have occasionally used both translations (p. 299), according to what seemed most appropriate in the context. The reader can of course make a substitution if she finds my choice in a given instance wanting.

LIST OF WORKS CONSULTED

The following works in the public domain were consulted for this translation.

Franckforter. *Theologia Germanica*. Translated by Susanna Winkworth. Boston: John P. Jewett and Co., 1857.

Goethe, Johann Wolfgang von. *The Natural Daughter*. Goethe's Works, Vol. II. Philadelphia: George Barrie, 1885.

Goethe, Johann Wolfgang von. *Iphigenia in Tauris, Torquato Tasso, Goetz von Berlichingen*. Translated by Anna Swanwick and Sir Walter Scott. Dramas of Goethe, Vol. XX. Boston: Francis A. Nicholls and Co., 1902.

Goethe, Johann Wolfgang von. *Faust*. Translated by Bayard Taylor. New York: The Modern Library, [1870] 1912.

Kant, Immanuel. *Critique of Practical Reason*. Translated by Thomas Kingsmill Abbott. London: Longmans, Green and Co., 1909.

Mainländer, Philipp. *Die Philosophie der Erlösung*. Berlin: Theobald Grieben, 1876.

Montaigne, Michel de. *The Essays of Michel de Montaigne*. 2 vols. Translated by Charles Cotton. New York: A. L. Burt Company, 1892.

Spence Hardy, Robert. *Eastern Monachism: An account of the origin, laws, discipline, sacred writings, mysterious rites, religious ceremonies, and present circumstances of the order of mendicants founded by Gotama Budha*. London: Partridge and Oakey, 1850.

Tasso, Torquato. *Jerusalem Delivered: A Poem*. Translated by Edward Fairfax. London: George Routledge and Sons, 1890.

Die Philosophie der Erlösung.

Von

Philipp Mainländer.

> Wer einmal Kritik gekostet hat, den ekelt für immer alles dogmatische Gewäsche.
> Kant.

> Die Philosophie hat ihren Werth und ihre Würde darin, daß sie alle nicht zu begründenden Annahmen verschmäht und in ihre Data nur Das aufnimmt, was sich in der anschaulich gegebenen Außenwelt, in den unseren Intellekt constituirenden Formen zur Auffassung derselben und in dem Allen gemeinsamen Bewußtseyn des eigenen Selbst sicher nachweisen läßt.
> Schopenhauer.

Berlin.
Verlag von Theobald Grieben.
1876.

The
Philosophy of Redemption

by

Philipp Mainländer

> Whoever has savoured critique once is forever disgusted by all dogmatic prattle.
>
> **Kant**

> Philosophy has its worth and dignity in the fact that it spurns all assumptions which cannot be justified and incorporates in its data only that which allows itself to be attested in the intuitively given external world, in the forms which constitute our intellect for the apprehension of that same world, and in the consciousness of one's own self, a consciousness which is common to all.
>
> **Schopenhauer**

Berlin
Theobald Grieben Press
1876

Foreword

Whoever investigates the course of the human mind's development, from the beginning of civilisation up to our own day, shall make a curious discovery. He shall find, namely, that reason at first grasped nature's undeniable power always in a fragmented manner and personified the discrete expressions of force, that is, formed gods; then melded these gods into a single God; then, by means of the most abstract thought, made this God into a being that could no longer be imagined in any way; finally, however, became critical, tore up its own subtle fabrication, and set the real individual—the fact of inner and outer experience—on the throne.

The stations of this path are:

1) polytheism;
2) monotheism – pantheism:
    a. religious pantheism,
    b. philosophical pantheism;
3) atheism.

Not all civilisations have walked the entire path. The mental life of most has halted at the first or second point of development, and only in two countries has the final station been reached: in India and in Judea.

The religion of the Indians was initially polytheism, then pantheism. (Later, very refined and eminent minds took possession of religious pantheism and developed it into philosophical pantheism—Vedanta philosophy.) At this juncture Buddha, the glorious prince, appeared, and in his sublime doctrine of karma he founded atheism on *faith* in the *omnipotence* of the individual.

Likewise, the religion of the Jews was at first crude polytheism, then strict monotheism. In monotheism as in pantheism, the individual lost his final trace of autonomy. As Schopenhauer very aptly remarks: Having sufficiently tormented his utterly powerless creature, Jehovah then threw it on the dung heap. Against this, critical reason reacted with unbridled force in the exalted personality of Christ. Christ restored the individual once more to his inalienable right, and on that right, and on *faith* in the motion of the world out of life into death (downfall of the world), he founded the atheistic religion of redemption. That pure Christianity in its deepest foundation is genuine atheism (i.e., *denial* of a *personal* God *coexisting* with the world, but *affirmation* of an immense, all-pervading breath sighed out by a godhead *which perished before it*) and only on its surface is monotheism, I shall prove in this work.

Exoteric Christianity became a world religion and, following its triumph, not a single civilisation more reached the endpoint of the developmental course described above.

In contrast, in the community of occidental peoples, occidental philosophy advanced alongside the Christian religion and is now approaching the third station. It took its lead from Aristotelian philosophy, which was preceded by the Ionian. In the latter, discrete *visible* individualities of the world (water, air, fire) were made into principles of the whole, in a manner similar to that of every primitive religion, wherein discrete observed agencies of nature were formed into gods. In the Middle Ages (pure Christianity had already gone astray long before), the simple unity which had been gained in Aristotelian philosophy through the condensation of all forms then became the philosophically pruned God of the Christian Church; for Scholasticism is nothing other than philosophical monotheism.

This monotheism then metamorphosed through Scotus Erigena, Vanini, Bruno, and Spinoza into philosophical pantheism, which, under the influence of a particular branch of philosophy (that is, of critical idealism: Locke, Berkeley, Hume, Kant) was shaped further: on one hand, into pantheism without process (Schopenhauer), and, on the other, into pantheism with development (Schelling, Hegel). That is, it was driven to extremes.

Most of the educated members of all civilised peoples whose foundation is occidental culture presently move within this philosophical pantheism (it is all the same whether the simple unity which pervades the world be called will or idea, or matter or the absolute)—just as the noble Indians did at the time of Vedanta philosophy. But now the day of reaction has come.

The individual demands, louder than ever, the restoration of his torn up and trampled but inalienable right.

This work is the first attempt to give him that right unconditionally.

The philosophy of redemption is the continuation of the doctrines of Kant and of Schopenhauer, and the confirmation of Buddhism and of pure Christianity. It amends and supplements those philosophical systems, and reconciles these religions with science.

As a philosophy it founds atheism not on some faith, as these religions do, but on *knowledge*, and so, for the first time, atheism has been given a scientific foundation.

Atheism will also become part of the knowledge of humanity, for humanity is ripe for it, humanity has come of age.

P. M.

Analytics of the Cognitive Faculty

The more widely known the data are, the harder it is
to combine them in a new and yet correct manner,
since an exceedingly large number of minds has
already dabbled at it and exhausted the possible
combinations of those data.

Schopenhauer

1.

True philosophy must be *purely* immanent, that is, its substance as well as its limit must be the world. It must explain the world starting from principles which can be cognised in that world by each man, and must call to its aid neither extramundane powers, of which absolutely nothing can be known, nor powers which, though they be in the world, would be intrinsically uncognisable.

True philosophy, furthermore, must be *idealistic*, that is, it must not ignore the cognising Subject and speak of things as if, independently of an eye that sees them and of a hand that feels them, they were precisely as the eye sees them and the hand feels them. Before such a philosophy ventures a step towards solving the riddle of the world, it must have investigated the cognitive faculty carefully and precisely. It may turn out:

   i. that the cognising Subject produces the world entirely out of its own means;
   ii. that the Subject perceives the world precisely as it is;
   iii. that the world is a product partly of the Subject, partly of a source of phenomena independent of the Subject.

To proceed from the Subject is therefore the starting point of the only sure path to truth. It is possible, as I might—indeed must—say here, that ignoring the Subject would also lead the philosopher onto that path; but to proceed in this way, leaving everything to chance, would be unworthy of a sober mind.

2.

The sources from which all experience, all cognition, all our knowledge flows are:

   1) the senses,
   2) self-consciousness.

There is no third source.

3.

Let us first consider sensory cognition. A tree standing before me throws back in straight lines the rays of light that strike it. A few of these enter my eye and make on the retina an impression, which the stimulated optic nerve conducts to my brain.

I handle a stone and the sensory nerves conduct the received sensations to my brain.

A bird sings and thus provokes an oscillating motion in the air. A few waves strike my ear, the tympanic membrane trembles, and the auditory nerve conducts the impression to my brain.

I inhale the scent of a flower. The scent touches the mucosa of my nose and stimulates the olfactory nerve, which brings the impression to my brain.

The senses' *function* is therefore: to conduct impressions to the brain.

Since, however, these impressions are of a very particular nature and are the product of a reaction which is likewise a function, a division of the sense into sensory organ and conductive apparatus suggests itself. The *function* of the sensory organ would therefore have to be placed simply in the production of the specific impression; and the function of the conductive apparatus, as stated above, in the conduction of the particular impression to the brain.

4.

The sense-impressions projected outwards by the brain are called *presentations*; the totality of these is the *world as presentation*, which may be divided into:

1) intuitive presentation or, in short, intuition;
2) non-intuitive presentation.

The first is based on the sense of sight and partly on the sense of touch (sense of feeling); the second on the senses of sound, smell, and taste, as well as partly on the sense of touch (sense of feeling).

5.

We have now to see how *intuitive* presentation, intuition, arises for us, and we begin with the impression that the tree made in my eye. Up to now, nothing more has happened. A certain change has taken place on the retina and this change has affected my brain. If nothing further happened, if the process were here concluded, then my eye would *never* see the tree; for how should the weak change in my nerves be able to be processed into a tree, and by what miraculous means should I see the tree?

But the brain reacts to the impression, and that faculty of cognition which we call the *understanding* becomes active. The understanding seeks the *cause* of the change in the sensory organ, and this transition from the effect in the sensory organ to the cause is the understanding's sole *function*: the *law of causality*. This function is innate in the understanding and lies in the understanding's essence *prior* to all experience, just as the stomach must be capable of digesting before it receives its first nourishment. If the law of causality were not the *à priori* function of the understanding, then we would never arrive at an intuition. After the senses, the law of causality is the first precondition of presentation and therefore lies within us à priori.

On the other hand, however, the understanding would never be able to begin functioning and would be a dead, useless faculty of cognition were it not stimulated by causes. Should the causes which lead to intuition, like the effects, lie *in* the senses, then they would have to be produced in us by a strange almighty hand beyond our ken—a notion which immanent philosophy must reject. There remains, therefore, only the assumption that causes entirely independent of the Subject produce changes in the sensory organs—that is, that autonomous *things-in-themselves* actuate the understanding.

As certain as it therefore is that the law of causality lies within us and, specifically, *prior* to all experience, it is on the other hand equally certain that, independent of the Subject, there exist things-in-themselves the *efficacy* of which actuates the understanding in the first place.

6.

The understanding seeks the cause of the sensation and, by following the direction of the light rays that have fallen upon my eye, finds it. However, the understanding would perceive nothing if there did not lie within it, *prior* to all experience, *forms* which it uses to mould the cause, as it were. One of these forms is *space*.

In speaking of space, it is usually emphasised that it has three dimensions: height, width, and depth, and that it is infinite, i.e, that it is impossible to think of space as having a limit, and the certainty that in measuring space we shall never come to an end is said to be precisely its infiniteness.

That infinite space exists independently of the Subject and that its confinement, called spatiality, belongs to the essence of things-in-themselves is a view originating in the childhood of humanity, one which has been overcome by critical philosophy and which it would therefore be a pointless labour to refute. Outside of the intuiting Subject there is neither infinite space nor finite spatialities.

But space is also not a pure à priori intuition of the Subject, nor has the Subject pure à priori intuition of finite spatialities through the joining together of which it could attain an intuition of an all-encompassing, single space.

Space *as a form of the understanding* (we are not now speaking of mathematical space) is a *point*—that is, space as a form of the understanding is only to be thought of in the image of a point. This point has the capacity (or is nothing less than the Subject's capacity) to delimit in three directions the things-in-themselves which have an effect on the relevant sensory organs. The essence of space is therefore the capacity to spread out indefinitely (IN INDEFINITUM) in three dimensions. Where a thing-in-itself ceases to have an effect, there space delimits it, and space has not the power *to impart extension* to it in the first place. Space behaves completely indifferently in regard to extension. It is as accommodating in delimiting a palace as a quartz granule, a horse as a bee. The extent to which it unfolds itself is *determined* by the extent to which the thing-in-itself has an effect.

If therefore, on one hand, (point-)space is a precondition of experience, an à priori form of our cognitive faculty; then, on the other, it is certain that each thing-in-itself has a *sphere of efficacy* totally independent of the Subject. This sphere of efficacy is not determined by space; rather, it solicits space to delimit it precisely where it ceases.

7.

The second form which the understanding calls to its aid in order to perceive the discovered cause is *matter*.

It is likewise to be thought of in the image of a point (we are not speaking here of substance). It is the capacity to *objectify* precisely and faithfully every quality of the things-in-themselves, every special efficacy of these within the shape described by space; for the *Object* is nothing other than the thing-in-itself which has passed through the Subject's forms. Without matter, no Object; without Objects, no external world.

Bearing in mind the division of sense previously made, into sensory organ and conductive apparatus, matter is to be defined as the point where the conducted sense-impressions, which are the processed specific efficacies of intuitive things-in-themselves, are unified. Matter is therefore the common form for all sense-impressions or, in other words, the sum of all sense-impressions of those things-in-themselves on which the *intuitive* world is based.

Matter is therefore a further precondition of experience, or an à priori form belonging to our cognitive faculty. It is paralleled by the sum of the efficacies of a thing-in-itself—or in a word, by *force*—which is completely independent of it. Insofar as a force becomes an object of a Subject's perception, it is *substance* (objectified force); in contrast, independently of a perceiving Subject every force is free of substance and *only* force.

For this reason it is worth remarking that, with however much precision and photographic fidelity the subjective form called matter may render the particular effects of a thing-in-itself, the rendering is yet TOTO GENERE different from the force. The shape of an Object is identical with the sphere of efficacy of the thing-in-itself which is that Object's foundation, but the expressions of force of the thing-in-itself as objectified by matter are not identical with those expressions of force in their essence. Nor is there any resemblance, for which reason an image can be used for clarification only with the greatest reservation, by saying something like: matter portrays the qualities of the things-in-themselves like a coloured mirror shows the objects presented to it, or: the Object relates to the thing-in-itself as a marble bust to a clay model. Force's essence is simply TOTO GENERE different from the essence of matter.

Certainly, the redness of an Object points to a particular quality of the thing-in-itself, but the redness and this quality are essentially unalike. It is beyond all doubt that two Objects, of which the one is smooth and malleable, the other coarse and brittle, are allowing differences to manifest which are rooted in the essences of the two things-in-themselves; but the smoothness, the coarseness, the malleability, and the brittleness of Objects on one hand, and the relevant qualities of the things-in-themselves on the other, are essentially unalike.

We have therefore to declare here that the *Subject* is a *principal factor* in the production of the external world, although it does not distort the efficacy of the thing-in-itself, but renders with precision only that which has an effect on it (that is, on the Subject). Accordingly, the Object is different from the thing-in-itself, the phenomenal appearance different from that which appears in it. Thing-in-itself and Subject together make the Object. But it is not *space* which distinguishes the Object from the thing-in-itself, and just as little is it *time*, as I shall soon show; rather, it is *matter* alone which produces the chasm between that which appears as phenomenon and its phenomenal appearance, although matter behaves quite indifferently and can from its own means neither deposit a quality in nor strengthen or weaken the efficacy of the thing-in-itself. Matter simply objectifies the given sense-impression, not caring whether the quality of the thing-in-itself which it has to bring to presentation is the foundation of the loudest red or the softest blue, the greatest hardness or the fullest softness; but it can present the impression only in keeping with *its own* nature, and so it is here that the knife must be applied in order to be able to make the correct, ever so important cut between what is ideal and what is real.

8.

The work of the understanding is concluded with the discovery of the cause of a given change in the sensory organs and with the moulding of this cause in the two forms of the understanding, space and matter (objectification of the cause).

Both forms are equally important and support each other. I emphasise that without space we would have no Objects positioned behind other Objects; but, on the other hand, that space can apply its dimension of depth only to the shaded colours supplied by matter, to shadow and light.

Accordingly, the understanding alone has to objectify sense-impressions, and no other faculty of cognition supports it in its work. But *finished Objects* the understanding cannot supply.

9.

The understanding objectifies sense-impressions not as whole but as partial presentations. As long as the understanding alone is active—which is never the case, since all the faculties of our cognition (the one more, the other less) are always functioning together, although for our present purpose we must deal with them separately—only those parts of the tree which strike the centre of the retina or such points as lie very near the centre will be seen clearly. For this reason we constantly change the position of our eyes while observing an Object. In one moment we move our eyes from the root to the farthest tip of the crown, then from right to left, then left to right, and finally we let them glide countless times over a small blossom, only so that each part is brought into contact with the centre of the retina. In this way we gain a set of discrete partial presentations which, however, the understanding cannot join together into one Object.

For this to happen, the understanding must pass them on to another faculty of cognition: to *reason*.

10.

Reason is supported by three auxiliary faculties: *memory*, *judgment*, and *imagination*. All the faculties of cognition, taken together, are the human *mind*, and yield the following scheme:

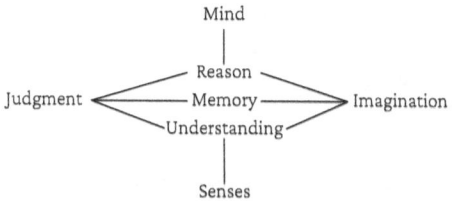

The *function* of reason is *synthesis* or conjunction understood as an *activity*. Hereinafter I shall use the word "synthesis" when speaking of the function of reason; the word "conjunction", in contrast, for the product, for what has been conjoined or synthesised.

The *form* of reason is: the *present*.

The *function* of memory is: to preserve sense-impressions.

The *function* of judgment is: to place together what belongs together.

The *function* of imagination is: to retain as an *image* that intuitive Object which has been synthesised by reason.

However, the *function* of the mind in general is: to accompany with consciousness the activity of all faculties, and to associate their cognitions in the point of self-consciousness.

11.

Together with judgment and imagination, reason maintains the closest relationship to the understanding for the purpose of producing *intuition*, with which we are still exclusively concerned.

Judgment first gives to reason those partial presentations which belong together. Reason conjoins these presentations (so, for example, those that belong to a leaf, a branch, a stem) little by little, always letting imagination retain what has been conjoined, adding to this image a new piece and again letting the whole be retained by imagination, and so on. Reason then conjoins in a similar manner those disparate elements which belong together—so, the bough, the branches, twigs, leaves, and blossoms—and, indeed, it repeats this process of synthesis upon presentations more partial or more whole, according to what is needed.

Reason exercises its function on the onwards-rolling point of the present, as it were, and time is not necessary for this; yet synthesis can also take place in time—more on this later. Imagination carries onwards, from present to present, that conjunction which is being progressively synthesised, and reason joins piece to piece, remaining always in the present, i.e., rolling onwards on the point of the present.

The customary view is that the understanding is the synthetic faculty; there are even many who in good faith claim: Synthesis does not take place at all, each object is immediately apprehended as a whole. Both views are incorrect. The understanding cannot synthesise because it has only one function: transition from the effect in the *sensory organ* to the cause. Synthesis itself, however, cannot ever be absent, even when the head of a pin is all we are observing, as a keen self-examination makes evident; for the eyes, though barely noticeably, will move. The deception originates mainly in the fact that although we are conscious of finished conjunctions, we carry out the synthesis almost always unconsciously: firstly, because of the great speed with which the most complete sensory organ, the eye, receives impressions and the understanding objectifies these, as well as the speed with which reason synthesises; secondly, because we forget that we, as children, had to learn gradually and with the greatest effort to carry out this synthetic process, just as we forget that the spatial dimension of depth was initially quite unknown to us. Thus, as adults, upon opening our eyes we instantly and faultlessly apprehend each object with respect to its own extension and its distance from us, while it is an undisputed fact that to the newborn the moon as well as the images in the parlour and the face of its mother float close before its eyes as smudges of colour on a single surface. Likewise, we now apprehend instantly at a glance the Objects, even the largest, as whole Objects, whereas in infancy we certainly saw only parts of Objects, and because of the limited exercise of our powers of judgment and imagination we could neither judge what belonged together nor retain the vanished partial presentations as an image.

The deception also arises from the fact that most objects, considered from a suitable distance, draw their complete image on the retina and the synthesis is thus made so easy that it eludes perception. To an attentive self-observer, however, it does become undeniably conspicuous when he encounters an object which he cannot view in its entirety—encounters it, that is, in such a way that perceived parts disappear from view as the synthesis proceeds. It becomes even more apparent when we pass close by a mountain range and want to appreciate its entire form. However, it is most clearly recognised when we ignore the visual sense and let the sense of touch function alone.

Synthesis is an à priori function of the cognitive faculty and as such an à priori precondition of intuition. Synthesis is paralleled by the unity of the thing-in-itself, which is completely independent of it and compels it to proceed in a very specific manner.

12.

Although we have not yet covered the entire domain of intuition, we must now leave it briefly.

The visible world arises for us in the manner specified. However, it ought to be remarked that through the synthesis of partial presentations into Objects, *thought* is not brought into *intuition* at all. The conjunction synthesised from manifold partial presentations given in intuition is certainly a work of reason, but it is no work in concepts or by means of concepts, neither by means of pure à priori concepts (categories), nor by means of customary concepts.

ANALYTICS

Reason, however, does not restrict its activity to the synthesis of partial presentations of the understanding into Objects. It exercises its function, which is always one and the same, in other domains as well. Of these we want first to consider the abstract domain, the domain in which the world is reflected in concepts.

The partial presentations of the understanding which have been synthesised into whole Objects or into whole parts of Objects are compared by the faculty of judgment. Whatever is similar or of a similar kind is placed together by that faculty, with the help of the imagination, and passed on to reason, which synthesises it into a collective unity, into a concept. The greater the similarity in what has been placed together, the closer is the concept to the intuitive source and the easier is the transition to an intuitive representative of that same concept. If, in contrast, the number of similar traits between the Objects becomes ever smaller and the concept thereby ever broader, then the concept stands that much farther from intuition. However, even the broadest concept is not entirely uprooted from its maternal soil, although it may be but a thin and very long filament which anchors it there.

In the same manner as reason reflects visible Objects in concepts, with the help of memory it also forms concepts out of all our other perceptions. Of these I shall speak in what follows.

It is clear that the concepts drawn from intuitive presentations are more easily and quickly realised than those which have their origin in non-intuitive presentations; for just as the eye is the most complete sensory organ, so the imagination is reason's most powerful auxiliary faculty.

In learning language—that is, in acquiring finished concepts—a child has to carry out the same operation which was generally necessary in order to form concepts. This operation is merely made easier for the child by having finished concepts. If it sees an object, then it compares it with the one it knows and places that which is of a similar kind together. It thus forms no concept, but merely subsumes under a concept. If an object is unknown to the child, then it is clueless and must be given the correct concept.

Reason then proceeds to synthesise the concepts themselves into judgments—that is, it conjoins concepts which have been assembled by the faculty of judgment. Reason further synthesises judgments into premises, from which a new judgment is drawn. In doing this, reason's process is governed by the four well-known laws of thought on which logic is constructed.

In this abstract domain reason *thinks* and, just as in the intuitive domain, it does so on the point of the present and not in *time*. But it is to time that we must now turn our attention. In doing so, we enter an extraordinarily important domain—namely, that of the *conjunctions* of reason on the basis of *à priori forms and functions of the cognitive faculty*. All the conjunctions with which we shall become acquainted have arisen on the basis of *experience*, thus à posteriori.

13.

Time is a conjunction of reason and not, as is usually assumed, an à priori form of the cognitive faculty. The child's faculty of reason produces this conjunction in the domain of presentation—that is, in the domain of outer experience—as well as on the inward path, the path of inner experience. We want now to let time arise in the light of consciousness, and to this end we choose the latter path, since it is the one most suited to philosophical investigation, although we have not yet dealt with the inner source of experience.

If we detach ourselves from the external world and sink into our inner being, then we find ourselves caught in a continuous rising and falling—in short, in an unceasing motion. The point where this motion touches our consciousness I want to call the *point of motion*. Upon it floats (or sits as if screwed on) the form of reason, i.e., the point of the *present*. Where the point of motion is, there too is the point of the present, and the latter is always positioned exactly *above* the former. The point of the present cannot rush ahead of the point of motion and cannot linger behind it. Both are inseparably connected.

Now, if we examine the process attentively, then we find that we are indeed always in the present, but always at the expense of or through the death of the present. In other words: We move from present to present.

Becoming conscious of this transition, reason lets imagination retain the disappearing present and conjoins it with the arising present. It slides a *solid* surface, as it were, beneath the onwards-rolling, flowing, intimately connected points of motion and of the present, a surface from which it reads off the path traversed and acquires a series of *filled* moments, i.e., a series of filled transitions from present to present.

In this way, reason acquires the essence and the concept of the past. If reason then, remaining in the present—for reason cannot release the present from and advance it beyond the point of motion—rushes on ahead of the motion and conjoins the coming present with the one that follows it, then it gains a series of moments which will be *filled*, i.e., it gains the essence and the concept of the *future*. If reason now conjoins the past with the future into an *ideal, solid* line of indeterminate length on which the point of the present rolls onwards, it has then synthesised *time*.

Just as the present is nothing without the point of motion on which it floats, so time, too, is nothing without the substrate of real motion. Real motion is completely independent of time, or in other words: *real succession* would also take place without *ideal succession*. Were there no cognisant beings in the world, then the existing cognitionless things-in-themselves would yet be in restless motion. If cognition arises, then time is only the prerequisite for *cognising* motion. We might say: Time is the *subjective* measure of motion.

In individual cognisant beings, the point of the present is situated above the point of motion. This point of individual motion stands *next to* the points of all other individual motions, i.e., all individual motions form a general motion of uniform succession. The present of any Subject is therefore always a precise index of the point of motion of all things-in-themselves.

14.

With this important à posteriori conjunction, time, now in hand, we return to intuition.

I have said above that the synthesis of partial presentations is independent of time, since reason accomplishes its syntheses on the moving point of the present, and imagination retains what is synthesised. Synthesis can, however, also take place in time, when the Subject directs its attention to doing so.

The Subject behaves no differently with *change*, which can be perceived on the point of the present.

There are two kinds of change. The one is *change of location* and the other is *inner change* (drive, development). Both are unified in the higher concept called *motion*.

Now, if the change of location is such that it can be perceived as displacement of the moving Object relative to resting Objects, then its perception does not depend on time, rather it is cognised on the point of the present, like the motion of a branch, the flight of a bird.

For reflecting reason, however, all changes without exception have a certain duration, like intuition itself; but like intuition, the perception of such changes of location is not dependent on the consciousness of time; for the Subject cognises them immediately on the point of the present—a fact worth noting. Time is an ideal conjunction; it does not elapse but is a solid line that is thought. Every moment that has passed is ossified, as it were, and cannot be moved by a hair's breadth. Likewise, every future moment has its particular fixed place on the ideal line. What, however, does move continuously is the point of the present: *it* elapses, *not time*.

It would also be completely wrong-headed to say: Precisely this elapsing of the present is time. For if we pursue only the point of the present, then we never arrive at the presentation of time, but remain always in the present. We must look backwards and forwards and in so doing have fixed reference points ashore, so to speak, to gain the ideal conjunction called time.

In contrast, changes of location which cannot be perceived immediately on the point of the present, and all developments, are only cognised by means of time. The movement of the hands on a clock eludes our perception. Now, if I am supposed to recognise that the *same* hand stood first at 6, then at 7, then I must become conscious of the succession—that is, in order to be able to attribute two contradictory predicates to the same Object, I require the conjunction time.

It is the same with changes of location which I, remaining in the present, could have perceived but did not perceive (displacement of an Object behind my back), and with developments. Our tree is blossoming. If we now imagine ourselves in autumn and give the tree fruit, then we need the conjunction time in order to recognise the blossoming and the fruit-bearing tree as the same Object. One and the same Object can be hard and soft, red and green, but it can only ever have *one* of these two predicates in a *single* present.

15.

We have now covered the entire domain of intuition.

Is this domain—that is, the totality of spatial-material Objects—the entire world of our experience? No! That totality is but an extract from the world as presentation. We have sense-impressions the origins of which are sought by the understanding in exercising its function, but which the understanding cannot shape spatially and materially. And yet we do also have the presentation of non-intuitive Objects, and only once we have these do we have the presentation of a collective unity, of the universe. How do we get to these?

Every way in which a thing-in-itself has an effect, insofar as it affects the senses on which intuition is based (visual and tactile senses), is objectified by the form of the understanding called matter, i.e., it assumes a material form for us. There is no exception at all, and matter is for this reason the ideal substrate of all visible Objects, a substrate which in and of itself is without qualities, in which however all qualities must appear, just as space is without extension but circumscribes all spheres of force.

In consequence of the ideal substrate of all visible Objects having no qualities in and of itself, manifold but homogeneous presentations are given to reason, and reason associates these into the unity called *substance*.

Like time, substance is therefore an à posteriori *conjunction* of reason on the basis of an à priori form. With the assistance of this ideal conjunction, reason now thinks matter into all the sense-impressions which do not allow themselves to be moulded in the forms of the understanding, and in this way arrives at the presentation of incorporeal Objects. These and corporeal Objects constitute a coherent whole of *substantial* Objects. Only now do the air, colourless gases, scents, and sounds (vibrating air) become Objects for us, even if we cannot exactly shape them spatially and materially. And so the proposition that everything which makes an impression on our senses is of necessity substantial is now unconditionally valid.

The unity of the ideal conjunction called substance is paralleled in the real domain by the universe, by the collective unity of forces, which is totally independent of it.

16.

The sensations of taste remain. They do not lead to new Objects, but to such Objects as have already arisen through impressions on other senses. The understanding seeks the cause only and then leaves everything else to reason. Reason simply exercises its function and conjoins the effect with the Object already existing—for example, the taste of a pear with the material morsel of it in one's mouth.

In general, it is only reason which can recognise the various effects emanating from an Object as flowing from a single sphere of force; for the understanding is no synthetic faculty.

If we now summarise everything, then we recognise that presentation is neither sensory nor intellectual nor rational, but *mental*. It is the work of the mind, i.e., of *all* the faculties of cognition.

17.

As I have shown above, all sense-impressions lead to Objects which in their totality constitute the objective world.

Reason reflects this entire objective world in concepts and thus gains, alongside the world of immediate perception, a world of abstraction.

Finally, reason attains yet a third world, the world of reproduction, which lies between the first two.

With the help of memory, reason reproduces, separately from the external world, everything that is perceived, and specifically it brings about either entirely new conjunctions or, with precise and yet faded and weak results, it presents to itself anew what has vanished. The process is entirely the same as that carried out with immediate impressions on the senses. Reason does not remember *entire* images, scents, sensations of taste, words, sounds completely, but only their *impressions on the senses*. With the aid of memory, it evokes in the sensory nerves (and, specifically, not at their tips but where they terminate in that part of the brain which we must think of as the understanding) an impression, which the understanding then objectifies. Take our tree: The understanding shapes the impressions which memory has preserved into partial presentations, judgment places these together, reason synthesises or conjoins what has thus been placed together, the imagination holds onto what has thus been synthesised, and a pale likeness of the tree stands before us. The extraordinary swiftness of the process must not, as I have already said, mislead us into assuming that an immediate recollection of the Objects is taking place. The process is just as complicated as the arising of Objects on the basis of real influences on the senses.

Dreams arise in a similar manner. They are complete reproductions. In general, they owe their objectivity to the repose of the sleeping individual and in particular to the complete inactivity of the ends of the sensory nerves.

18.

We have now to consider the remainder of the important conjunctions which reason, on the basis of à priori functions and forms of the cognitive faculty, brings about.

The function of the understanding is the transition from the effect in the *sensory organ* to the cause. It exercises this function unconsciously, for the understanding does not *think*. It also cannot exercise its function in reverse and go from the cause to the effect, for only an effect makes it active, and as long as an object has an effect on it—that is, as long as the understanding is active at all—it can concern itself with nothing beyond the discovered cause. Assuming that the understanding could think and wished to go from the cause to the effect, then in that moment the Object would disappear, and it could only be regained by the understanding searching once again for the cause of an effect.

The understanding can therefore expand its function in no way. Reason, however, can.

Firstly, reason cognises the function itself—that is, it cognises the fact that the function of the understanding consists in searching for the cause of a change in the sensory organs. Reason then travels the path from the *cause* to the effect. It therefore cognises two causal relations:

1) the law of causality, i.e., the law that every change in the *sensory organs* of the Subject must have a cause;
2) that things-in-themselves have an effect on the Subject.

The causal relations of undisputed validity are thus exhausted, for the cognising Subject cannot know whether other beings cognise in the same way, or whether they are subject to other laws. However, as praiseworthy as critical reason is for proceeding so cautiously, it would be as blameworthy if it here gave up further inquiry into the causal relations. It does not allow itself to be misled and, first of all, stamps the body of the cognising Subject as an Object amongst Objects. On the basis of this cognition it arrives at an important third causal relation. Namely, it expands the law of causality (relation between thing-in-itself and Subject) into general causality, which I formulate thus:

> Thing-in-itself has an effect on thing-in-itself and every change in an Object must have a cause which precedes the effect in time.

Here, too, I intentionally keep thing-in-itself and Object separate, since although we recognise that thing-in-itself has an effect on thing-in-itself, things-in-themselves can be perceived by the Subject only as Objects.

By means of *general causality* reason therefore associates Object with Object, i.e., general causality is a prerequisite for cognising the relation in which things-in-themselves stand to each other.

Here, now, is the place for establishing the concept of cause. Since thing-in-itself has an effect on thing-in-itself, there are only ever effective causes (CAUSAE EFFICIENTES), which can be subdivided into:

1) mechanical causes (pressure and impulse),
2) stimuli,
3) motives.

Mechanical causes appear principally in the inorganic realm, stimuli mainly in the plant kingdom, motives only in the animal kingdom.

Furthermore, since man, by means of time, can see the approach of what is coming, he can set goals for himself, i.e., for man and only for man are there final causes (CAUSAE FINALES) or ideal causes. They are, like all other causes, *effective*, because they can only ever have an effect when they stand on the point of the present.

The term "occasional cause" is to be restricted to denoting the occasion that one thing-in-itself gives to another to have an effect on a third. If a cloud obscuring the sun moves away and my hand becomes warm, then the movement of the cloud is the occasional cause, not the cause itself, of the warming of my hand.

19.

Reason further expands this third causal relation, general causality, which connects two things-in-themselves (the effective thing and the suffering thing), into a fourth causal relation, which encompasses the efficacy of *all* things-in-themselves. This fourth causal relation is *community* or *interaction*. This fourth relation says that all things-in-themselves continually have an effect, directly and indirectly, on all other things of the world, and that *at the same time* all other things continually have an effect, directly and indirectly, on it; whence it follows that no thing-in-itself can be absolutely autonomous in its efficacy.

Just as the law of causality led to the positing of an efficacy independent of the Subject, and general causality led to the positing of the influence of things-in-themselves on each other independently of the Subject; so community is only a subjective association by means of which the *real, dynamic coherence of the universe* is *cognised*. This coherence would also exist without a cognising Subject; the Subject, however, could not cognise it if it did not have within itself the capacity to produce the conjunction of community, or in other words: The causal relation called community is the prerequisite for apprehending the dynamic coherence of the universe.

20.

It now remains for reason to produce just one final conjunction: *mathematical space*.

(Point-)space is fundamentally distinguished from the present by the fact that it is sufficient to produce intuition, whereas the present is not sufficient to cognise all of the motions of the things-in-themselves.

It may therefore appear altogether useless to proceed to the construction of mathematical space, which, like time, is a conjunction à posteriori. This, however, is not the case; for mathematical space is indispensable for human cognition, because mathematics is based on it, and even he who is no friend of mathematics shall willingly acknowledge its great value. Not only is mathematics the indestructible basis of various sciences, above all of astronomy, which is so overwhelmingly important for the culture of the human species; it is also the cornerstone of art (architecture) and the foundation of technology, which in its continuing development will totally reshape the social conditions of human beings.

Mathematical space arises when reason (rather than a thing-in-itself) determines point-space to spread out, and then synthesises any number of pure spatialities into a whole of *indeterminate* extension. Reason proceeds here, as with the formation of whole Objects, from partial presentations.

Mathematical space is the only conjunction resting on an à priori basis which no thing-in-itself has a role in determining. Accordingly, in the real domain it is not a thing-in-itself, nor a totality of such things, but *absolute nothingness* which parallels mathematical space, and this absolute nothingness we can imagine in no other way than by means of empty, mathematical space.

21.

To the multiple relationships which reason has to the understanding is added finally this one: to remedy *illusion*, i.e., the errors of the understanding. Hence we see the moon as larger when it is on the horizon than when it is high in the sky; a staff held in the water as broken; a star that has already gone extinct; in general all stars in places where they are not actually located (because the earth's atmosphere refracts all light and the understanding can search for the cause of the sense-impression only in the direction of the rays falling into the eye); hence we believe, furthermore, that the earth does not move, that the planets now and then stand still or move in a retrograde orbit, and so on—all of which is corrected by thinking reason.

22.

We now want to summarise concisely the foregoing observations. The human cognitive faculty has:

1. Various à priori functions and forms, specifically:
    a. the law of causality;
    b. (point-)space;
    c. matter;
    d. synthesis;
    e. the present,

which are paralleled in the *real* domain, entirely independently, by the following determinations of the thing-in-itself:

   a. efficacy in general;
   b. sphere of efficacy;
   c. pure force;
   d. the unity of every thing-in-itself;
   e. the point of motion.

The human cognitive faculty has:

2. Various *ideal* conjunctions or, as the case may be, connections, contrived by reason on the basis of à priori functions and forms:
   a. time;
   b. general causality;
   c. community;
   d. substance;
   e. mathematical space.

Corresponding to the first four in the *real* domain are the following determinations of the things-in-themselves:

   a. real succession;
   b. the influence of one thing-in-itself on another;
   c. the dynamic coherence of the universe;
   d. the collective unity of the universe.

Mathematical space is paralleled by absolute nothingness.

We have found, furthermore, that the Object is the phenomenal appearance of the thing-in-itself, and that *matter alone* produces the difference between them.

23.

The thing-in-itself, so far as we have investigated it up to now, is *force*. The world, the totality of things-in-themselves, is a whole of pure forces, which become Objects for the Subject. The Object is the phenomenal appearance of the thing-in-itself, and although it depends on the Subject, we have seen that it in no way distorts the thing-in-itself. We may therefore rely on experience. Now, what force in itself may be need not now concern us. We remain for the time being in the world as presentation and consider force in general, anticipating the Physics as little as possible.

The law of causality, the function of the understanding, only ever seeks the cause of a change in the *sensory organs*. If nothing changes in these organs, then the law of causality remains at rest. If, in contrast, a sensory organ is modified by a real influence, then the understanding immediately becomes active and seeks the cause of the effect. If the understanding has found the cause, then the law of causality steps aside, so to speak.

The understanding, and this should be noted, never finds itself in the situation of applying the law of causality further and, for instance, asking after the cause of the cause, for the understanding does not think. It will therefore never abuse the law of causality; and it is also obvious that no other faculty of cognition can do this. The law of causality merely mediates presentation, i.e., the perception of the external world.

If, before my eyes, the discovered Object changes, then the law of causality serves only to seek the cause of the new change in the *sensory organ*, *not* of the change in the Object; it is as if an entirely new thing-in-itself had exerted an effect on me.

On the basis of the *law of causality* we can therefore never ask, for example, after the cause of the motion of a branch that was previously motionless. On that basis we can only perceive the motion, and only because the *sensory organ* was modified as a consequence of the transition of the branch from a state of rest to one of motion.

Now, are we unable to ask after the cause of the branch's motion at all? Certainly we can, but only on the basis of *general causality*, an à posteriori conjunction of reason; for only by means of general causality can we cognise the influence of Object on Object, whereas the *law of causality* merely spins the thread between *Subject* and thing-in-itself.

We therefore ask with every right after the cause of the branch's motion. We find it in the wind. If we like, we can then ask further: firstly, after the cause of the wind, then after the cause of this cause, and so on—that is, we can form *causal chains*.

But what happened when I asked after the cause of the moving branch and found this cause? I sprang down, as it were, from the tree and took hold of a different Object, the wind. And what happened when I found the cause of the wind? I simply abandoned the wind and stand now by something quite different, perhaps by sunlight or heat.

From these considerations it follows with utmost clarity:

1) that the application of general causality always *sets out* from the things-in-themselves,
2) that chains of causality are only ever the association of the *efficacies* of things-in-themselves, and therefore never contain the *things themselves* as links.

If we (each man for himself) attempt to pursue further the foregoing chain of causality which we broke off at the phenomenon of heat, then it shall become clear to us all:

3) that it is just as difficult to form *correct* causal chains as it seems in the first moment to be easy; indeed, that it is quite impossible for the Subject, starting from some modification, to produce a correct causal chain A PARTE ANTE, which would progress unimpeded IN INDEFINITUM.

The *things-in-themselves* therefore *never* lie within a chain of causality, and I can ask after the cause of the *being* of a thing-in-itself neither with the aid of the law of causality, nor with the aid of general causality; for if a thing-in-itself which I have found as an Object by means of the law of causality changes, and if I ask by means of general causality after the cause of the change, then general causality leads me at once away from the thing-in-itself. The question: What is the cause of some thing-in-itself in the world?, not only may not, but simply *cannot* be posed at all.

From these considerations it becomes clear that causal relations can never lead us into the *past* of the things-in-themselves, and to deem the so-called infinite causal chain to be the best weapon against the famous three proofs of God's existence shows an incredible lack of reflection. It is the bluntest weapon which can possibly exist, indeed it is no weapon at all: it is Lichtenberg's knife. And strangely, it is precisely what makes this weapon into nothing that also makes the mentioned proofs untenable! Namely: Causality. The opponents of the proofs claim without hesitation that the chain of causality is infinite, without ever having attempted to form a series of fifty *correct* links; and the authors of the proofs, without hesitation, made the *things-in-themselves* of this world into *links* in a causal chain and then, with extraordinary naïveté, ask after the cause of the world. It must be explained, as above, to both parties: General causality *never* leads into the *past* of the things-in-themselves.

The seed is not the *cause* of a plant, for seed and plant are related not *causally*, but *genetically*. In contrast, one can ask after the causes which brought the seed in the earth to germination, or after the causes which made the foot-high plant into one of six feet in height. If these questions are answered, however, then everyone shall find what we found above—namely, that each of these causes *derives from* the plant. In the end the plant shall be found cocooned entirely in the links of causal chains in which, however, the plant itself never appears as a link.

Now, is there no means at all of inquiring into the past of the things-in-themselves? The mentioned genetic relationship between seed and plant answers the question affirmatively. Reason can form *developmental chains*, which are something quite different from *causal chains*. The latter arise with the help of *causality*, the former merely with the help of *time*. Chains of causality are the concatenated efficacies not of one, but of many things-in-themselves; developmental chains, in contrast, have to do with the being of *one* thing-in-itself and with its changes. This result is very important.

24.

If, on the basis of natural science, we now proceed further down this *sole* path which leads into the *past of the things-in-themselves*, then we must trace all the chains of organic forces back to the chemical forces (carbon, hydrogen, nitrogen, oxygen, iron, phosphorous, and so on). That we shall also succeed in tracing these simple chemical forces, the so-called elemental substances, back to fewer substances, is an unshakeable conviction of most natural scientists. However, whether this shall happen or not remains quite irrelevant for our investigations, since it is an unalterable truth that we shall, in the *immanent* domain, *never* overcome *multiplicity* to arrive at *unity*. It is thus clear that even three simple chemical forces would bring us no further than a hundred or a thousand. Let us therefore keep to the figure that contemporary natural science specifies.

In contrast, we find in our thinking not only no hindrance, but in fact a logical compulsion to bring, at the very least, the multiplicity to its simplest expression, the *duality*; for that which, for reason, underlies all Objects is force, and what could be more natural than that reason, exercising its function, valid for the present as well as all of the future, synthesised the forces into a metaphysical unity? Not even the diverse efficacies of the forces could hinder reason in this pursuit, for reason has in view only what is general, the efficacy as such of each thing-in-itself, therefore the essential likeness of all forces; and reason's function consists solely in conjoining the manifold but homogeneous presentations which are given to it by the faculty of judgment.

However, we must not here yield to reason but must, by means of powerful restraint and while keeping the truth firmly in view, preserve reason from certain downfall.

I repeat: In the immanent domain, in this world, we can never get beyond multiplicity. Even in the past we are not permitted, as honest investigators, to annihilate multiplicity, but must ultimately come to a stop at the logical duality.

Nevertheless, reason does not allow itself to be kept from pointing time and again to the necessity of a simple unity. Reason's argument is the one already presented, that for it *all* forces which we keep separated are, as forces, at root essentially alike and for this reason must not be separated.

How is this dilemma to be solved? This much is clear: The truth must not be repudiated and the immanent domain must be preserved in its complete purity. There is only one way out. We already find ourselves in the *past*. Let us then allow the final forces, which we were not permitted to touch lest we succumbed to wishful thinking, flow together in the *transcendent domain*. It is a domain that *has passed, vanished*, that *was but is no more*, and with it the *simple unity*, too, *has passed and vanished*.

25.

By fusing the multiplicity into a unity, we have above all destroyed *force*; for force has validity and significance only in the immanent domain, *in* the world. From this fact alone it is evident that we can form for ourselves no presentation, let alone a concept, of the *essential nature* of a *pre*mundane unity. The utter uncognisability of this premundane unity becomes quite clear, however, when we parade before it in succession all the à priori functions and forms and all the à posteriori conjunctions of our mind. It is the head of Medusa, which turns them all to stone.

First the senses give up their service, for they can react only to the efficacy of a force, and the unity has no effect in the manner of a force. Then the understanding remains completely inactive. Here—indeed, in principle only here—the expression "the understanding stands still" is completely valid. The understanding can neither apply its law of causality, since no sense-impression is present, nor can it make use of its forms, space and matter, for a content for these forms is lacking. Powerless, reason then collapses. What is it supposed to conjoin? Of what use to it is synthesis? Of what use is its form, the present, which lacks the real point of motion? Of what use to it is time, which, in order to be anything at all, requires real succession as a substrate? Confronted with the simple unity, what is it supposed to do with general causality, whose task is to associate the efficacy of one thing-in-itself, as cause, with the influence on another, as effect? Can reason make use of the important conjunction called community where there is no simultaneous interlocking of different forces, no dynamic coherence, but rather where a simple unity gazes upon it with the unfathomable eyes of the Sphinx? Finally, of what use is substance, which is only the ideal substrate of the diverse efficacies of many forces?

And so they all become paralysed!

We can therefore define the simple unity only negatively, and specifically, from our current standpoint, as: inactive, extensionless, undifferentiated, unfragmented (simple), motionless, timeless (eternal).

But let us not forget and let us take due note of the fact that this enigmatic, simple unity which is utterly uncognisable has vanished with its transcendent domain and *exists no more*. From this insight we want to take heart and, with renewed courage, return to that domain which persists, to the only one still valid, to the clear and distinct world.

26.

From what we have so far said, it follows that all developmental chains, regardless of our point of departure, issue A PARTE ANTE in a transcendent unity, which to our cognition is entirely sealed, an x, equivalent to nothingness, and we may therefore certainly say that the world has arisen out of nothingness. Yet since, on one hand, we must attribute to this unity a positive predicate, that of *existence*, although of this kind of existence we can form for ourselves not even the most beggared concept; and, on the other, it is utterly impossible for our reason to think of an arising out of nothingness; we are therefore dealing with a *relative* nothingness (NIHIL PRIVATIVUM), which must be described as a passed, incomprehensible, primordial being in which everything that is was contained in a manner inconceivable for us.

From this it is evident:

1) that all developmental chains have a beginning (which, incidentally, already follows with logical necessity from the concept of development);
2) that there cannot therefore be any infinite causal chains A PARTE ANTE;
3) that all *forces* have *arisen*; for whatever they were in the transcendent domain, in the simple unity, eludes our cognition entirely. We can say only this: That they had mere existence. We can further say, apodictically, that they were not, in the simple unity, force; for force is the essence, the ESSENTIA, of a thing-in-itself in the *immanent* domain. However, what the simple unity, in which everything now existing was once contained, essentially was—that, as we have clearly seen, is for all time shrouded from our minds by an impenetrable veil.

The transcendent domain, in fact, no longer exists. If, however, we go back into the past using our imagination, up to the beginning of the immanent domain, then we can figuratively place the transcendent alongside the immanent domain. Yet both are then separated by a chasm which can never be crossed by any means of the mind. Only a single, fine thread bridges the fathomless abyss: it is *existence*. On this fine thread we can get *all* the forces of the immanent domain across into the transcendent. This load the thread can bear. But as soon as the forces have arrived in the latter domain, they also cease to be forces for human thought, and for this reason the following important proposition holds:

Although everything that is has not arisen from nothingness, but already existed *prior* to the world; still everything that is, every force, insofar as it is a force, has indeed arisen—that is, it had a definite beginning.

27.

At these results we therefore arrive when we proceed backwards from some being in the present into its past. We now want to examine the behaviour of things on the onwards-rolling point of the present.

We first look at the inorganic realm, the realm of *simple* chemical forces, such as oxygen, chlorine, iodine, copper, and so on. As far as our experience reaches, it has never transpired that any one of these forces has, under the same circumstances, shown different qualities; likewise, we know of no case where a chemical force would have been *annihilated*. If I let sulphur enter into all possible compounds and leave all possible compounds, then once it has left it shows again its old qualities and its quantum has been neither augmented nor diminished; at least everyone, in the latter regard, can be resolutely certain that it is so—and rightly so: for Nature is the sole source of truth and her statements alone are to be heeded. She never lies and, whenever queried about the present topic, answers each time that no *simple* chemical force can cease to be.

Nevertheless, we must concede that skeptical attacks can be made against this statement. Suppose I took a quite general approach, without adducing a single feature of matter from which the impermanence of the force objectifying itself in matter could be inferred; what would be the response if, for example, I then said: It is correct that still no case has as yet been known in which a simple substance has been annihilated, but can you claim that experience in all of the future shall teach the same? Can anything at all be stated about *force* à priori? Not at all, for force is entirely independent of the cognising Subject, is the genuine thing-in-itself. From the nature of limitations of mathematical space—even if mathematical space only exists in our imagination—the mathematician may well draw propositions of unconditional validity for the *formal* aspect of things-in-themselves; he may do this because the point-space underlying mathematical space has the capacity to spread out in three dimensions, and because every thing-in-itself is extended in three dimensions. It is, furthermore, all the same whether I am speaking of a particular *real* succession in the essence of a thing-in-itself, or whether I translate that real succession into *ideal* succession, i.e., relate it to time; for ideal succession keeps pace with real succession. But the natural scientist may, from the nature of the *ideal* conjunction called substance, deduce nothing which would concern force; for I cannot repeat often enough that the essence of matter is, in every regard, TOTO GENERE different from the essence of force, although force impresses its qualities down to the smallest detail upon matter. Where *real* force and *ideal* matter come into contact, there precisely is the important point through which the boundary between the ideal and the real must be drawn, where the difference between Object and thing-in-itself, between phenomena and the foundation of phenomena, between the world as presentation and the world as force, is obvious. As long as the world is, so long shall the things-in-themselves be extended in it in three directions; as long as the world is, so long shall these spheres of force be in motion. But do you know what new—new for you, not newly arising—laws of nature future experience shall let you discover, laws which shall let the essence of force appear to you in an entirely new light? For it is a resolute fact that a statement about the innermost essence of force can never be made à priori, but only on the basis of *experience*. But has all your experiencing reached its end? Have you all the laws of nature already in hand?

What response might be given to me?

Now, that such skeptical attacks on the above proposition can be made at all must put us in a very cautious mood and compel us to leave the question open for the Physics, particularly for the Metaphysics, in which the threads of all our investigations in the purely immanent domain shall come together. Here, however, in the Analytics, where we have encountered the thing-in-itself as something entirely general, where we therefore assume the lowest standpoint on the thing-in-itself, we must endorse unconditionally Nature's pronouncement that a *simple* chemical force *never ceases to be*.

If, in contrast, we take a chemical compound such as hydrogen sulphide, then this force is already transient. It is neither sulphur, nor hydrogen, but a third thing, a sphere of force firmly self-contained, but a force that can be destroyed. If I decompose it into its basic forces, then it is annihilated. Where, now, is this idiosyncratic force which made on me a very distinct impression that was different from sulphur as well as from hydrogen? It is *dead*, and we can certainly imagine that this compound, under particular circumstances, will altogether vanish from the world of phenomena forever.

In the organic realm it is the same through and through. The difference between chemical compound and organism will occupy us in the Physics; here it does not concern us. Every organism consists of simple chemical forces which, like sulphur and hydrogen in hydrogen sulphide, are merged in a single, higher, entirely self-contained and unified force. If we bring an organism into the chemical laboratory and analyse it, then, be it an animal or a plant, we shall always find in it only simple chemical forces.

Now, what does Nature say when we ask her about the higher force living in an organism? She says: The force is there as long as the organism lives. If it dissolves itself, then the force is *dead*. She gives no other testimony, because she is unable to. It is testimony of the utmost importance, which only a dim mind can distort. If an organism dies, then the forces bound up in it are liberated once more without the slightest loss, but the force which dominated the chemical forces up to that point is dead. Is it supposed to live on still, separated from them? Where is the destroyed hydrogen sulphide? Where the higher force of the burned plant or of the killed animal? Do they float between heaven and earth? Did they fly onto a star in the Milky Way? Only Nature, the sole source of truth, can apprise us of the facts, and Nature says: They are *dead*.

As impossible as it is for us to imagine an arising from nothingness, we can as easily imagine all organisms and all chemical compounds forever annihilated.

From these considerations we draw the following conclusions:

1) all *simple* chemical forces, as far as our experience reaches at present, are indestructible;
2) all chemical compounds and all organic forces, in contrast, are destructible.

The confusion of substance with the simple chemical forces is as old as philosophy itself. The law of the persistence of substance is:

Substance is unarisen and intransient.

According to our investigations, substance is an *ideal* conjunction on the basis of the à priori form of the understanding called matter, and nature is an entirety of forces. The previously stated law would in our language therefore be:

All forces in the world are unarisen and intransient.

In contrast, we have found through our honest investigation:

1) that *all* forces, without exception, have *arisen*;
2) that only a *few* forces are intransient.

At the same time, however, we also reserved our final judgment on these matters until the intransience of the chemical forces has been re-examined in the Physics and the Metaphysics.

28.

We have seen that every thing-in-itself has a sphere of force, and that this sphere of force is no vain illusion which the à priori form called space conjures out of its own means. Furthermore, we have, by means of the extraordinarily important association called community, cognised the extremely intimate, dynamic coherence of these forces, and we thus arrived at a totality of forces, at a collective unity firmly self-contained.

In doing this, however, we have claimed the *finiteness of the universe*, which we now have to justify more closely. Before doing so, let us make clear to ourselves the significance of what is at issue. We are not concerned here with a self-contained, *finite* immanent domain surrounded on all sides by an *infinite* transcendent domain; rather, since the transcendent domain in fact no longer exists, we are concerned with an immanent domain which alone still exists and is supposed to be *finite*.

How can this ostensibly bold claim be justified? We have only two paths before us. Either we supply the proof with the aid of presentation, or we do so purely logically.

Point-space, as I said above, is equally accommodating in delimiting a grain of sand and a palace. The sole precondition is that it be solicited to do so by a thing-in-itself or, lacking this, by a reproduced sense-impression. Now, we have before us a world: our earth beneath us and above us the starred heavens, and so to a man of naïve disposition it may well appear that the presentation of a finite world is possible. Science, however, destroys this delusion. With each new day, it extends the universe's sphere of force or, subjectively expressed, it daily compels the point-space of the understanding to lengthen its three dimensions. Thus, for now, the world is still immeasurably large, i.e., the understanding still cannot delimit it. Whether the understanding shall accomplish this we must leave undecided. Accordingly, we must refrain from making intuitive models of the universe in microcosm, akin to those plastic imitations we make of our earth to render its form comprehensible; and we must simply state that we shall not by way of presentation arrive at our objective: proving intuitively the world's finiteness. All that then remains for us is inexorable logic.

And, in fact, it is extraordinarily easy for logic to prove the finiteness of the world.

The universe is not a single force, a simple unity, but a totality of finite spheres of force. Now, to none of these spheres of force can I give infinite extension; for in doing so I would firstly destroy the concept itself, then I would turn multiplicity into unity, i.e., I would be striking experience in the face. Alongside a single eternal sphere of force there is no room for any other sphere of force, and the essence of nature would simply be done away with. A totality of *finite* spheres of force must, however, necessarily be *finite*.

It could here be objected that, although in the world only finite forces are to be met with, infinitely many finite forces may be present, such that the world is no totality, but is infinite.

The response to this must be: All of the forces of the world are either simple chemical forces or compounds of the same. The former are countable and, furthermore, all compounds can be traced back to these few simple forces. No simple force, as elaborated above, can be infinite, if we are also to be allowed to designate each one summarily as immeasurably large. Consequently, the world, at bottom, is the sum of the simple forces, which are all finite, i.e., the world is finite.

Now, why does something within us resist this result time and time again? Because reason abuses the form of the understanding called space. Space has significance only for experience; it is only an à priori precondition of experience, a means for cognising the external world. Reason, as we have seen, is justified in letting space spread out (like one who presses the release which lets a sword be drawn from a cane) only when it is reproducing a sense-impression or has to produce for mathematics the pure intuition of a spatiality. It is clear that the mathematician has need of such a spatiality in the smallest dimensions merely in order to demonstrate all of his proofs; but it is also clear that precisely this production of mathematical space for the mathematician is the cliff at whose edge reason becomes perverse and goes too far. For when we endeavour to capture the logically assured finiteness of the world in an image (as well as that can be expected to go) and, to this end, allow space to spread out, then perverse reason immediately gives space occasion to extend its dimensions beyond the world's limits. The complaint is then raised: We do indeed have a finite world, but in a space which we can never complete because the dimensions are constantly being lengthened (or better: We do indeed have a finite world, but *in absolute nothingness*).

There is only one remedy for this. We have to rely heavily on the logical finiteness of the world and on the awareness that point-space, forced to extend itself into a limitless mathematical space, is a thing of thought, exists only *in* our heads and has no reality. In this way we are rendered invulnerable as if by magic, and resist with critical sobriety the temptation to indulge in solitary ecstasies of the mind and, in so doing, to betray truth.

29.

It is likewise only critical sobriety that can protect us against other great dangers, which I now want to describe.

Just as it is in the nature of point-space to spread out from *nought* in three dimensions IN INDEFINITUM; it is also in its nature to let any given pure (mathematical) spatiality become ever smaller until it is again point-space, i.e., nought. Just as the snail draws its feelers in, so point-space draws its three dimensions back into itself and becomes again an inactive form of the understanding. This subjective capacity called space cannot be thought of as having any other constitution, for it is a precondition of experience and is constituted for the external world alone, without which it has no significance at all. But even the stupidest person will see that a form of cognition which is supposed on one hand to delimit things-in-themselves of the most varied kinds (the largest and the smallest, and *in one moment* the largest, *in the next* the smallest) as Objects, on the other hand to help apprehend the totality of all things-in-themselves, the universe, in proceeding from as well as in receding to nought—even the stupidest person, I say, will see that such a form of cognition must be *unconstrained*; for if its capacity to spread out were limited, then beyond this limit it could not shape a real sphere of force; and if, in retreating, it had a limit before nought, then all those spheres of force which lie between this limit and nought would be absent to our cognition.

In the last section, we saw that reason can abuse the limitlessness of point-space in spreading out and thereby arrive at the notion of a finite universe in an infinite space. We have now to illuminate reason's abuse of this limitlessness in withdrawing to nought, or in other words: We now confront the *infinite divisibility* of mathematical space.

Let us imagine a spatiality, approximately a cubic inch; we can then divide this IN INDEFINITUM, i.e., the dimensions are always *prevented* from retreating all the way to the nought-point. We might divide a year, a century, a millennium long—we would always be faced with a residual spatiality, which can again be divided IN INFINITUM. To this the so-called infinite divisibility of mathematical space is due, just as the infiniteness of mathematical space is due to the spreading out of point-space IN INFINITUM.

But what are we doing when we start from a particular spatiality and relentlessly divide it? We are playing with fire, we are big children whom every sober-minded person should rap on the knuckles. Or are we somehow not proceeding in the manner of children who, in the absence of their parents, handle a loaded pistol, which has a very specific purpose, with no purpose at all? Space is only intended for the cognition of the external word; it is supposed to delimit every thing-in-itself, be it as large as Mont Blanc or as small as an animalcule: that is its purpose, just as that of the loaded pistol is to bring down an intruder. But when we toy dangerously with space in this way, unfettering it from the external world, we are, in Pückler's words, as I already said above: indulging in "solitary ecstasies" of the mind.

30.

The division IN INDEFINITUM of a given *pure* spatiality has, by the way, also an innocent side so long as what is being divided is a thing of thought, a spatiality which is only in the head of the individual making the divisions and which has no reality. Its dangerousness, however, is doubled when the infinite divisibility of mathematical space is, with utter impropriety, transferred to the force, the thing-in-itself. And on the heels of this senseless beginning follows the punishment: logical contradiction.

Every chemical force is divisible; against this view no objection can be raised, for it is taught by experience. But *before* being divided it does not consist of parts, is no *aggregate* of parts, for the parts first become *effectively* so in the division itself. The chemical force is a homogeneous simple force of thoroughly uniform *intensity*, and this is the basis of its divisibility, i.e., each separated part does not even in the slightest differ essentially from the whole.

If we now turn our gaze from real division, which Nature according to her laws as well as man in organised work accomplishes for practical purposes, and the results of which are always definite spheres of force, then there remains *idle, frivolous* division.

Perverse reason takes some part of a chemical force, a cubic inch of iron for example, and divides it in thought continuously IN INDEFINITUM, and finally becomes convinced that, though it—that is, perverse reason—might go on dividing a billion years long, the dividing would never come to an end. At the same time, however, logic says to reason that a cubic inch of iron, a *finite* sphere of force, cannot possibly be composed of *infinitely* many parts, indeed that it is entirely unwarranted to speak of *infinitely* many parts of an Object; for the foundation of the *concept of infinity* consists *merely in the unimpeded activity* IN INDEFINITUM *of a cognitive faculty*—here, therefore, in the unimpeded progression of division—*never, never* in the *real* domain.

Perverse reason can thus venture into the darkness at the hand of unrelenting division, but, once there, it must also continue ever onwards. To the finite sphere of force from which it set out it can no longer return. In this desperate situation it violently tears itself free of its guide and postulates the atom, i.e., a sphere of force which is supposed to be divisible no further. Of course, through the compounding of such atoms reason can now return to the cubic inch of iron, but at what price? It has stumbled into contradiction with itself!

If he wishes to remain honest, then the thinker must be sober-minded. Sobriety is the sole weapon against the abuse which perverse reason is disposed to commit with our cognitive faculty. In the present case, therefore, the *divisibility* of chemical forces in the real domain shall not be called into question by us at all. However, we shall certainly strive with all our might, firstly, against the *infinite* divisibility of forces, because such a divisibility can only be claimed if, in the most lunatic manner, the essence of a faculty of cognition (a faculty, moreover, that has been abused) is transferred to the thing-in-itself; secondly, against the *composition* of force out of *parts*. We therefore reject both the infinite divisibility of force *and* the atom.

As I said above, a faculty of cognition which is supposed to delimit all the forces which can be present in an experience must be so constituted that it can spread out without constraint and, on the way back to nought, encounters no limit whatever. If, however, we apply this faculty one-sidedly—that is, unfettered from experience, for which alone it is intended—and make conclusions which we drew from its nature binding for the *thing-in-itself*, then we fall into contradiction with pure reason—a great evil!

31.

Finally, we still have to escape by means of a critical mind one danger which arises out of time.

Time, as we know, is an *ideal* conjunction à posteriori, gained on the basis of the à priori form called the present, and is nothing without the foundation of *real* succession. With time's powerful guidance we arrived at the beginning of the world, at the boundary of a vanished premundane existence, of the transcendent domain. Here, time becomes powerless, here it issues in an *eternity* which has passed, and this word—eternity—is merely the subjective label *for the lack of each and every real succession*.

Critical reason humbles itself; perverse reason does not, but revives time and spurs it onwards IN INDEFINITUM *without* a foundation in reality, not minding the eternity there presiding.

Here more than anywhere, the abuse which can be committed with a faculty of cognition is exposed. *Empty moments* are ceaselessly conjoined and a line is continued which, up to the transcendent domain, certainly had a solid, sure foundation, namely, real development, but which floats now in the air.

We have, then, nothing else to do in this situation but to rely on pure reason while simply forbidding foolish excesses.

Now, even though real motion, whose subjective measure is time alone, had a beginning A PARTE ANTE, this does not mean that it must have an end A PARTE POST. The solution of this problem depends on the answer to the question: Are the simple chemical forces indestructible? For it is clear that real motion must be infinite if the simple chemical forces are indestructible.

From this it therefore follows:

1) that real motion had a beginning;
2) that real motion is infinite.

We render the latter judgment while reserving the right to revise it in the Physics and the Metaphysics.

32.

These and the earlier investigations of our cognitive faculty establish, I am convinced, the genuine *transcendental* or *critical idealism*, which does not with *words* alone but *truly* gives the things-in-themselves their empirical reality—that is, grants them *extension* and *motion*, *independently of the Subject*, of *space* and *time*. The emphasis of this idealism is on the *material* objectification of *force*, and it is in this regard *transcendental*, a word which denotes the dependence of the Object on the Subject.

It is, on the other hand, *critical* idealism because it restrains perverse reason (PERVERSA RATIO) and does not allow it:

a) to abuse *causality* for the production of *infinite* chains;
b) to unfetter *time* from its indispensable foundation, real development, and to make it into a line of *empty* moments which comes out of eternity and hastens onwards into eternity;
c) to consider *mathematical space* and *substance* to be anything more than mere *things of thought*, and
d) beyond that, to impute to this real space infinity and to this real substance absolute persistence.

Furthermore, critical idealism permits perverse reason even less the arbitrary *transference* of such figments of the brain onto the *things-in-themselves* and annuls its bold claims that:

a) the pure *being* of things-in-themselves is included in the infinite causal chains;
b) the universe is infinite and the chemical forces are infinitely divisible or they are an aggregate of atoms;
c) the development of the world has no beginning;
d) *all* forces are indestructible.

The two judgments which we had to render:

1) that the *simple* chemical forces are indestructible;
2) that the development of the world has no end,

we declared to stand in need of revision.

As an important positive result we have then still to mention the fact that transcendental idealism brought us to a transcendent domain which, because it no longer exists, can no longer trouble the investigator.

In this way, critical idealism frees every honest and true observation of nature from inconsequence and vacillation and makes nature once more the *sole* source of all truth, which no-one, tempted by deceptive forms and mirages, can abandon with impunity—for in the desert he must languish.

> A fellow who speculates,
> Is like an animal on an arid heath,
> Led in circles by an evil spirit,
> And round about lies beautiful green pasture.

Goethe

33.

Of the foregoing investigations, the result most important for the investigations yet to come is: that the things-in-themselves are for the Subject substantial Objects and, independently of the Subject, are moving forces with a definite sphere of efficacy. We attained this result through careful analysis of the *outwards* directed faculties of cognition, thus entirely on the territory of the objective world; for we could just as well have produced the conjunction time (which we gained on the inward path) with reference to our body or through our consciousness of other things.

However, the recognition that the thing-in-itself underlying the Object is a force of a particular extension and with a particular capacity for motion is all that can be achieved on the outward path. What the force is in and for itself, how it has its effect, how it moves—all this we cannot cognise outwardly. Here, too, immanent philosophy would have to come to an end if we were only cognising Subject; for what immanent philosophy on the basis of this one-sided truth would have to say about art, about the actions of man, and the motion of humanity as a whole, would be of dubious worth: it could be so and it could also not be so—in short, immanent philosophy would lose the firm ground beneath its feet and it would lose all courage, and for that reason would have to abandon its investigations.

But the outward path is not the *only* one open to us. We can penetrate into the innermost heart of force; for every man belongs to nature, is himself a

THE PHILOSOPHY OF REDEMPTION

force and, specifically, a self-conscious force. The essence of force *must* be there in self-consciousness to be apprehended.

Thus, we now want to draw from this *second* source of experience, from *self-consciousness*.

If we sink deeply enough into our inner being, then the senses and the understanding (the outwards directed cognitive faculty) cease to function entirely; they become dormant, as it were, and only the higher faculties of cognition remain active. In our inner being we have no impressions for which we would first have to seek a cause that is different from them; furthermore, we cannot on the inside shape ourselves spatially and are completely immaterial, i.e., within us the law of causality finds no application and we are free from space and matter.

Although we are now completely unspatial—that is, we cannot attain an intuition of a shape of our inner being—we are not for this reason a mathematical point. We *feel* our sphere of effect precisely as far as it reaches, we lack only the means of shaping it. The general feeling of force reaches as far as the outermost tips of our body, and we feel ourselves neither concentrated into a point nor diffusing IN INDEFINITUM, but rather in a quite definite sphere. This sphere I shall henceforth call the *real individuality*: it is the first pillar of purely immanent philosophy.

If we examine ourselves further, then we find ourselves, as already described above, in ceaseless motion. Our force is essentially restless and unceasing. Never, not even for the duration of the smallest part of an instant, are we in absolute rest; for rest is death, and the smallest conceivable interruption of life would entail the extinguishing of life's flame. We are therefore essentially restless; yet we feel ourselves in motion only in self-consciousness.

The state of our innermost essence as the real point of motion is effectively always in contact with consciousness, or, as I said earlier, the present floats *on top of* the point of motion. We are constantly aware of our inner life in the present. If, in contrast, the present had primacy and so the point of motion stood on it, then my essence, during every intermission of my self-consciousness (in fainting, in sleep) would have to rest totally, i.e., death would touch my essence and it would not be able to rekindle its life. The assumption that the point of motion is actually dependent on the present (and real motion actually dependent on time) is like the assumption that space lends extension to things-in-themselves—as absurd as it was necessary for the developmental course of philosophy, by which I mean to say that there can simply be no higher degree of absurdity.

By becoming aware of the transition from present to present, reason gains, in the manner previously discussed, the form called time and with it real succession, which I shall from now on, in relation to the real individuality, call *real motion*; it is the second pillar of immanent philosophy.

The greatest illusion in which we can be caught is to believe that we would on the inward as on the outward path be cognising, and that that which cognises would be paralleled by that which is cognised. We find ourselves in the midst of the thing-in-itself, there can be no more talk at all of an Object, and we apprehend immediately the core of our essence, through self-consciousness, in *feeling*. It is an immediate awareness of our essence by means of the mind, or more accurately, by means of sensibility.

Now, what is this force that unveils itself in the core of our inner being? It is the *will to life*.

Whenever we step onto the inward path—whether we meet ourselves in apparent rest and equanimity, or shudder blissfully under beauty's kiss; whether we dash and dive in wildest passion or dissolve in compassion; whether we "raise a cry to the heavens" or "are saddened to death"—we are always the will to life. We want to exist, always to exist; because we *want* existence, we *are*, and because we want existence, we remain in existence. The will to life is the innermost core of our essence; it is always active, though often not on the surface. To be convinced of this, let the most exhausted individual be brought into genuine mortal peril and the will to life will unveil itself, wearing with appalling clarity on all its features the desire for existence: its ravenous appetite for life is insatiable.

When, however, a man genuinely wills life no more, then he annihilates himself at once through the terminal deed. Most only *wish* death upon themselves, they do not *will* it.

This will is a developing individuality which is identical with the moving sphere of efficacy found from outside. But it is thoroughly *devoid of matter*. I consider this immediate apprehension of force, on the inward path, as free of matter to be a seal of approval impressed by Nature upon my epistemology. Not space, not time distinguish the thing-in-itself from the Object, but matter alone makes the Object into a mere phenomenon which stands and falls with the cognising Subject.

As the most important result of the Analytics we hold the *individual, moving* will to life, which is totally independent of the Subject, firmly in hand. It is the key that leads into the heart of the Physics, Aesthetics, Ethics, Politics, and Metaphysics.

Physics

Magnetic mystery, explain to me this!
No greater mystery than love and hate.

Goethe

Search within yourselves and you will find
everything and be glad when out there,
whatever you may call it, there lies a nature
which gainsays nothing that you have found
within yourselves.

Goethe

1.

As the foundation stone of the Physics I take not the species floating invisible between heaven and earth, the metaphysical concept of type without marrow and blood; still less the so-called physical forces such as gravity, electricity, and so on; but the *real individual* will to life gained in the Analytics. In the innermost core of our essence we have apprehended this will to be that which underlies force (as cognisable from the outside), and since everything in nature unceasingly has an effect, and efficacy is force, we are justified in concluding that every thing-in-itself is an individual will to life.

2.

"Will to life" is a tautology and an explanation; for life is not to be separated from will, not even in abstract thought. Where there is will, there too is life; and where life, will.

On the other hand, if explanation entails attributing what is less familiar to what is more familiar, then the will is explained by life; for we perceive life as a continuous flux on the pulse of which we can in any moment lay our finger, whereas the will becomes obvious to us only in voluntary actions.

Furthermore, life and motion are interchangeable concepts; for where there is life there is motion and vice versa, and life that were not motion could not be grasped with human thought.

Life, in turn, is explained by motion; for motion is the characteristic of life that is cognised or felt.

Motion is therefore essential to the will to life; it is the *sole, genuine predicate* of that will and we must take our bearings from it in order to be able to take the first step in the Physics.

A clear-eyed look into nature reveals to us individual wills of the most diverse kinds. This diversity must be founded in the essence of these wills, for the Object can only manifest what lies within the thing-in-itself. Now, the difference reveals itself to us most distinctly in *motion*, so if we begin by investigating this motion more closely, then we will gain the first general classification of nature.

If the individual will has a uniform *undivided* motion, because it itself is whole and *undivided*, then as an Object it is an *inorganic individual*. It goes without saying that we are here speaking only of the drive, of the *inner* motion, within a particular individuality.

If, in contrast, the will has a *resultant* motion in consequence of its having *divided* itself, then as an Object it is an *organism*. The part which has arisen from this division and is distinct from the residual motion is called an organ.

Organisms are then differentiated from each other as follows.

If the motion of the organs is only *irritability*, which merely reacts to *external* stimuli, then the organism is a *plant*. The resultant motion is *growth*.

If, further, the individual will has within itself separated *into parts* such that one of those parts of its motion is further divided into a portion that is moved and a portion that does the moving, into a controlled and a controlling portion, or in other words into irritability *and sensibility*, which taken together once again form *the entire part* of the motion; then, as an Object, it is an *animal*. Sensibility (and so the mind) is therefore nothing more than a part of the motion essential to the will and, as such, is just as much a manifestation of the will as irritability or the residual whole motion. There is but one principle in the world: *individual will* to life, and there is no other principle besides.

The larger a part resulting from the division of the whole motion is—that is, the larger the intelligence is—the higher is the rung on which the animal stands and the greater is the significance which the controlling portion has for the individual; and the less favourable the ratio of the controlling portion—that is, sensibility—to the residual undivided motion is, the greater is this residual whole motion, which here appears as *instinct*, of which the *drive to artifice* is a branch.

Finally, if through a further division of the residual whole motion *thought in concepts* emerges in the individual will, then that individual will is a *man*.

The resultant motion manifests itself in animals, as in man, as *growth and voluntary motion*.

The controlling portion on one hand and, on the other, the controlled portion and the undivided motion I would depict as a seeing rider and a blind horse whose bodies have fused. The horse is nothing without the rider, the rider nothing without the horse. Yet it ought to be noted that the rider also has not the merest *direct* influence on the will and cannot, for instance, direct the horse at his discretion. The rider only suggests the directions; the horse alone determines the direction in which it moves. In contrast, the indirect influence of the mind on the will is of the greatest significance.

3.

The mind stands to the will of the animal in a two-fold, to that of man in a three-fold relationship. The relationships which they have in common are the following. Firstly, the mind *controls*, that is, it indicates various directions and takes the one chosen by the will. Secondly, it chains the will to *feeling*, which it can intensify into the greatest pain and the greatest lust.

The third relationship, which is present with man alone, is that the controlling portion, by means of *self-consciousness*, gives the will the ability to look into its innermost essence.

The two latter relationships can give the mind's influence, although it is an indirect one, great power and completely reshape its original relation to the will. The slave that has only to obey becomes first a sentinel, then an advisor, and finally a friend, into whose hands the will confidently lays its fate.

4.

Accordingly, *only motion* belongs to the will's essence, and not presentation, feeling, and self-consciousness, which are phenomenal appearances of a particular *divided* motion. – *Consciousness* manifests itself in man:

1) as feeling,
2) as self-consciousness.

Presentation as such is an unconscious work of the mind, a work of which the mind first becomes conscious through the relationship to feeling or to self-consciousness.

The will to life is therefore to be defined as an originally blind, intense compulsion or drive, which through the division of its motion becomes cognisant, feeling, and self-conscious.

Insofar as the *individual* will to life is subject to the law of one of the kinds of motion elaborated above, it reveals its essence in general, which, as such, I call its *idea* in general. We thus have

1) the chemical idea,
2) the idea of the plant,
3) the idea of the animal,
4) the idea of man.

However, insofar as one speaks of the particular essence of an individual will to life, of its unique character, of the sum of its qualities, I call that individual will quite simply an *idea*, and so we have just as many *ideas* as there are *individuals* in the world. Immanent philosophy places the idea's centre of gravity where nature places it, namely, in the real individual, not in the species, which is nothing other than a concept, like chair and window; nor in an intangible, dreamt-up transcendent unity in, above, or behind the world and co-existing with it.

5.

We have now to approach the ideas in general and the particular ideas more closely, and specifically in the reverse order of that given above, because we apprehend the idea of man most immediately. It would be called "explaining the form of a thing on the basis of its shadow" if we wanted to make the organic ideas understandable to ourselves through chemical ones.

We achieved the above differentiation of ideas according to the type of their motion with the aid of the fact, found in self-consciousness, of motion without rest. Now if, in seeking to apprehend immediately the essence of the things-in-themselves, inner experience is also preferred to outer experience, then, in contrast, when seeking to cognise the *factors* of the motion, outer experience is preferred to inner. Within myself I always find only the individual will to life in a particular motion, and am conscious of a particular state of that motion. I receive only the resultant of many activities; for inwards I do not conduct myself in a cognising way. I neither cognise my bones, my muscles, my nerves, my vessels and innards, nor do their individual functions enter my consciousness: I only ever feel one state of my will.

For the complete cognition of nature it is therefore necessary to call on presentation, and we must draw from both sources of experience; yet in doing so we must not forget that on the outward path we shall never find our way into the essence of things, and that for this reason, if we had to choose between both sources of experience, inner experience would be decidedly preferred. I want to make this clear with an image.

A locomotive can be considered in three ways. The first is a precise investigation of every part and how they all fit together. The furnace, the boiler, the valves, the pipes, the cylinders, the pistons, the rods, the cranks, the wheels, and so on, are inspected. The other way is much easier. One simply asks: What do all of these particular parts achieve overall?, and is entirely satisfied by the answer: The simple motion of the complicated, puffing contraption forwards or backwards on straight rails. Whoever declares himself satisfied with the cognised interrelationship of the parts and, astonished by the wonderful mechanism, overlooks the motion of the whole is inferior to another who has only the motion of the whole in view. But superior to both is he who makes clear to himself first the motion of the whole and then the composition of its parts.

We therefore also want now, from a very general perspective, to supplement through presentation what we have found on the basis of inner experience.

The human body is an Object, that is, it is the idea of man that has passed through the forms of cognition. Independently of the Subject, man is pure idea, individual will.

Therefore, what we, with only motion in view, called the *controlling portion* is, on the outward path, a *function of the nerve mass* (therefore of the brain, spinal cord, of the nerves and of the ganglia); and the *controlled portion* (irritability) is a *function of the muscles*. All organs are formed from the blood, have precipitated from it. Thus, the entire will does not lie in the blood, and the motion of the blood is only a *residual whole motion*.

Accordingly, *every organ* is the objectification of a particular striving of the will which, as blood, it cannot fulfil but can only actuate. The brain is therefore the objectification of the will's striving to cognise the external world, to feel and to think; the digestive and procreative organs are therefore the objectification of the will's *striving* to maintain itself in existence, and so on.

Yet even if the blood, considered in itself, is not the objectification of the entire will, in the organism it is still the *main issue*, the master, the prince; it is genuine will to life, although weakened and constrained.

In contrast, the entire organism is the objectification of the entire will: it is the unfurling of the entire will. From this point of view, the entire organism is the will's sphere of force become presentation, objectified; and every action of the organism, be it digestion, respiration, speech, grasping, walking, is a *whole* motion. Thus, the grasping of an object is first of all the combination of nerve and muscle into a whole partial motion, the act however in itself is a combination of this partial motion with the residual whole motion of the blood into a whole motion of the will. The unified motion of chemical force is a simple action, the motion of an organism a composite, resultant action. Fundamentally, both are identical, just as it is all the same whether ten people together or one strong person raises a load.

Just as we were only able to divide the motion of the human will into sensibility and irritability on one hand, and residual whole motion on the other; so the factors of motion present themselves in the organism as nerves and muscles on one hand, and as blood on the other. Everything else is a side issue. And of these three factors, the blood is the most important and that from which nerve and muscle originally precipitated. It is the intuited, undivided will to life, the objectification of our innermost essence, of the *dæmon*, which plays in man the same role as instinct in the animal.

6.

It ought however to be observed that although the nerve mass, like every other part of the body, is the objectification of the will, it nevertheless assumes a quite exceptional position in the organism. We have already seen above that it stands in a very important relationship to the dæmon and, although in total dependence on the dæmon, encounters it as a stranger. In any case, the muscles are significantly closer to the blood, that is, they contain the larger part of the divided motion, which is already evident from their colour and chemical composition. Added to this is the fact that no organ can function without nervous stimulus, whereas the *brain* only works with the aid of the blood. For these reasons alone—we will later find much more important reasons—it is already at this juncture advisable to highlight at least this part of the nerve mass (the objectified mind) and to place the idea of man in an inseparable combination of will and mind; in doing so, however, always keeping in view that everything which belongs to the body is nothing other than the objectification of the *will*, of the sole principle in the world, which I cannot impress upon the reader enough.

7.

The idea of man is therefore an inseparable unity of will and mind, or an inseparable combination of a particular will with a particular mind. I have already dissected the *mind* in the Analytics. It encompasses the faculties of cognition unified into an inseparable unity.

In each man it is a particular mind, because its parts can be deficiently, little, or highly developed. If we go through the faculties, then firstly individual senses can be extinguished or weakened. The understanding always exercises its function—transition from the effect to the cause—and, specifically, with the same speed in every man, a speed which is so incomparably great that any deviations from it must be completely imperceptible. Its forms, space and matter, also objectify equally in all men; for possible imperfections such as fuzziness of the outlines and false determinations of colour are to be attributed to the defective constitution of the relevant sensory organs (short-sightedness, limited capacity of the retina to divide its activity qualitatively).

What distinguishes the dunce from the genius must therefore be sought in the higher cognitive faculty. In reason alone that distinction cannot lie, for reason's function, synthesis, like the function of the understanding, can in no man be stunted, but is unified in reason with reason's auxiliary faculties: memory, judgment, and imagination. For of what help to me is synthesis, i.e., the faculty of conjoining IN INDEFINITUM, if, having arrived at the third thought, I have already forgotten the first one, or when I want to memorise a figure and, arriving at the neck, am missing the head, or when I am unable quickly to place like with like, same with same? For this reason the highly developed auxiliary faculties of reason are indispensable prerequisites for a genius, whether he manifest himself as thinker or artist.

On one hand, there are people who cannot speak three words coherently because they cannot think coherently, and, on the other, there are people who can read a great work once and never again forget its train of thought. There are people who can contemplate an object for hours and yet cannot remember its form clearly; in contrast, there are others who let their clear eye glide once slowly over a wide landscape and from then onwards carry it distinctly within themselves for all time. The former have a weak, the latter a strong memory; the former a weak, the latter a highly gifted fancy. Yet it must be taken into account that the mind cannot always reveal itself fully, because its activity depends on the will, and it would be perverse to conclude from the stuttering speech of an anxious, timid man that he lacks wit.

It must further be observed that genius, though certainly a phenomenon of the brain, does not rest solely on a quantitatively and qualitatively good brain. Just as a large pile of coal cannot melt metal when only the conditions for prolonged burning are present, whereas an efficient bellows leads quickly to this goal; so the brain can only manifest high genius when actuated by an energetic circulation, which in turn is essentially dependent on an efficient digestive system and strong lungs.

8.

If we turn to the *will* of man, then we have first to define his individuality as a whole. It is a closed being-for-itself or *egoism* (selfishness, I-ness). Where the ego ceases, the not-ego begins, and the following propositions obtain:

> OMNIS NATURA VULT ESSE CONSERVATRIX SUI.
> PEREAT MUNDUS, DUM EGO SALVUS SIM.

Fundamentally, the human will, like everything in the world, wants existence as such in the first instance. But it then also wants it in a particular way, i.e., it has a *character*. The most general form of character, which is, as it were, the internal aspect of the ego (the skin of the will), is *temperament*. As is well known, four temperaments are generally distinguished:

1) the melancholic,
2) the sanguine,
3) the choleric,
4) the phlegmatic,

which are fixed points between which many varieties lie.

Now, within the temperament there are *qualities of the will*. The principal ones are:

            Envy — Good will
          Greed — Generosity
         Cruelty — Mercifulness
         Avarice — Prodigality
        Falseness — Fidelity
      Haughtiness — Humility
        Defiance — Pusillanimity
    Imperiousness — Meekness
       Immodesty — Modesty
        Vulgarity — Nobility
      Inflexibility — Malleability
       Cowardice — Audacity
         Injustice — Justice
        Obduracy — Candour
      Malevolence — Uprightness
       Impudence — Shamefacedness
       Sensuality — Temperance
         Villainy — Aspiration
          Vanity — Holiness

and between each of these pairs there are gradations.

The qualities of the will are to be seen above all as formations of the will to life. They are all of them off-shoots of egoism, and since every man is will to life encased, as it were, in egoism, so in every man there also lies the germ of every quality of the will. The qualities of the will are to be compared with grooves which can expand to become channels, into which the will can flow upon the merest inducement. Yet here already it must be observed that the human will enters life already as character. Remaining with this imagery we may say, then, that the infant already shows, besides mere grooves, deep depressions; however, the former can be widened and deepened, the latter narrowed and flattened.

9.

From the qualities of the will the *states* of the will are to be strictly distinguished. In them, as I have already often said, we apprehend our innermost essence alone. We apprehend it immediately and do not cognise it. Only by bringing our states, which are nothing other than *felt motions*, into reflection do we become cognisant and do the states at the same time become objective for us. Thus, not until we engage in abstract thinking do we find that what lies at the foundation of our states is the will to life, and then, by directing the utmost attention to those motives which put our will at all times in a particular motion, extrapolate from the constantly returning states to the constitution of our character, whose traits I have called qualities of the will. And so we can, furthermore, define our temperament only by means of abstract classification and the composition of many states.

We have now to cognise reflectively the principal states of our will as we *feel* them on the inward path, and in doing so we shall, where necessary, use presentation to assist us.

The basic state from which we must proceed is the normal *feeling of life*. We feel ourselves, as it were, not at all, the will is completely satisfied: nothing disturbs its clear surface, neither pleasure nor unpleasure. If we glance at the body, it is completely healthy: all organs function without disruption, we nowhere sense either a relaxation or an intensification of our feeling of life, neither pain nor ecstasy.

One could also call this state, in the mirror of the Subject, the normal-*warm* and mild-*luminous* state; for the impression of the body on our tactile sense is objectified by matter (substance) as warmth, and the impression on the eyes, in which so to speak the inner motion is revealed, is objectified by matter as bright, soft light. That light and warmth in themselves are nothing but *phenomena of motion* is now an undisputed scientific truth. In contemplating the chemical ideas, we will approach light and warmth more closely, and it will then also turn out that they are not phenomena of a mysterious aether's motion but of the ideas familiar to all; for in the world there are only individual wills, and there is in it no place for essences which cannot be perceived with the senses and whose logical definition scorns all natural laws.

All other states of the will are based on this normal one (which one might also call equanimity) and are only *modifications* of this normal state.

The principal modifications are: *joy* and *sorrow*, *courage* and *fear*, *hope* and *despair*, *love* and *hatred* (*affects*). The last two are the strongest; they are modifications of the highest degree. They are all to be attributed to the transformation of the normal state, which the will brings about under the stimulus of a corresponding motive. Nothing mysterious, extrasensory, or foreign forces its way into the will's individuality, asserts itself and reigns in that individuality: not the powerful spirit of a dreamt-up species, no God, no devil; for the individuality is sovereign in its home. Just as chemical force is impenetrable, so man is a closed sphere of force which, to be sure, can be forced from without to show itself in this way or that, or to transition from this state to that; but the motive still only ever effects stimulation and the will merely reacts in accordance with its nature, its character, out of *its own force*.

10.

If I now proceed to label the mentioned states of the will, then it is clear that I can only present the results of a self-observation, which lay no claim to infallibility; for this kind of self-observation is extraordinarily difficult. What is required is that, for example, in the highest affect which overwhelms the entire mind one yet remain clear- and sober-minded enough to cognise this motion—a demand nigh impossible to fulfil.

In the normal state the will moves, as it were, like a calmly flowing current. If we think of the will as a sphere, then the motion would be a uniform, ring-like motion about a centre: a circular motion that is calm within itself.

All other motions previously mentioned, in contrast, flow either from the centre to the periphery or vice versa. The difference between them lies in the way in which that path—from centre to periphery or periphery to centre—is covered.

Joy is a jumping, fitful gushing from the centre, powerful one moment, weak the next, in waves that are long one moment and short the next. One speaks of the heart hopping, the heart jumping for joy, and often the motion also manifests itself externally: we hop, dance, laugh. For the joyful man, his individuality is too narrow; he cries:

> Be embraced, ye millions!

Courage is a calm, serene efflux in short regular waves. A courageous person appears firm and sure.

Hope, in contrast, always covers the path in *one* wave. It is a blissful, gentle motion from the centre outwards. One speaks of being on the wings of hope, blissful with hope, and often the hopeful person spreads his arms out as if he were already at his goal and could lay his hands on it.

Love I compare to an intense outburst from the centre towards the periphery; it is the most powerful efflux: the waves overrun each other and form whirlpools. The will would like to break through its sphere, it would like to become the entire world.

Hatred, in contrast, is the most intense backward flux of the will from the periphery to the centre, as if every extension were anathema to it and as if it could not have its cherished ego concentrated, compressed and compacted enough. Like an army in retreat, so this feeling knots itself together.

Despair covers the path to the centre as if in a single leap. Man, abandoned by all, convinced that he is beyond saving, flees into his innermost core, to whatever is left for him to cling to, and even this shatters. Such a man, it is said, has surrendered himself.

Fear is a trembling inward motion. The individual wishes to make himself as small as possible, he wishes to disappear. It is said that anxiety drives one into a mouse hole.

In *sorrow* the will moves in large regular waves towards the centre. One looks for oneself, one seeks in one's innermost the consolation that can never be found. One speaks of sorrow rallying the spirits, of the heart being mended through sorrow.

For "state" we often substitute the word "humour" and say: He is in a solemn, hopeful, courageous, sorrowful humour; one also says "ill-humoured" to denote the fact that the circling motion is no longer proceeding regularly.

11.

We want now to cast a brief glance at the qualities of the will which, upon stimulation by motives, primarily evoke the states of hatred and love.

Quite generally it can be said that in love one strives to extend one's individuality, whereas in hatred one essentially strives to limit it. Since, however, neither the one nor the other of these aims can be realised, the individual can only aspire to enlarge or constrain his *external* sphere of efficacy.

Man initially extends his individuality *dæmonically* through the sex-drive (lust) and here love appears as *sexual love*. It is the most aroused state of the will and in that state its feeling of life attains the highest degree. The individual in the grip of sexual love endures the greatest pains with resolve, achieves the exceptional, patiently clears obstacles from his way and in some circumstances does not even take fright at certain death, because he wants to live on purely dæmonically (unconsciously), only in combination with a particular other will.

Through sexual love man extends his individuality to the family.

He extends his external sphere further and puts himself in a state of love through the quality of the will called imperiousness or ambitiousness. He subordinates to himself other individuals and makes his will a law unto them. Love here appears as a *feeling of pleasure in power*. The man who stands at the centre of the greatest sphere says proudly: A wave of my hand and hundreds of thousands cast themselves to their deaths, or: My will is a law unto millions.

Love also manifests itself as love for money, due to avarice.

Love further manifests itself as a *feeling of pleasure in mental superiority*, on the basis of that quality of the will called desire for fame. The sphere is extended by means of the mind's children, who storm through every land and subordinate other minds to that of the father.

Here, too, friendship must be mentioned, which rests on the quality of the will called fidelity. When the relation is genuine, it effects a restricted extension of the sphere.

Finally, love also appears as *love for humanity*, which I will deal with in the Ethics.

In contrast to all of this, the individual, through envy, narrows his external sphere and puts himself in the state of hatred. Such an individual feels repelled and thrown back on himself by the apparent happiness of other individuals.

The individual's sphere is also narrowed through hatred towards distinct parts of the world: towards people above all, towards certain social classes, towards women and children, towards priests, and so on, due to respective qualities of the will.

Hatred then also appears in a characteristic form, namely as hatred of man towards himself, and I will touch on this more closely in the Ethics.

12.

Between the principal states introduced above there are many gradations; apart from these, there are many other states which, however, I pass over, since I must not dwell on particulars. What is more, we will in the Aesthetics and Ethics become acquainted with even more states which are important.

However, we have still to consider a second kind of motion of the will, which I want to call *double motions*, to differentiate them from the simple motions investigated so far.

In hatred, the individual withdraws into his innermost core. He concentrates himself, he would like to be extensionless. Now, if the hatred is very great, then it often recoils in the opposite direction, i.e., the will flows suddenly towards the periphery, not to embrace lovingly, but rather to annihilate. This motion is *wrath*, *ire*, the FUROR BREVIS. In it the individual annihilates his opponent either with words, assailing him with a torrent of invective, insults, curses; or he turns to acts of violence, which may end with death blows and murder.

In the Aesthetics and Ethics we will become acquainted with several other double motions.

13.

It remains for me to say a few words about *intoxication* and *sleep*.

Intoxication is a heightened life of the blood of which the individual grows all the more conscious the more the senses and with them the understanding slacken. Intoxication is complete in anaesthesia by means of narcotic agents (nitrous oxide, chloroform, and the like). The senses are entirely inactive and the understanding is taken out of service; in contrast, self-consciousness is a very clear mirror. With extraordinary clarity the anaesthetised person becomes conscious of his circulation; he senses distinctly how the blood races and rages and presses against his vessels as if it wanted to burst them asunder. He reflects on this and certainly thinks, but with miraculous speed.

Sleep is necessary first of all for the organism. The organism's force, which in commerce with the external world consumes itself so intensely, must be renewed and disorder in the organs must be removed. For this reason, the senses are closed off and the will, restricted entirely to its sphere and restless as ever, sets its house in order and prepares itself for new actions. A ceasefire now presides over the struggle for existence.

Sleep is also also necessary for the dæmon itself. It must from time to time become stateless in order not to despair; and it can become stateless only in deep sleep:

> Is it not true, sleep is God himself, who embraces tired men?
> **Hebbel**

And:

> Methought I heard a voice cry 'Sleep no more;
> Macbeth does murder sleep, the innocent sleep,
> Sleep that knits up the ravelled sleeve of care,
> The death of each day's life, sore labour's bath,
> Balm of hurt minds, great nature's second course,
> *Chief nourisher in life's feast.'*
> **Shakespeare**
> (Macbeth, Act II, Scene II)

14.

All states of the *will* are united by immanent philosophy in the concepts of *pleasure* and *unpleasure*. Pleasure and unpleasure are *immediate* states of the dæmon, they are whole, undivided motions of the genuine will to life or, expressed objectively, states of the blood, of the heart.

Pain and *lust*, in contrast, are *mediate* states of the will; for they rest on vivid sensations of the *organs*, which are precipitates of the blood and claim a certain independence with respect to the blood.

This distinction is important and must be noted. Here I append a few observations in the objective domain.

The states of pleasure are expansion, those of unpleasure concentration of the will. I already alluded above to the fact that the individual in the former states wants to show, from within himself and to the entire world, how blissful he is. Thus, he expresses his state with his entire body, in gestures, movements (embracing, hopping, jumping, dancing) and in particular through laughing, crying out, cheering, singing, and through language. All of this is to be attributed to that one striving of man to manifest his state and to share himself with others and, were it possible, with the entire world.

In contrast, in the states of unpleasure the individual is cast back upon himself. The spark of his eyes is extinguished, his countenance becomes serious, his limbs become motionless or are drawn together. He furrows his brow, his eyes are closed, his mouth turns mute, his hands ball themselves convulsively into fists and the man cowers, he falls into himself.

Crying, too, is worth mentioning. It is as if the receding blood no longer exerted the necessary pressure on the lachrymal ducts and these, in consequence, emptied themselves. Crying is preceded by a convulsion of the heart, and one senses immediately the flowing-back of the will towards the centre. In impotent fury, in contrast, the tears are forcefully pressed out.

Finally, I draw attention to the characteristic phenomena of light in the eyes, determined by faint or intense inner motions, and the sensations of heat and cold. The poets speak correctly of glowing, passionate, luminous, phosphorescent eyes; of a sombre fire in the eyes; of their uncanny twinkling; of blazes of fury; of a lighting up, a blazing up of the eyes. They say also that the eyes throw out sparks, that there is a storm in the eyes, and so on. Furthermore, there are many expressions which denote the cessation of these phenomena, such as "the light of the eyes has been extinguished", "the eyes have lost their fire", and "tired souls, tired eyes". In the last expression, one skips over the phenomenon and emphasises only what occasions it.

However, it must be noted that all of these phenomena in the eyes (to which the darkening of the iris, specifically of the blue iris, when the individual becomes furious also belongs) are due to modifications of the organ. The excitations of the will modify the tension of the parts of the organ (cornea, iris, pupils, etc.) such that the light is *reflected* in a manner essentially different from that in the normal state, or in other words: The internal motions of man, insofar as they reveal themselves in the eye, only modify the usual light, they are not themselves independent sources of light.

The sensations of heat and cold are very numerous. We feel an icy shudder, we are chilled; in contrast we glow, hot blazes engulf us, we burn, we melt, we seethe, the blood boils in our veins.

But we do not only have these inner feelings, our body also exhibits a modified temperature. The extremities become cold in states of unpleasure, they die off; and, on the other hand, the body, in states of pleasure or in the outwards-flowing part of a double motion like fury, exhibits greater heat. *Fever*, too, belongs here.

15.

We now leave man and descend into the animal kingdom, and specifically we concern ourselves first of all with the higher animals, those which are nearest to man, his "immature brothers".

Like man, the animal is a combination of a particular will with a particular mind.

The animal's *mind* has first and foremost the same senses as man; however, in many individuals these are keener, i.e., have a greater receptivity to impressions, than those of man. The animal's understanding is also the same. It searches for the cause of every impression and shapes that cause in accordance with its forms, space and matter. Furthermore, like man, the animal has *reason*, i.e., the capacity to conjoin or synthesise. It also has, more or less, a good memory but weak powers of imagination and of judgment, and it is to this incompleteness that the great difference existing between man and animal is to be attributed.

The first consequence of this incompleteness is that the animal combines the partial presentations of the understanding usually only into parts of Objects. Only such Objects as delineate themselves in their entirety on its retina will be apprehended as whole Objects; all others do not exist as whole objects for the animal, since its imagination is incapable of retaining *many* disappearing partial presentations. It can therefore be said that the cleverest animal, standing close to a tree, will not gain the whole image of the tree.

The animal also lacks the important conjunctions contrived by reason on the basis of à priori forms and functions. It cannot construct time and therefore lives exclusively in the present. To this fact is joined a second: that the animal only cognises such motions as are perceptible on the point of the present. The *entire course* of an Object's change of location, an imperceptible change of location, and all inner motions (developments) escape its mind. Furthermore, the animal will not be able to connect one Object's influence with the change in another, for the animal lacks general causality. The cognition of a dynamic coherence of things is, of course, entirely impossible for the animal. With the aid of memory it will cognise only the causal connection between its body and such things whose influence on its body it has already experienced—therefore the *second* causal relation introduced in the Analytics, yet fundamentally constrained. Since it also lacks substance, its world as presentation is defective and fragmentary.

Finally, the animal can form no concepts. It therefore cannot think in concepts, and its mind lacks that ever so important point which is only to be attained through thought: self-consciousness. Its consciousness expresses itself:

1) as feeling;
2) as a feeling of self (ordinary feeling of individuality).

Now, if we cannot attribute abstract thought even to the higher animals, then, in contrast, we must attribute to them a form of thought in *images*, on the basis of judgments in images. A fox caught in a trap which bites through its leg in order to free itself makes, by holding the free leg figuratively next to the other, two correct judgments and draws from them a correct conclusion: all this by means of images (without concepts), helped by immediate intuition.

The animal's faculty of reason is therefore one that has been formed one-sidedly and its mind in general is fundamentally limited. Now, since the mind is nothing more than a part of a divided motion, the remaining whole motion of the animal's will must as a result be more intense, therefore instinct must be significantly more pronounced in the animal than the dæmon is in man. And, in fact, the controlling portion of the animal is powerfully supported by instinct wherever it cannot cognise concatenated efficacies and future relations on which the animal's preservation depends. It is therefore instinct which determines when migratory birds must leave the north and which impels other animals in autumn to gather nourishment for the winter.

16.

If we turn now to the will of the animal, then its individuality as a whole, like that of man, is a closed being-for-itself or egoism.

Furthermore, like man, the animal wants to live in a particular way, i.e., it has a *character*.

PHYSICS

Now, regarding the animal's temperaments and the qualities of its will, it is clear that they must be less numerous than those of man; for the animal's mind is less perfect, and only in combination with a developed mind can the will shape itself in manifold ways, i.e., disclose itself. Therefore, in speaking of the higher animals, the correct perspective will be found by limiting their temperaments to two qualities of the will, vitality and inertia. Only with a few domestic animals whose intelligence and character have been awakened and trained through thousands of years of interaction with human beings does one encounter human temperaments, and here we have to mention the horse above all other animals.

How important this interaction with man is for animals is shown by feral horses and dogs. The latter, as Humboldt reports, often bloodthirstily attack the man in whose defence their fathers fought. In such feral animals a regression has taken place whereby the intelligence has been reduced and by this means the whole motion of the blood (instinct) has become more intense, the character simpler.

Of the qualities of the will all those shall fall away which have the human mind as a prerequisite, such as avarice, justice, resoluteness, shamefacedness, and the like. The remaining qualities, such as envy, falseness, fidelity, patience, meekness, spite, and the like are shown by monkeys, elephants, dogs, foxes, horses, most animals. Often the entire character of an animal can be described with a single quality of the will, often not even that and all that remains is the character of the individuality in general: the egoism.

The animal's capacity to feel, because of its relatively smaller nerve mass and also because of this nerve mass's cruder constitution, is weaker than that of man. The animal's sensations of pain and lust are for that reason more dampened and less intense than those of man.

Even the states of pleasure and unpleasure in the animal are weaker and less numerous than those of man; for their deepening and duration depend on abstract thought. Only animals of the highest order are familiar with the states of joy and grief. Very probably only the dog can grieve as persistently and experience joy as intensely as man.

Furthermore, despair disappears and in only a few animals will a state of expectation assume the place of hope, which presupposes the concept of the future. In contrast, every animal knows fear, for animals in general are cowardly. The animal is only courageous when it has instinctively decided in favour of extended individuality (males fighting over females, defence of the brood). The dog alone is courageous out of faithfulness and in so being appears to be the noblest of animals.

Finally, hatred and love are manifested by all animals more or less distinctly. Love appears as sexual love (*heat*) and, because it is rooted in the life of the blood, and instinct is much more intense than the dæmon, is a wilder and more exclusive state with animals than with man. In love, the feeling of life attains its highest level. The body bristles, the motions become livelier and the intense inner arousal is propagated as sound. Birds sing, cluck, whistle, trill; cattle bellow; cats cry; foxes bark; deer bleat; reindeer beckon; a stag in heat raises a loud cry audible in the distance. The excitement manifests itself further in the sultry, rolling eyes, in the unceasing movement of the ears, in stamping with the feet and in digging up the earth with the antlers or, as the case may be, with the horns. The animal in heat barely acknowledges danger and often forgets hunger, thirst, and sleep.

Love then also appears as the feeling of pleasure in power. Bull and ram, cock and drake move with a certain pride within their families.

Hatred shows itself as disinclination, indeed as enmity of the sexes after copulation and, on the basis of egoism (for a single quality of the will can seldom support hatred) as hatred towards the whole environment or, when existence is at stake, towards individuals.

Like man, so too the animal transforms the normal motion into all of the other states out of its own force. Heat is the most aroused state.

The further one descends in the animal kingdom, the simpler does the individual will appear, owing to the increasingly unfavourable relation of the intelligence to the will and owing to the ever simpler mind. Entire senses are lacking, the forms of the understanding atrophy, and the understanding's function is solicited ever more infrequently, and finally the higher faculties of cognition fall away entirely.

17.

We enter now the silent kingdom of plants. No sensibility, i.e., no presentation, no feeling, no feeling of self, no self-consciousness: these are the characteristics by which the plant is distinguished from the animal.

The plant has a *resultant* motion. It is two *whole* partial motions which join together into a resultant motion. The one partial motion has not, as with the animal, divided itself again, but has remained whole, and for this reason the plant has no sensibility and is barren of all the phenomena which accompany sensibility.

Plant irritability therefore still contains *sensibility*, so to speak, and is thus essentially different from animal irritability. It reacts *immediately* to external stimulus and in the process is actuated by the original residual whole motion.

If we call presentation to our aid, then the *sap* is the genuine will of the plant. But it is not the objectification of the entire will. Roots, stems, leaves, and reproductive organs are excretions of the sap and, with the sap, form the objectification of the plant's entire will. The great difference between plant and animal lies in the fact that the sap immediately actuates the organs, just as the blood actuates the brain, while the remaining organs of the animal could not function at all through the mere actuation of the blood. With these organs, the combination of nerve and muscle is necessary first of all, and only by this means, as was explained above, can the blood effect the entire motion.

18.

The plant is an individual will to life and is a closed being-for-itself. It wants life in a very particular way, i.e., it has a *character*. But this character is very simple. It does not separate out into qualities of the will but, understood from within, is for all plants a blind urge, growth of a particular intensity. In contrast, considered from without, it shows impressive character of its own or, in other words, it shows us its character as an Object: it makes a show of it.

In plants only three *states* can be distinguished which correspond to the normal state, to love and to hatred in animals, namely: *growth*, *blossoming*, and *wilting*. Under wilting I here understand *concentration*.

In the state of blossoming the plant has attained its highest life. It "glows and shines" and the majority of plants, in the urge to extend their sphere even further, exude fragrance. It is as if they wanted to inform the entire world of their bliss; yet this comparison presupposes consciousness, which we must quite decisively deny the plant. What speech is for man, and sound for the animal, that is fragrance for the plant.

In this regard I want to mention that the deep arousal of the plant in the state of blossoming very often makes itself known in an elevation of its temperature, which in individual cases is downright astonishing. So, for example, the blossom of *Arum cordifolium* at an ambient temperature of 21°C exhibits a warmth of 45°C (Burdach I, 395).

In the state of wilting the plant narrows its sphere. (One can consider the bending back of the filaments after fertilisation as analogous to animal hatred after copulation.) The filaments, the petals, the leaves wilt; the fruit falls off the plant and the idea of the plant concentrates itself in the sap.

With yearling plants and others such as the sago palm, *Agave americana*, and *Furcraea longaeva*, wilting is identical with dying off. In these instances, the idea of the plant concentrates itself entirely in the *fruit*.

The states of the plant's will, as all states of the individual in general, are due to the self-actuated transformation of its normal motion, i.e., a transformation effected out of its own force.

To be sure, the life of the plant, owing to its lack of sensibility, is a dream-life; however, precisely because of this it is extraordinarily intense. Only ostensibly is it peaceful and gentle. Think of the effusive fecundity which reveals the intense drive of the plant to maintain itself in existence; and of the famous experiment of Hales, according to which the grapevine's sap flows out with a force five times stronger than that with which the blood moves in the great crural artery of the horse.

19.

We now enter the inorganic realm, the realm of the inorganic or chemical ideas, whose distinguishing feature is *undivided* motion.

The chemical idea, like all individual wills, is a closed being-for-itself. The genuine individuality in the inorganic realm is the *whole* idea. Since, however, every part has the same essence as the whole, so every closed sphere of a homogeneous chemical force encountered in nature is an individual.

The chemical idea wants life in a particular way, i.e., it has a *character*. The same character, grasped from within, is a ceaseless, simple, blind urge. All activities of the chemical idea are to be attributed to this one urge. It reveals itself clearly, like that of the plant, in its externalities: it leaves a complete impression in the Object.

Nothing can be more absurd than to deny a chemical idea *life*. In the same moment that a piece of iron, for example, lost its inner motion, which is the sole distinguishing feature of life, it would not simply disintegrate but would actually become nothing.

20.

Now, chemical ideas are firstly the so-called elemental substances such as oxygen, nitrogen, iron, gold, potassium, calcium, and so on—pure, without mixture. Then we have all pure compounds of elemental substances with each other, such as carbon dioxide, water, hydrogen sulphide, ammonia, iron oxide, manganese oxide, and the combinations of these with each other, such as sulphate calk, potassium chromate, nitrate; therefore, all simple substances, acids, bases, and simple salts are particular ideas.

Particular ideas are also those compounds which, at the same (percentage) composition, show different characteristics, and which have been called polymeric substances. Thus, pentathionic acid (S_5O_5) is essentially different from disulphur dioxide (S_2O_2), although sulphur and oxygen appear together in the same percentwise proportion in both compounds.

Furthermore, the organic chemical compounds are autonomous ideas, therefore the radicals and their compounds, such as aethyl ($C_2H_5 = Ae$) and aethyl oxide (AeO), aethyl iodide (AeI), sulphuric aether ($AeOSO_3$), as well as the polymeric organic substances such as aldehyde ($C_4H_6O_2$) and acetic aether ($C_8H_8O_4$).

Finally, all double salts and the conserved remains of organisms, such as bone, wood, and so on, are particular ideas because they are particular chemical compounds.

In contrast, mixtures as such are not particular ideas.

Within this framework which we have given to the inorganic realm are contained not merely the chemical preparations; it is no framework for the chemical formulas alone; rather, it encompasses all the individuals of inorganic nature. It would therefore be false, for example, not to separate aragonite and calcite, which have an entirely different crystal structure; for each difference in the Object points to a difference in the thing-in-itself, and the particular ideas are to be defined according to such deviations too.

I conclude this general part with the observation that it is quite irrelevant for immanent philosophy whether the number of simple chemical substances and their compounds will be multiplied or diminished as science progresses. The philosopher is not permitted to constrain and bind the natural sciences. His task is merely: to sift through the material gathered by natural researchers and to bring it under general perspectives. He must only define the chemical ideas, without caring whether the Objects united under particular concepts are multiplied or diminished.

21.

We must now, on the basis of three quite definite *states*, classify the Objects of the inorganic realm and then investigate the character of the Objects of each class.

All bodies are either *solid*, *liquid*, or *gaseous*.

Common to all is *extension* and *impenetrability*, which means nothing more than that every inorganic body is an *individual* will to life. It has a sphere of force and asserts itself in life, which it wills.

The *solid bodies* exhibit *heaviness*, i.e., they have a principal striving: to reach the centre of the earth. Each individual of the inorganic realm wants to be in the centre of the earth: that is its general character. Its specific character is the *intensity* with which it asserts this striving, its *cohesion*, or also its *specific heaviness* (specific weight).

In exercising this striving, which the solid body always has and never loses, it exhibits *inertia*.

Every solid body, furthermore, is more or less extensible or compressible. In accordance with this one determines its *extensibility* and *compressibility*, its *hardness*, *brittleness*, *elasticity* and *porosity*—in short, its so-called physical qualities, which are in no regard ideas or autonomous forces, but only determine the essence of chemical ideas more closely. They are read off from the Object (the thing-in-itself that has passed through the subjective forms) and are justifiably related to the foundation of phenomena. Independently of a chemical idea they are not even thinkable: they stand and fall with the idea.

A few of these characteristics are based on a modification of the aggregate state, which can likewise be called the normal state. Extensibility through heat implies merely that a body, through foreign excitation, has transitioned into a *more aroused* state, into a more intense inner motion, and seeks to extend its sphere within that motion. The body has not become warmer because a part of a particular idea, called heat, has in the most miraculous way penetrated into the body's individuality, become the master within it, or even entered into a combination with it; rather, it has become warmer because it has, upon foreign stimulation certainly, but out of its very own force, modified its motion and in this new motion now makes on the observer's sense of touch an impression different from before.

On the other hand, a body compresses itself and becomes smaller because either the foreign stimulation has ceased or the body, affecting other bodies, loses its more aroused motion. It leaves the more agitated state and returns to the normal one, and we now say it has become colder because in its new state it also makes a particular, new impression on our senses.

The *gaseous bodies* show a striving, a motion, which is the exact opposite of heaviness. While the solid body strives only towards the centre of the earth or, expressed in entirely general terms, towards a particular, ideal point that lies outside of itself, the gaseous bodies want to disperse ceaselessly in all directions. This motion is called *absolute expansion*. It forms, as mentioned, the direct opposite of heaviness, and I must therefore reject decisively the claim that gases are subject to heaviness. That they are heavy I do not deny; this, however, is due, firstly, to the fact that they have an effect in all directions, therefore also where their weight is being determined and, secondly, to the coherence of all things, which does not permit uninhibited extension.

Between the solid and the gaseous bodies lie the *liquid* bodies. Liquid exhibits a single undivided motion, which is to be defined as a flowing apart in the striving towards an ideal centre that lies outside of itself. This motion is restricted expansion or also modified heaviness.

The various strivings of solid, liquid, and gaseous bodies manifest themselves most clearly when they are impeded. Thus, a stone only presses on its surface because it has but the one direct striving towards the centre of the earth; in contrast, a liquid presses, so far as it can, upon all parts of the vessel because it has an effect in all directions which lie beneath its surface; finally, a gas completely fills out a closed balloon and stretches it until it is taut because its striving presses in all directions.

22.

If we compare the so-called aggregate states with each other according to their intensity, then every man will immediately describe the motion of the gaseous idea as the most intense and most powerful. If we speak of uprisings, wars, revolutions, then seldom will we fail to weave such words as "storm", "explosion", "outbreak" into our speech. Seldomer will we invoke the imagery of liquids and speak, for instance, of the force of deluges, of overflowing mountain streams, and of downpours. The efficacy of solid bodies is not invoked at all. Likewise, we speak of outbreaks of fury, volcanic eruptions of individual passion and also say: to burst, to explode with rage.

The dogged pursuit of a single objective is very sensibly compared with heaviness, the flexibility of a character with waves, individualistic conduct with steam; and, just as sensibly, we speak of the solidity of an individual in the good sense, of his inertia in the critical sense, of his multifacetedness and capriciousness. The French say: *une femme vaporeuse* and the Italians often apply the word *vaporoso* to a character that pursues no particular objectives, wants this today and that tomorrow and nothing sincerely.

According to degree of intensity, therefore, the gaseous state is the most intense, followed by the liquid state, and the least intense is the solid state.

23.

The aggregate state is the normal state of an inorganic body. This normal state can be modified by every chemical idea, upon external inducement, without being entirely lost. The state of a glowing piece of iron is one essentially different from that of a piece at the usual temperature, and yet the glowing iron has not left its aggregate state. Within this limit, however, its motion is more intense than before. The same applies to liquids and gases, for example, to boiling water and compressed air.

Now, apart from these normal states and their modifications we find in the inorganic realm two more: the *positive-* and the *negative-electric* state.

The chemical idea in the normal state is indifferent, i.e., it exhibits neither positive nor negative electricity. If, however, it is stimulated in a particular manner, then it transforms its state into the positive- or negative-electric state.

If the excitation brings about an expansion of the individuality, then the force is positive-electric; otherwise it is negative-electric, and for this reason, in my view, the formation of chemical compounds is quite unjustly attributed to affinity or elective affinity. The process resembles more closely an act of rape than a loving union. The one individuality wants a new motion, wants another life in a third; the other struggles with all its power against this, but is conquered. In any case, a chemical compound is the product of *procreation*. Both individuals live on in what has been procreated, but bound together such that what has been procreated exhibits quite different characteristics. The simple chemical compound is something procreated, which can in turn procreate. In this way the salts arise, and specifically the base is the genuine procreative principle, because it always behaves electropositively towards the acid.

That during the compounding of chemical ideas something takes place which, were it accompanied by consciousness, we would call rape and violent subjugation, not a mutual longing search, seems to me to be confirmed by the fact that the same force is in one moment positive-, in another negative-electric, depending on whether it plays the main role in procreation. Thus, in procreative moments sulphur behaves positively with respect to oxygen, negatively with respect to iron. When the calk of chalk combines with salt acid and carbonic acid escapes, then one may speak—not unfittingly, I would contend—of a liberation.

If two metals touch each other and become oppositely charged, then this of course is not an instance of procreation, rather each individual exhibits only a large excitation, as with dog and cat.

That the formation of chemical compounds is only possible in the excited electric state of the bodies is clearly evident from the fact that by cooling, therefore by annihilation of the necessary stimulus, the formation of compounds can be impeded. The one force does not attain the energy for attack, the other does not attain the resistive capability and both therefore remain indifferent.

The decomposition of chemical compounds through heat is due to the fact that the external stimulus has an uneven effect on the bound forces. The suppressed force enters a more excited and more powerful state than the previously stronger one and can now liberate itself. The same thing takes place during decomposition by means of electric current.

The three principal modifications of elective affinity:

1) Simple: $Fe + ClH = FeCl + H$
2) Double: $FeO + ClH = FeCl + HO$
3) Predisposing: $Fe + HO + SO_3 = FeOSO_3 + H$

can be explained simply based on the desire of every electropositive force to have a particular new motion or mode of existence. In the last case iron decomposes water because iron wants to be compounded as an oxide with sulphuric acid, and the sulphuric acid stimulates it to the decomposition of water.

Finally, a further expansion of individuality takes place through simple attraction, i.e., the individual expresses *adhesion*. Compounding through adhesion is the inorganic analogue of the expanded external sphere of man.

24.

If we now look back at the path we have so far taken in the Physics, then we everywhere see—no matter which way we turn—a single principle, the fact of inner and outer experience: *individual* will to life and its *states*.

The individuals which belong to our empirical world divide themselves initially into four large groups according to the particular type of their motion. Then, within those groups, they are further differentiated from each other:

a) within the inorganic realm and plant kingdom, grasped from within by analogy, they are differentiated through greater or lesser intensity of drive, an intensity which reveals itself externally in physical qualities or, as the case may be, in a great diversity of forms;
b) within the animal kingdom and in man, they are differentiated through greater or lesser unfolding of the will (qualities of the will) and of the mind (above all, of the auxiliary faculties of reason).

All individuals are in ceaseless motion, and each motion evokes a particular state. All states are modifications of a normal state, which are brought about by the will out of its own force, and only upon foreign stimulation.

The elements of the sequences:

sexual love – heat – blossoming – positive electricity;
human hatred – animal hatred – wilting – negative electricity,

are not identical, though they are arguably very closely related to each other.

25.

We have now to consider the life of the chemical ideas, then the procreation and life and death of the organic ideas.

The simple chemical ideas exist, and according to all observations that have been made, they neither modify their essence nor can they be annihilated. However, since they can be compounded with each other they are, as materialism says, caught in a ceaseless (not eternal) cycle. Compounds arise and disappear, arise again and disappear again: it is an endless exchange.

If we hold only the compounds in view, then we can arguably speak of procreation, life and death in the inorganic realm as well.

If one simple chemical idea is compounded with another, then a new idea with a character of its own arises. This new idea, in turn, has procreative power; it can, together with other ideas to which it stands in an elective affinity, form a new idea which in turn has a character of its own. Let us take an acid, a base, and a salt—say, SO_3, FeO, and $FeOSO_3$. Iron oxide is neither iron nor oxygen; sulphuric acid is neither sulphur nor oxygen; sulphuric acid iron oxide is neither sulphuric acid nor iron oxide; and, nevertheless, the individual ideas are contained entirely in each compound. The salt, however, no longer has any procreative force.

In the inorganic realm, procreation is fusion, i.e., the individuals are merged entirely into what is procreated. Only by temporarily sacrificing themelves in their entirety, or better: only by the one temporarily sacrificing itself in its entirety and the other being entirely sacrificed can the former swing itself onto a higher level, i.e., give itself a different motion, which is what everything comes down to with procreation.

The life of a chemical force is its persistence in a particular motion, or, if the circumstances are favourable, in the expression of the longing for a new motion. This longing is immediately realised if a stronger individual does not prevent it (just as the touching of copper with iron makes use of the former in such a way that it cannot be compounded with the carbonic acid of the air into carbonic acid copper oxide). This persistence is made possible only by constant resistance, and already here the truth that life is a struggle becomes obvious.

Finally, the death of the chemical compound manifests as a return of the simple substances bound within it to their original motion.

26.

In the organic realm, sexual procreation in general and the sexual procreation of man in particular is the most important, and for this reason we want to consider the latter alone.

A man and a woman, each with a particular character and a particular mind, copulate. If fertilisation occurs, then one individual (or more) arises with the predisposition to a particular character and a particular mind.

That the man's seed fertilises the woman's egg, although the seed cannot get directly into the ovaries, is a fact. The egg and the seed are secretions from the innermost core of the individual and contain, like an after-image, all of its qualities. Thus each procreator enters into the copulation, which proceeds with the greatest arousal. Now, the *state* in which each procreator finds him- or herself determines in the second place the type of fruit, and this is a very important factor; for according as the woman or the man is more passionate, more firm, more energetic in copulating, the new individual will manifest more of the individuality of the woman or of the man. It must also be kept in mind that the woman, ablaze with passionate love for the man, will essentially heighten his influence, just as the man, conversely, out of great love for the woman, can leave the field open for her determining activity.

In this way certain qualities of the will of the procreators are strengthened, weakened, or completely bound; others are transmitted unmodified to the child and at the same time determine the child's mental abilities. Yet the constitution of the germ is not absolutely invariant; for now the individual is carried in the mother's body, under the direct influence of which it remains for quite some time. And what cannot happen in this period! Heavier physical labour or more diligent care, disinclination or heightened inclination towards the man, mental stimulation, love for another man, sickness, the most intense but brief arousal, or an enduring state of fever through wars, revolutions: all of this, if it occurs, will not flow past the embryo without leaving a trace but will affect it more gently or more strongly. It may be assumed that the German people after the French reign of terror and the French people after the great revolution and the Napoleonic Wars acquired a generally modified character; the German more determination, the Frenchman more inconstancy, and both more mental excitability; and it may also be assumed that this is to be attributed not to the state of the procreators during copulation alone, but also to the influences during the woman's pregnancy.

The new individual is nothing other than a *rejuvenation of the parents*, a living-on, a new motion of the parents. Nothing can be in it that was not in the parents, and the poet is right when he says of himself:

> From father I have my stature,
> My earnest way of living;
> From mother my cheerful nature,
> And love of storytelling.
> Forefather charmed the prettiest girls,

> Sometimes that spirit's with me;
> Foremother treasured gold and jewels,
> Sometimes that love can sway me.
> Such elements are intertwined
> In every individual.
> What is it then in me, or mine,
> That can be called original?
>
> **Goethe**

That the character traits, stature, hair and eye colour of the grandparents here and there break through in the children finds its explanation in the fact that a constrained quality of the will, through favourable circumstances, can become free again and reveal itself.

These ever so simple relations, which only those who do not want to see fail to see, are forcefully turned by many into something thoroughly mysterious, so that one might reluctantly cry out with Goethe:

> Is the world not already sufficiently full with riddles, that one should also make riddles of the simplest phenomena?

In one moment the inconceivable, powerful species is supposed to become active during the business of procreation, in the next an extramundane principle is supposed to determine the nature of the child, and then the character of the newborn is supposed to be utterly without qualities. The most superficial observation must lead one to reject these chimeras and to recognise that the parents live on in their children.

On the diversity of the parents' states during copulation, in which age also has an influence, rests the diversity of the children. The one is more intense and more alert, the other gentler and dreamier; the one more prudent, the other more stupid; the one more selfish, the other more generous. It is not at all miraculous that children occasionally exhibit characteristics entirely different from their parents', because the neutralisation and alteration of qualities of the will can, in some circumstances, become very pronounced.

If we enter the animal and plant kingdoms, then we will find that the farther we go, the narrower the difference between child and parent becomes; because the individual will spreads out in ever fewer qualities, the number of its states becomes ever smaller and the states themselves ever simpler. It is then usually said that the individual has only the character of the species, from which it is to be understood that the individuals of a species are all similar. That the procreated things are nothing other than the rejuvenated parents is clearly on display with some insects, which die immediately after copulation or, as the case may be, after laying their eggs; and it is even very clearly on display with the annual plants and those perennial plants which die off after seed formation.

27.

The individual therefore enters life as a particular individuality. As I already said above, we must attribute to him, alongside prominent qualities of the will, also the germs of all other qualities. They can wither or unfold themselves. Apart from that we must also give to the individual's mind a capacity for education that is not too scantily apportioned; for though one may never succeed in making a genius from a simpleton through the most careful rearing, still the powerful influence of circumstance on the higher mental powers, causing them either to wither or awaken, is not to be misjudged.

The world takes on the new individual and trains him up. He is initially ravenous will to life, an intense simple compulsion; but he soon expresses his inborn individuality, exhibits individual character, and immediately other individuals impose on him in a restrictive way. He has an insatiable thirst for existence and wants, in accordance with his particular nature, to slake that thirst; but the others have a similar thirst and similar striving. Out of this arises the struggle for existence, in which the individuality develops, hardens or weakens itself, and is either victorious or succumbs, i.e., wrests for itself a freer motion or becomes more bound. The inborn individuality metamorphoses into an acquired individuality, which under certain circumstances can be identical with the former and to which—though within narrow limits—we must concede the capacity for further modification, as I will show in the Ethics.

28.

Every organism dies, i.e., its idea is destroyed. The type, which during life, persisting amidst change, assimilated to itself the simple chemical ideas which constituted it and then excreted them again, itself disintegrates.

Standing before a corpse, the immanent philosopher has to pose the question to Nature: Is the idea annihilated or does it live on? Nature will always answer: It is dead and it lives on. It is dead if the individual has not rejuvenated himself through procreation, and it lives on if in his time he looked upon his own children.

Not only does this answer satisfy the *immanent philosopher*, but for some whose character must be taken for a simple fact—such as that of the domineering, or of the ambitious, or of the lustful man (who cannot take three steps without falling into a brothel)—the first part of the answer even offers the most comforting of all comforting words. Some day it shall do so for all.

29.

Our earth is a small collective unity in an immeasurably large but finite sphere of force, the universe. The probable constitution of our planet, the constitution of the universe, and finally the motion of the celestial bodies shall now concern us.

The deeper one penetrates into the earth's interior, the greater becomes the heat, i.e., the more intense becomes the motion of the chemical ideas that we encounter. Hence, already at a depth of only thirty-four miles no metal can persist any longer in a solid state and becomes liquid. From this we may conclude that at a particular distance from the periphery the liquid state can likewise no longer be preserved and the core of the earth is filled with gases, and specifically with extremely compressed gases, upon which everything liquid floats. The liquid part would then be contained by the solid crust of the earth.

This hypothesis, proposed by Franklin, must be adopted as the best by immanent philosophy; for it is clear that our earth, indeed the entire universe, can *persist* only by virtue of the fact that the striving of every chemical idea *never* finds complete satisfaction. Even an inch, a line away from the ideal mathematical centre of the earth, a solid or liquid body would still have to fall; for it wants only to be in this centre: that constitutes its entire essence. Now, if such a body succeeded in attaining the centre of the earth, then it would have lost its striving, and thus its entire efficacy, its entire essence, and it would in the moment of its arrival actually become nothing.

In contrast, the centre of the earth stands in an entirely different relation to the gaseous ideas. These ideas have no relationship to it at all, for they always strive in *all* directions, never in a single one. If therefore a gas is located in the centre of the earth, then it continues to carry out its activity, for its striving has not been fulfilled.

From this it is evident that if we had first to create our earth from the material at hand we could not find any other arrangement than the one existing, i.e., we would have to place compressed gases on the inside of the sphere, solid bodies at its surface, and between both a sea of molten chemical ideas.

Thus immanent philosophy—which has a single principle which is found innermost in self-consciousness and is thoroughly confirmed by nature: the individual will to life—agrees on one hand with the empirical fact that the temperature increases the deeper one penetrates into the earth, and on the other hand with the Kantian-Laplacian theory. This agreement makes Franklin's hypothesis very convincing indeed.

30.

If we look at the universe, the immeasurably large but finite universe, then a single sphere of force shows itself to us, i.e., we gain the concept of a collective unity of innumerable individual ideas, of which each has its effect on every other and simultaneously experiences the efficacy of all others. This is the dynamic coherence of the universe, which we cognise with the form of general causality extended to community. Now since, on one hand, our experience has up until now not been able to overstep a particular sphere and is essentially limited and, on the other, the atmosphere of our earth shows all the phenomena of limited activity, we must assume a dynamic continuum and posit chemical ideas—about whose nature, however, we can make no judgment—as existing between the individual celestial bodies. The best we can do is to subsume them under the familiar concept of *aether* while staunchly repudiating the assumption that it is imponderable.

We have, above, already attributed heat and electricity to the *state of ideas* and have seen that they are only phenomena of motion; for motion is the sole predicate of the individual will, and the most diverse states of a particular will are merely modifications of its normal motion. There is neither *free* heat nor *free* electricity, also no bound (latent) heat. If a body is warm and it loses its heat to another body, then this only means that it heightens the state of the other and, in acting as a stimulus, has lost force, i.e., has weakened its own state. Latent heat expresses on the one hand only the capability (the native force) of the will to modify its state upon a corresponding stimulus; and on the other hand it expresses the return of the will from a stimulated state to its normal one. Like heat and electricity, magnetism, too, is no transcendent essence lurking behind things, which in one moment falls upon them and brings them under its yoke, in another leaves them again *cavalièrement* and withdraws into its abode (an abode which could only be characterised as an "everywhere and nowhere"), and the same applies to light.

Light is nothing other than the very intense motion of ideas become visible, or the impression (objectified by the Subject) of an intense motion upon the visual sense. The recognition that light is not the perceived oscillations of an aether surrounding all bodies, but is the body itself, gains ever more ground and will become an uncontested scientific truth. This view must have a completely convincing effect upon all those who cannot think of the world as anything but finite and, contemplating the dynamic coherence of countless things with the most diverse strivings, recognise that everything is caught in ceaseless action and reaction and gain a universe of the most violent tension. Wherever within the universe a motion takes place, no thing will remain untouched by that motion: it will suffer the influence of that motion and react to it.

Now, the sun is for our system a centre, from which is propagated in all directions the most intense motion, the sources of which are to be sought in combustion processes of the utmost intensity, in the violent impact exerted by cosmic masses plunging into the sun, and in the contracting of the sun itself.

When, however, a motion which is propagated on all sides can modify the state of our air at a distance of 20 million miles in such a way that it gives rise to an impression on the sense of sight which, objectified, is white blinding light; when, furthermore, that same motion makes, in the tropics, an impression on the sense of touch that, objectified, is a blazing heat that almost annihilates us; then it must be a motion of such violent force that we lack every measure to ascertain its magnitude; for in the way in which our organs react to these stimuli we as little find a standard as we find one for the immense air pressure suffered by our bodies in the playful ease with which we move our limbs.

From this we conclude:

1) that sunlight on our earth is only a perceived characteristic motion of the air (perhaps only of its oxygen), which motion in the end, if one skips over the links in the chain, has its basis in the motion resulting from the processes on the sun—just as sound is only a characteristic motion of the air perceived by the ear;
2) that, when one has in view merely the violence with which the original motion is propagated, one can *figuratively* call sunlight an extraordinarily great *force*.

31.

According to the Newtonian theory, the earth is moved around the sun by two different forces: by an original, the centrifugal force, and by the attractive force of the sun. The former alone would push the earth onwards in one straight line or another; the latter alone would attract the earth towards the sun in a straight line. However, through the combined effect of both forces, the earth describes a curved line about the sun.

These forces were simply postulated by Newton and taken as given. Their essence is completely unknown and we know only the laws according to which they have their effect. The law of inertia is:

> A body which is once in motion will without the influence of external forces continue its motion with unchanging velocity, in unchanged direction, until that motion is abolished by external hindrances.

And the law of gravitation is:

> The attraction of every body is related directly to its mass and indirectly to the square of its distance, or: the attraction of a body is the same as its mass divided by the square of its distance.

It is beyond all doubt that all of celestial mechanics, all motions of the heavenly bodies can be explained according to these two laws. Whatever the true causes of the motion may be, they must have their effect according to these laws.

What, however, is of extraordinary interest to us is precisely the causes of the motion, and attempting at least to discover its ultimate basis is a task that immanent philosophy must not reject. The attempt in itself will be of service even if it does not succeed. Posterity will hardly be able to believe that we had so long contented ourselves with the laws and had not investigated the true forces. When, however, they consider how in the relevant period everything inexplicable was imputed to transcendent essences, their astonishment will cease.

That immanent philosophy must not content itself with the two unknowable forces, those of attraction and repulsion, is clear. It must discard them as it discards all other apparent forces of nature which are supposed to be everywhere and nowhere and which, for the purpose of revealing their essence, quarrel over so-called objective matter; it must discard them as it discards the extrasensory species of things that is supposed to live behind the real individuals and fill now the one, now the other with its overwhelming power; it must discard them as it discards every simple unity that is supposed to exist in, beside, or behind nature—in short, it must discard them as it discards everything that can becloud our view of the world, confuse our judgment about the world, and abrogate the purity of the immanent domain.

The "first impulse" from which the astronomers derive the tangential force must straight away arouse the most serious concerns in the mind of every clear thinker; for they conceive that impulse: as the *external* impetus of a *foreign* force. To immanent philosophy, in contrast, the first impulse presents no difficulties, because it does not have to attribute it to a foreign force but can derive it from the *first motion* of which all motions that were, are, and will be are merely continuations. This first motion is the *disintegration of the transcendent unity into the immanent multiplicity*, a *transformation of essence*. When the simple premundane unity (i.e., absolute rest and the transcendent domain) perished, multiplicity (i.e., motion and the immanent domain), the world arose. The motion which every individual will then had was a first impulse, but not a foreign one; for though we may never be able to explain the nature of the premundane unity from the essence of the individual will, it is yet certain that the essence of the unity, though modified, is present in this world, and motion, the sole predicate of the individual will, arose from *within*, it did not settle upon the will from *without*. On this basis one may then conceive, with the aid of the Kantian-Laplacian theory, the motion of a complete earth.

Not so the astronomers. For them, as stated, the first impulse is the effect of a foreign force. Supposing, however, that we had contented ourselves with this blatant *petitio principii*, then we would be immediately startled to attention by the question which Littrow captures in the words:

Since the bodies, as we assume, cannot move themselves without the effect of an external force, how are they then, according to the same assumption, supposed to maintain themselves in this motion without external force?

Here is a difficulty that can only be resolved when we place the impulse within the essence of the body itself and either make that impulse itself into a force having a constant effect or allow it to be *continually maintained* by means of a demonstrable foreign force that likewise has a constant effect.

Just like the first impulse by means of a foreign force, *gravitation* too cannot withstand a critical investigation. It is the extension of the heaviness so familiar to us all into universal heaviness. As we have seen above, heaviness is not to be sought outside of the solid and liquid bodies, but inside them. It is their inner drive and only expresses the fact that every solid and liquid body wants to be at the earth's centre. The intensity of this drive, which objectively constitutes its specific heaviness, is the body's special character.

The physicists and astronomers claim the very opposite; in doing so, they turn the matter on its head and tie themselves up in the greatest contradictions, as I will now show.

Firstly, they are forced to dissolve heaviness from bodies, to make it into a force foreign to them which has its effect on them from outside and compels them to obey it. Since, moreover, it is not conceivable that this mystic force should, at a distance of only a line from the earth's centre, cease to have its effect, the physicists must therefore also place the seat of this force in the earth's centre, and this centre is necessarily extensionless. "He that is able to receive it, let him receive it."

Let us suppose we were satisfied with this, then we could certainly explain the real phenomena on our earth and the hypothetical ones within it, or in other words: for simple heaviness the seat of the attractive force at the centre of the earth is sufficient. However, the issue changes immediately when one transitions from heaviness to general heaviness, i.e., to the force of attraction in our solar system. Now the mass of the attractive celestial body becomes an element of the attractive force, which demands a sufficient explanation. There the seat of the force in the ideal centre of the world body is no longer sufficient. In their embarrassment, the astronomers do not pause long to think. They simply do away with the seat of the attractive force outside of the bodies and displace it into the entire sphere of force of those bodies.

This is an act of confusion. On earth, heaviness is not supposed to inhere in the body; in the solar system, in contrast, the heaviness is supposed to lie in the bodies.

This obvious contradiction perplexes every thinking person. Even Euler, in his *Letters to a German Princess*, found fault with gravitation; he sought to explain it on the basis of a burst of the aether upon the bodies, "which would be more rational and more appropriate to those people who love clear and conceivable principles." At the same time, he speaks of "a characteristic inclination and desire of the bodies," to which I shall soon return.

Even Bessel could not ally himself with gravitation, although not for the reason that it is contradictory in itself, but because it could not explain to him processes in the light cone of Halley's comet:

The core of the comet and its emanations gave the appearance of a burning rocket whose tail is being turned sideways by the wind. (Humboldt, *Cosmos*, Vol. 1)

Bessel concluded from numerous measurements and theoretical observations:

that the emanating light cone *deviated* considerably to the left as well as to the right of the line to the sun, but that it always *returned* to this line in order to pass over to the other side of it.

From this he convinced himself:

of the existence of a polar force, of the effect of a force that is significantly different from gravitation or the usual attractive force of the sun, because those parts of the comet that form the tail experience the effects of a *repulsive force of the solar body*.

Thus, whereas the laws of the tangential and attractive forces are correct and do indeed explain all motions (even those of Halley's comet, as shall be shown), the forces themselves must be decisively discarded by philosophy. But what should we then put in their place?

I remind the reader that heaviness is the drive, or as Euler says, the "inclination and curiosity" of solid and liquid bodies to be in the centre of the earth. In contrast to this, expansion is the inclination and curiosity of the gaseous bodies to extend themselves on all sides, or also their shyness of any particular point. We have for compelling reasons had to declare Franklin's hypothesis about the earth's constitution to be the best, and have adopted it. If we place it at the foundation of our attempt to explain the earth's motion about the sun, then our earth is a collective unity of individual wills which have diametrically opposed strivings. Furthermore, every individual exercises its striving with a particular intensity. With such a constitution, with such varied motions of the individuals there must however arise in every moment a resultant motion of the whole, which we want to characterise as curiosity towards the centre of the sun.

On the other hand, we have seen that sunlight is nothing other than the intense motion of our air become visible, which is to be traced back to forceful expansions of the gases surrounding the sun, and we therefore called light, figuratively, an extraordinarily great force. It is clear that it can only be a repulsive force because we are dealing here with the state of gases, the essence of which consists precisely in absolute expansion. They always want to spread themselves out, in all directions, and we have to imagine light as the appearance of a force which, as with a gunpowder explosion, in the forceful striving outwards from ideal centres exercises the most intense repulsive pressure.

If we summarise these observations, then the elliptical motion of the earth around the sun would be the result of two motions: of the motion of the earth towards the centre of the sun and of the force of repulsion of the sun or, figuratively, of the light.

The roles would therefore be completely exchanged. Whereas in the Newtonian theory the earth, in consequence of its tangential force, flees from the sun and the sun, in consequence of its force of attraction, wants to draw the earth towards itself; according to our hypothesis, the earth wants to fall into the sun and the sun repels it.

Furthermore, the laws for the two motions would have to be formulated as follows:

1) the striving of the earth towards the sun varies directly as the intensity of its drive and inversely as the square of its distance;
2) the repulsion of the sun varies directly as the intensity of the expansion it effects and inversely as the square of its distance.

The congruity of the laws according to which the light and the attraction have their effects astonishes all who concern themselves with nature. Here is a hypothesis which derives the motion of the heavenly bodies from two forces whose efficacy partly finds its expression in one and the same law, to be precise, in the law of light and of gravitation. At the same time, all absurdities fall away, for these forces are no metaphysical, mystical essences, but only strivings of the sole real thing in the world, of the individual will or, as the case may be, of dynamically cohering individuals. The rotation of the earth upon its axis and the progressive motion of its centre connected therewith—motions which are only natural consequences of the first impulse (of the collapsing of the unity into multiplicity)—are simply *maintained* by means of the repulsive force of the sun: this is the tangential force that continues to have its effect constantly; in contrast, the earth wants at the same time to fall into the sun: that is gravitation. Both effect the rotation of the earth about the sun in a curved line.

The variable speed with which the earth moves about the sun can, furthermore, be explained in the most unforced manner: for the closer the earth is to the sun, the greater is its curiosity towards the sun's centre, but at the same time the greater is the sun's repulsive force, and vice versa. The greater, however, the sides of the force parallelogram are, the greater is the diagonal and vice versa.

In this way the mentioned peculiar motion of Halley's comet is also adequately explained, without recourse to a new force, a polar force; for the force of the sun is essentially repulsive, not attractive.

We could also abandon the curiosity of the earth and in its place simply put the reaction to the repulsive action of the sun. (Newton's third law.)

But here I must leave the matter. That in a physics which is built entirely on a new principle, the individual will to life, and which spurns all such comfortable auxiliary principles as the simple unity, the absolute, the idea, the eternal, the eternal laws of nature, the "eternal all-extending force" and so on; that in such a physics, I say, the motions of the heavenly bodies cannot be left untouched, let that be my apology for the above hypothesis. I recognise its weakness. I know that it would be very difficult to explain, among other things, the deviations of the planets amongst themselves and the motions of the satellites around the planets, although it is not a matter of light, but fundamentally of the intensity of violent convulsions in a universe which finds itself in *thoroughgoing tension*, and of the reactions to those convulsions. And yet it seems to me as if in this direction, although not long enough, I had seen the face of truth unveiled. May someone stronger than me, whose specialist areas are physics in the narrow sense and astronomy, reach the end of that path.

32.

The first motion and the arising of the world are one and the same. The transformation of the simple unity into the world of multiplicity, the transition from the transcendent to the immanent domain, was precisely this first motion. It is not the task of physics to explain the first motion; physics has to accept it as a fact that has been found already in the Analytics, in the immanent domain but close to the boundary of the transcendent, which is added on in thought. This is why even in the Physics the final expression for this first motion cannot be gained, and we must simply characterise it, from our current perspective, as the disintegration of the simple unity into a world of multiplicity.

All subsequent motions were only continuations of this first motion, i.e., they could not be anything other than, again, the disintegration or further fragmentation of the ideas.

In the first ages of the world, this further disintegration was only able to express itself through real division of the simple substances and through being compounded. Every simple chemical force was obsessed with extending its individuality, i.e., with modifying its motion, but in every other force it stumbled upon the same obsession, and so arose the most terrible struggles of the ideas against each other in the most intense, excited states. The result was always a chemical compounding, i.e., the victory of the stronger over a weaker force and the entry of the new idea into the ceaseless struggle. The striving of the compound was at first directed at maintaining itself, then, when possible, at extending its individuality further. But against both strivings there entered from all sides other ideas, first to dissolve the compound, then to compound themselves with the divided ideas.

In the continuation of this ceaseless fight of the imperishable ideas which lay at the foundation of all compounds, the celestial bodies were formed, of which our earth gradually became ripe for organic life. If we here interrupt our development and take the present individuals and their states as final products, then the question immediately forces itself upon us: What has happened? All the ideas from which our earth was composed at that time were in the fiery primordial nebula on which the Kantian-Laplacian theory is based. There a wild struggle of gases, vapours, chaos; here a closed heavenly body with a solid crust whose depths were filled by a hot sea; and above all of it a vaporous, nebulous, carbon-dioxide-containing atmosphere.

What has happened? Or better: Are the individual wills of which this earth is constituted, this earth which has been liberated from becoming, the very same wills which spun in the fiery primordial nebula? Certainly! The *genetic* context is there. But is the *essence* of some individuality still the same one that it was at the beginning of the world? No! It has changed. Its force has *lost intensity*. It has become *weaker*.

This is the great truth taught by geology. A gas, according to its innermost essence, its drive, is stronger than a liquid and this in turn is stronger than a solid body. Let us not forget that the world has a *finite* sphere of force, and that for this reason some idea or other whose intensity abates cannot be strengthened again without another idea losing force. A strengthening is nevertheless possible but always at the expense of another force, or in other words: If, in the struggle of the inorganic ideas, one of these is weakened, then the objectified sum of forces in the universe is weakened, and for this deficiency there is no substitute precisely because the world is finite and came into existence with a particular force.

If we therefore assume that our earth should some day explode like that planet between Mars and Jupiter which broke into pieces, then the earth's entire solid crust can certainly melt again and all liquid become vapour, but at the cost of the ideas which provide the stimuli to such events. Thus, even if the earth were thrown back into what seemed a more intense state by means of such a revolution, it has still become *weaker as a whole*, as a particular sum of force.

And if today the powerful processes on the sun ceased and all the bodies of our solar system were thereby reunited with the sun, and sun and planets blazed up in an immense celestial fire, then it would seem that the forces that constitute the solar system had transformed into a more excited state, but at the expense of the total force contained in our solar system.

Even now it is no different in the inorganic realm. The ideas struggle ceaselessly with each other. Without interruption new compounds arise and these are violently divided again, but the divided forces unite with others straight away, partly compelling the union, partly being compelled into it. And here, too, the result is *weakening of force*, although this result, because of its slow development, lies not in the plain light of day and eludes perception.

33.

In the organic realm, from the moment it arose, there reigned and reigns evermore as a continuation of the first motion: disintegration into multiplicity. The striving of every organism is directed merely towards maintaining itself in existence and, following this drive, it struggles on one hand for its existence and provides on the other hand, by means of procreation, for its maintenance after death.

That this growing fragmentation on one hand, and the struggle for existence that thereby becomes more intense and terrible on the other, must have the same result as the struggle in the inorganic domain—namely, weakening of the individuals—is clear. That the strongest individual (in the broadest sense) remains the victor in the struggle for existence and the weaker individual surrenders only seems to speak against this fact; for the stronger may usually gain the victory, to be sure, but in every new generation the stronger individuals are less strong, the weaker individuals weaker than those in the previous generation.

Just as geology is the important record for the inorganic realm, so for the organic it is palaeontology, from which is drawn the truth, raised beyond all doubt, that in the struggle for existence the individuals do indeed perfect themselves and scale ever higher rungs of organisation, but in the process become *weaker*. This truth forces itself upon anyone who peruses this record and in so doing draws comparisons with our current plants and animals. The record can teach this only because it reports on extraordinarily long chains of development or, translated into subjective terms, on modifications in incomprehensibly long periods of time, because that record joins final to initial links by very long chains of intermediate links and can thereby make the difference conspicuous. Direct observation of the weakening is not possible. And yet proof of the weakening of the organisms can be supplied, even without penetrating into the primordial world and calling palaeontology to our aid—but only in the Politics, as we shall see. In the Physics we cannot supply the direct proof and must content ourselves with having found the great law of the weakening of organisms on an indirect route, in the stony record of the terrestrial crust.

We thus see in the organic as in the inorganic realm a fundamental motion: disintegration into multiplicity, and in the former as in the latter we see as the first consequence: conflict, struggle, and war, and as the second consequence: the weakening of force. But the disintegration into multiplicity as well as the two consequences of this disintegration are in every respect greater in the organic realm than in the inorganic.

34.

Here the questions are forced upon us: In what relations do the two realms stand to each other? And is there between them really a chasm that cannot be bridged?

We have in fact already answered both questions at the start of the Physics; nevertheless, we must treat them once again, more extensively.

We have seen that there is in the world but one principle: individual moving will to life. Whether I have before me a piece of gold or a plant, an animal, a person, regarding their essence in general it is all the same. Each of them is individual will, each lives, strives, wills. What separates them from each other is their character, i.e., their *motion* or the manner in which they want life.

This must appear false to many; for if they place a person next to a block of iron, then they see here dead rest, there mobility; here a homogeneous mass, there the most miraculously complex organism; and, if they consider the matter more acutely, here a dumb, simple drive towards the centre of the earth, there many capabilities, many qualities of the will, constant change of states, a rich life of the soul, a magnificent life of the mind—in short, a delightful play of forces in a closed unity. At this they shrug their shoulders and say: The inorganic realm cannot after all be anything other than the firm, solid ground for the organic realm, the same thing that the well-timbered stage is for the actors. And if they say "organic realm", then they are already very unprejudiced people, for most people set human beings apart and let all of nature exist for these glorious lords of the world alone.

Such people, however, are doing what I earlier described with regard to a locomotive: losing themselves in the minutiae and forgetting the main issue, the resultant motion. A stone, like a man, wants to exist, wants to live. Whether life in one instance is a simple, obscure drive, in another the result of the activities of a unified will which has separated out into organs; as regards life alone, it is all the same.

If, however, this is the case, then it seems to be certain that every organism is fundamentally only a chemical compound. This must be tested.

As I presented the matter above, two simple chemical ideas that stand in elective affinity can create a third, which is different from each of the individual ones. They are totally bound to each other and in their being thus compounded become something entirely new. If ammonia (NH_3) had self-consciousness, then it would feel neither like nitrogen nor like hydrogen, but like *unified ammonia* in a particular state.

Simple compounds can in turn create, and the product is again a third compound, something totally different from each individual element. If ammonium chloride (NH_3HCl) had self-consciousness, then it too would not feel like chlorine, nitrogen, and hydrogen, but simply like hydrochloric ammonia.

Seen from this standpoint, there is no difference at all between a chemical compound and an organism. The latter and the former are each a unity in which a certain number of simple chemical ideas are blended together.

But the chemical compound, considered in itself, is, as long as it exists, constant: it discharges no constituent and accepts no new element, or in short: no exchange of material takes place.

Furthermore, procreation in the inorganic realm is essentially limited, and not only this, but also the individual which procreates perishes in what is created; the type of a compund rests on the individuals bound together, it stands and falls with them, it does not float above them.

An organism, in contrast, discharges from its compound first this, then that substance and assimilates to itself what replaces the discharged substance, while constantly maintaining its type; it then procreates, that is, the parts separated from it have in some way the organism's type and likewise unfold themselves while constantly maintaining the same type.

This motion which separates the organism from the chemical compound is growth in the broadest sense. We must therefore say that every organism is indeed fundamentally a chemical compound, but *with an entirely different motion*. But if the difference lies merely in the motion and if we are dealing here, as there, with individual will to life, then there is also no chasm at all between organic and inorganic ideas; rather, both realms border directly on each other.

It is the organs which customarily cloud the eye of the researcher. Here he sees organs, there none; and so he supposes in the best faith that there is an immeasurable chasm between a stone and a plant. He is simply assuming a standpoint that is too low, from which the main issue, the *motion*, is not visible. Every organ exists only for a particular motion. The stone needs no organs because it has a unified undivided motion; the plant, in contrast, needs organs because the particular motion wanted by it (resultant motion) is only to be brought about by means of organs. It is the motion, not how it arises which is the heart of the matter.

There is in fact no difference between the organic and the inorganic.

It might however still seem that the difference itself remains a fundamental one even when one views the organs as a side issue and places oneself on the higher perspective of pure motion.

In physics, however, this is not the case. From the standpoint of pure motion there is at first no greater difference between a plant and hydrogen sulphide than, on one hand (entirely within the inorganic realm), between water vapour and water, between water and ice; or, on the other (entirely within the organic realm), between a plant and an animal, an animal and a human being. Motion in all directions, motion towards the centre of the earth, growth, motion upon intuitive motives, motion upon abstract motives—all of these motions explain *differences* between the individual wills. For me at least, the difference between the motion of water vapour and of ice can be no more miraculous than the difference between the motion of ice and the growth of a plant.

Thus the matter presents itself from without. From within it simplifies itself even further. If I could anticipate subsequent chapters, then I could solve the problem with a single word. But we are still assuming the lower standpoint of physics, and however much we may, with each step we take in the Physics, yearn for a metaphysics, we must still keep both disciplines from flowing into each other, which would cause hopeless confusion.

Now, in physics, as we know, the first motion presents itself as disintegration of the transcendent unity into multiplicity. All motions that followed it bear the same character. Disintegration into multiplicity, life, motion—all of these expressions describe one and the same thing. The disintegration of unity into multiplicity is the fundamental law in the inorganic as well as the organic realm. In the latter, however, it finds a much more extensive application: it cuts much deeper, and its consequences—the struggle for existence and the weakening of force—are greater.

We thus return once more to the point from which we set out, but with the result that no chasm separates the inorganic bodies from organisms. The organic realm is only a higher rung of the inorganic; it is a *more complete form* of the struggle for existence, i.e., *of the weakening of force*.

35.

As frightful, indeed as ludicrous as it may sound to say that man is fundamentally a chemical compound and differs from such a compound only insofar as he has a different motion, it is yet a true result of physics. It loses its repellent character when one keeps firmly in view the fact that wherever we may investigate nature, we always find but one principle, the individual will, which wants but one thing: to live, to live. The essence of a stone is simpler than that of a lion, but only on the surface; fundamentally it is the same: individual will to life.

By tracing the organic realm back to the inorganic, immanent philosophy does indeed teach the same thing as materialism, but it is not for that reason identical with materialism. The fundamental difference which exists between them is the following.

Materialism is no *immanent* philosophical system. The first thing that it teaches is *eternal matter*, a *simple unity*, which no one has yet seen and no one shall ever see. If materialism wanted to be immanent, i.e., *merely* to be honest in the contemplation of nature, then above all it would have to declare matter to be a *collective* unity independent of the Subject and say that matter is the *sum* of so and so many simple substances. This, however, it does not do, and although no one has yet succeeded in making hydrogen from oxygen, gold from copper, materialism still places *behind* every simple substance the mystical simple essentiality: undifferentiated matter. Neither Zeus nor Jupiter, neither the God of the Jews, Christians, and Mohammedans, nor the Brahma of the Indians, in short: no uncognisable, transcendent essentiality has been so devoutly believed in from the depths of the human heart as that mystical divinity of the materialists: matter. For with the materialists, because it is undeniable that everything organic can be traced back to the inorganic realm, the head stands in league with the heart and sets it aflame.

However, despite the extraordinary assumption of simple matter, an assumption which strikes all experience in the face, it is yet insufficient to explain the world. Thus, once again, materialism must deny the truth, once again it must wax transcendent and posit various mystical essences, the forces of nature, which are not identical with matter and yet are connected with it for all time. In this way, materialism rests on *two* primordial principles, or in other words: it is *transcendent dogmatic dualism*.

In immanent philosophy, by contrast, matter is *ideal*, in our heads, a subjective capacity which enables us to cognise the external world, and *substance*, though an *undifferentiated unity*, is in the same sense *ideal*, in our heads, a conjunction à posteriori gained by synthetic reason on the basis of matter, without the slightest reality and existing only in order to cognise *all* objects.

Independently of the Subject there is only *force*, only individual will in the world: a single principle.

Therefore, whereas materialism is transcendent dogmatic dualism, immanent philosophy is *pure, immanent dynamism*: a difference than which no greater can be conceived.

To call materialism the *most rational* system is thoroughly absurd. Every transcendent system is EO IPSO *not* rational. Materialism, conceived only as a theoretical system of philosophy, is worse than its reputation. The truth that the simple chemical ideas are the sea from which everything organic has emerged, from which it arises and into which it sinks back, casts a purely immanent light on materialism and thereby gives it a seductive charm. But critical reason does not allow itself to be deceived. It investigates precisely, and thus finds behind the dazzling illusion that old chimera: the transcendent unity in or above or under the world and coexisting with it, which appears now in this, now in that, but always in fantastical attire.

36.

We have now to check the relation of the individual essence to the totality, to the world.

Here an immense difficulty arises. Namely: If the *individual* will to life is the sole principle of the world, then it must be thoroughly autonomous. If, however, it is autonomous and thoroughly independent, then a dynamic coherence is not possible. Now, experience teaches precisely the opposite: It forces the dynamic coherence upon every true observer of nature and at the same time shows him the dependence of the individual on that dynamic coherence. Consequently (so one is tempted to conclude), the *individual* will cannot be the principle of the world.

In the artificial language of philosophy, the problem presents itself as follows: Either the discrete essences are autonomous substances, in which case the INFLUXUS PHYSICUS is an impossibility; for how should one autonomous essence have an effect on another, compel modifications within it? Or the discrete essences are not autonomous substances, and then there must be one simple substance which actuates the discrete essences, from which the discrete essences have life as vassals their fief, so to speak.

The problem is extraordinarily important; indeed, one can declare it the most important problem of all philosophy. The autocracy of the individual is in the greatest danger and it seems, according to what has been presented above, as if it were irrecoverably lost. If immanent philosophy cannot here succeed in saving the individual whom it has hitherto so faithfully protected, then there is a logical compulsion to deem it a marionette and return it unconditionally to the almighty hand of some transcendent essence. The only possibilities are then: monotheism or pantheism. Nature is then *lying* and pressing fool's instead of genuine gold into our hands when she *everywhere* shows us *only individuals* and *never a simple unity*; we are then deceiving ourselves when, in our innermost self-consciousness, we apprehend ourselves as an uneasy or stubborn, blissful or suffering ego; there is then no purely immanent domain, and for that reason too an immanent philosophy can only be a work of lies and deception.

If, in contrast, we succeed in rescuing the individual will, the fact of inner and outer experience, then, however, there is also a logical compulsion to break definitively and forever with all transcendent chimeras, though they may appear in the mantle of monotheism or pantheism or materialism; then—and in fact for the first time—*atheism has a scientific foundation*.

It is apparent that we are standing before a very important question.

However, one should not forget that the Physics is not the place where the truth can let all of her veils fall away. Only later will she show us her noble visage, in all its fair clarity and beauty. In the Physics, questions such as the present one can at best only be half resolved. But this will do for now.

I shall be very brief. We have not, in the Analytics, obtained the transcendent domain surreptitiously. We have seen that no causal relation, neither the law of causality nor general causality, can lead us back into the *past* of things, but only *time* can do this. On the basis of time we pursued the *chains of development* A PARTE ANTE, but found that in the immanent domain we can never get beyond multiplicity. Just as airships never reach the limit of the atmosphere but, however high they climb, will always be surrounded by air, so the fact of inner and outer experience, the individual will, never left us. By contrast, our reason rightly and relentlessly demanded a simple unity. From these dire straits there was but one escape: to let the individuals flow together into an inconceivable unity beyond the immanent domain. We found ourselves not in the *present*, in which one can never, never get beyond the *being as such* of the Object, but in the *past*. And when, for this reason, we declared the transcendent domain that we had found to be no longer existing but to be premundane and downfallen, we were carrying out no *coup-de-main* but were being faithful servants of the truth.

Thus, everything that now is once was in a simple premundane unity, before which, as we will recall, all of our cognitive faculties collapsed. We could make for ourselves "neither simile nor any comparison" of it, and thus could gain no presentation of the manner in which the immanent world of multiplicity had once existed in the simple unity. But we gained *one* irrevocable certainty, namely, *that* this world of multiplicity had once been a simple unity, besides which nothing else was able to exist.

Here, now, lies the key to the solution of the problem with which we are concerned.

Why and how the unity disintegrated into multiplicity, these are questions that may not be asked in any physics. Here we can say only this: that, to whatever the disintegration may be traced back, it was the act of a simple unity. When in the immanent domain we therefore find only *individual* wills and the world is nothing other than a collective unity of these individuals, then these very individuals are nevertheless not thoroughly autonomous, *since prior to the world they were a simple unity* and the world is the deed of this unity. Thus, like a reflex, this premundane unity lies over the world of multiplicity; thus all discrete essences are embraced by one invisible, unbreakable bond, as it were, and this reflex, this bond, is the *dynamic coherence of the world*. Each will works on every other either directly or indirectly, and every other will works directly and indirectly on it, or all ideas are in "pervasive interaction".

We thus have the *half autonomous* individual, half active out of its own force, half suffering through the other ideas. It encroaches upon the development of the world autocratically, and the development of the world encroaches upon its individuality.

All fetishes, all gods, demons, and spirits owe their genesis to the one-sided contemplation of the world's dynamic coherence. If, in grey antiquity, things were going well for man, he did not think of fetishes, gods, demons, and spirits. The individual felt his force and, not detecting the unresting influence of the other ideas because of its momentary mildness, considered only himself to be active and behaved like a god. But if, in contrast, the other ideas attacked man in their dreadful, appalling efficacy, then *his* force disappeared *entirely* from his consciousness, then he saw in the efficacy of the other ideas the all-destroying omnipotence of a wrathful transcendent essentiality, and before effigies of wood and stone he fell down in agonies, his whole body trembling, in ineffable spiritual anguish. Nowadays it is arguably different.

From then on—before the transcendent domain was separated from the immanent and, specifically, in such a manner that the former was declared to exist *only prior* to the world, the latter to exist *only now*—one rightly passed the disjunctive judgment: Either the individual is autonomous, in which case the INFLUXUS PHYSICUS (the dynamic coherence) is impossible, or the individual is not autonomous, in which case the INFLUXUS PHYSICUS is the efficacy of some simple substance. Now, however, this either-or is no longer justified. The individual will to life, despite its half-autonomy, is rescued as the sole principle of the world.

Yet this result of half-autocracy is unsatisfying. Every clear, unprejudiced mind demands *completion*. We shall have it in the Metaphysics.

37.

In the Analytics we defined the character of the premundane simple unity negatively in accordance with the faculties of cognition. We found that the unity was inactive, extensionless, undifferentiated, unfragmented (simple), motionless, timeless (eternal). We have now to define it from the standpoint of the Physics.

Whatever kind of Object of nature we may contemplate, be it a gas, a liquid, a stone, a plant, an animal, a man, we always find it in relentless striving, in a ceaseless inner motion. To the transcendent unity, however, motion was foreign. The opposite of motion is rest, of which we can form for ourselves no notion; for we are not here speaking of apparent *external* rest, which in relation to the change of location of an entire Object or parts of the same we are indeed very much in a position to imagine, but of inner, absolute motionlessness. We must therefore attribute *absolute rest* to the premundane unity.

If we then reflect seriously on the dynamic coherence of the universe on one hand and on the definite character of the individuals on the other, then we recognise that everything in the world moves of *necessity*. Whatever we may contemplate: the stone dropped by our hand, the growing plant, the animal that moves upon intuitive motives and inner compulsion, the man who must surrender himself without resistance to a sufficient motive—they all are subject to the iron law of necessity. In the world there is no room for freedom. And, as we will see clearly in the Ethics, it must be so if the world is to have a sense at all.

What freedom is in a philosophical sense (LIBERUM ARBITRIUM INDIFFERENTIAE) we can indeed define with words and say, for example, that it is the capacity of a man of a particular character to will or not to will in the face of a sufficient motive; but if we also reflect but a moment on this combination of words which is so easily contrived, we recognise immediately that we will never obtain real evidence of this freedom, even if it were possible for us to examine the actions of all men to their very foundation over millennia. For us, therefore, the matter stands with freedom as it stands with rest. But we must attribute freedom to the simple unity, precisely because it was a simple unity. With it the compulsion of motive, the one factor of every motion known to us, falls away, for the unity was unfragmented, entirely alone, solitary.

The immanent scheme:

world of multiplicity – motion – necessity

is therefore paralleled by the transcendent scheme:

simple unity – rest – freedom

And now we must take the final step.

In the Analytics we already found that *force*, as soon as it has passed via the thin thread of existence from the immanent into the transcendent domain, ceases to be *force*. It becomes for us as completely unfamiliar and uncognisable as the unity into which it becomes submerged. As we proceeded in that chapter, we found that what we call force is *individual will*, and in the Physics we have finally seen that the *mind* is only the function of an organ that has precipitated from the will and in its deepest foundation is nothing other than a part of a divided motion.

The fundamental principle, the will, which is so intimate, so well-known to us in the immanent domain, and the secondary principle which is subordinated to it and likewise so intimate, the mind, lose (like force) all meaning for us as soon as we allow them to pass over to the transcendent domain. They forfeit their nature completely and elude our cognition entirely.

We are therefore compelled to conclude that the simple unity was neither *will*, nor *mind*, nor an idiosyncratic *interpenetration of will and mind*. In this way we lose our final point of reference. We press to no avail upon the springs of our elaborate, miraculous apparatus for cognising the external world: senses, understanding, reason—all go lame. Vainly we hold up the principles found within ourselves, in self-consciousness—will and mind—as a mirror towards the mysterious, invisible essence on the opposing elevation of the divide, and we hope that essence will reveal itself in that mirror: yet the mirror reflects no image. But now we also have the right to give this essence that familiar name which from time immemorial has designated what no imaginative power, no flight of the boldest fancy, no thinking however deep or abstract, no composed, devout soul, no ecstatic mind rapt on high has ever attained: *God*.

38.

But this simple unity *was*; it *is* no more. It has fragmented itself, changing its essence utterly into a world of multiplicity. *God has died and His death was the life of the world.*

Herein lie for the sober-minded thinker two truths which deeply gratify the mind and uplift the heart. We have firstly a *pure, immanent* domain, in or behind or above which no force resides (call it what one will) which has the individuals do now this, now that, like the concealed puppeteer his puppets. We are then uplifted by the truth that everything which now is existed *prior to* the world *in God*. We existed in Him, we can use no other word. If we wanted to say: we lived and moved in Him, then this would be false, for we would be transferring activities of the things of this world onto an essence which was totally inactive and motionless.

Furthermore, *we are no longer in God*; for the simple unity is dead and destroyed. On the contrary, we are in a world of multiplicity, whose individuals are compounded into a solid collective unity.

From the primordial unity we have already derived in the most unforced manner the dynamic coherence of the universe. In the same way we now derive from it the *purposiveness* in the world, which no reasonable person will deny. We remain standing before the disintegration of the unity into multiplicity, without now brooding over why and how this disintegration was accomplished. The fact itself is enough. The disintegration was the deed of a simple unity, its *first* and *last*, its *sole* deed. Every will now existing acquired its essence and motion in this single deed, and for this reason everything in the world encroaches on everything else: purpose pervades the world.

Finally, we derive indirectly from the primordial unity and directly from the first motion the developmental course of the universe. The disintegration into multiplicity was the first motion, and all motions that followed it—however far they may separate, intertwine, seem to become entangled and in turn disentangled—are merely its continuation. The *one* motion of the world, which results *continually* from the actions of all dynamically cohering individuals, is the *fate of the universe*.

God therefore became the world, whose individuals pervasively interact. Since, however, the dynamic coherence consists in the fact that every individual will has an effect on the whole and experiences the efficacy of the whole, but efficacy is motion, so *fate* is nothing other than the *becoming* of the world, the motion of the Orphic conjuncture, the resultant of all individual motions.

Here I can say no more about fate. However, we have now to connect the questions left unanswered in the Analytics with fate.

The propositions which we reserved for further examination were:

1) The *simple* chemical forces are indestructible;
2) The real motion had a beginning, but it is endless.

The foregoing discussion makes clear that physics is not in a position to overturn these propositions, or in other words: The two open questions about the annihilation of the simple chemical ideas and about the end of the world related thereto cannot be answered in the Physics. Accordingly, the fate of the world still presents itself to us here for the time being as an *endless* motion of the world: in the inorganic realm we see an endless chain of connections and disconnections, in the organic an endlessly progressing development of lower into higher forms of life (organisms).

But this view must be modified by the important factor of *the weakening of force* of which we have become aware. We have therefore to summarise the above propositions as one, which is:

> The world is indestructible, but the sum of force contained within it *weakens continually* as an endless motion proceeds.

We will take this proposition in hand once again when we arrive at the Metaphysics, in order to attempt, with the aid of those results which we have gained in that exclusive domain of humanity, to answer definitively the important question about the world's end.

39.

I here conclude the Physics by repeating the observation that it is the first attempt to explain nature with inner and outer experience, with the individual will to life *alone* (without the aid of any suprasensory force). In saying this it is at the same time likely that in some places I was too timid and have overlooked important details.

One ought also to be mindful of what it means to be the master of all disciplines, the present state of natural science being what it is. The burden of the empirical material is downright oppressive, and only with the magic wand of a clear, irrefutable philosophical principle can the sifting in some way be accomplished, like the chaotic masses of stone which arranged themselves into symmetrical structures according to the sounds of the Orphic lyre.

Such an irrefutable principle is *the individual will to life*. I press it like a gift into the hands of every true and honest investigator of nature, wishing that it yield for him better explanations of the phenomena in his delimited field than he has hitherto arrived at. In general, however, I hope that this principle opens up a new path to science on which it is as successful as it was on that one which Bacon opened up to it by means of his inductive method.

I further consider the *pure, immanent* domain, totally freed from the spectre of transcendent essentialities, to be a second gift that I am making to the investigators of nature. How peacefully they shall be able to work in that domain!

I foresee (and I may say this, because the end result of my philosophy is the sole light which imbues my eyes and in them holds my entire will enchained): The complete separation of the immanent from the transcendent domain, the separation of God from the world and of the world from God will have the most beneficial influence on the course of humanity's development. This separation was to be effected only on the basis of genuine transcendental idealism; the correct cut through the ideal and real had to be made first.

I see the dawn of a beautiful day.

Aesthetics

EST ENIM VERUM INDEX SUI ET FALSI.

Spinoza

1.

Aesthetics deals with a *specific state* of the human will which is produced by a *specific mode of* contemplating ideas, and it is a *science*, because it brings together numerous cases under particular perspectives and fixed rules. In constructing the Aesthetics, we want always to keep present to our minds the fact that there is but one principle in nature: individual will to life, and that this will, independent of the Subject, is thing-in-itself; dependent on the Subject, is an Object.

2.

Every man wants life in a particular way because he has a particular will and a particular mind, i.e., a particular motion. Now, if he regards things in the usual way, then he is either indifferent to them or they awaken in him a yearning, or they repel him. In short, his interest is the standard against which he measures them, and he judges them according to the relation in which they stand to his will. There can be no talk of a distinct and clear reflection of the Object; just as little does man cognise the complete efficacy of a thing-in-itself or the sum of its relations, because he regards only one of these and does so by way of his own interests, therefore falsely, deforming, exaggerating, or undervaluing it.

Now, if he is supposed to reflect the Object purely, to apprehend its relations correctly, then *his* relation to the Object must experience a *modification*, i.e., he must enter into a completely *disinterested* relation to it, it can only be *interesting* for him.

In aesthetics, therefore, as has just been remarked, we are dealing with a very specific relation of man to the world which establishes a specific state of his will. This relation I call the *aesthetic relation* and this state the *aesthetic state* or *aesthetic joy*. It is essentially different from the usual joy.

Every man is capable of entering into the aesthetic relation; yet the transition into this relation takes place in the one man with greater ease, in the other with less, and what it offers the one is more complete and richer, what it offers the other more limited and poorer.

The farmer who of an evening, when the day's work is done, casts his gaze over nature and, for example, contemplates the form, the colours, and the procession of the clouds without thinking of what use or harm the rain shall be to his crop; or who is gladdened by the undulation of the cornfields and by the vibrant redness of the ears at sundown without estimating the yield of the harvest—he is contemplating things aesthetically. The harvester who exposes a lark's nest and disinterestedly contemplates the beautifully formed and speckled little eggs or the chirping chicks and the parents, their great anxiety making itself known in unsettled gazes and restless fluttering to and fro, has put aside the usual mode of cognition and finds himself in the aesthetic state. The hunter who forgets to shoot at a magnificent deer that has stridden suddenly into view because the composure, the form, the gait of the beast captivate his mind has entered into an aesthetic relation to the Object.

Although we are dealing here with pure, to a certain extent free cognising, we are in no way dealing with an autonomous life of the mind freed from the will. The will is ever and always the sole thing that we encounter; we may search where we want, we may rifle through nature as deeply and as often as we want; always the will is there and only its *states* change.

3.

The ideas reveal their essence in the Object in very diverse ways. If we take the highest idea known to us, that of man, then it reveals its essence:

1. in his form and shape;
2. in the motion of his limbs;
3. in the play of his features and in his eyes;
4. in words and sounds.

In this order, what is internal becomes ever more distinctly evident in what is external; in words and sounds it is objectified most distinctly. For we have in the world always to do with *Objects* and only we ourselves, internally, are for ourselves not Objects. This distinction is also very important for aesthetics. The phenomena of sound and word have their foundation in the will's oscillations, in its motion, which imparts itself to the air. This idiosyncratic continuation of the motion in a foreign idea is sensibly perceived by us and objectified in *substance*.

Sounds and words are therefore Objects like everything else; and even when the state of an idea reveals itself in them in the lightest of veils, it is still never the thing-in-itself being revealed to us immediately. Only he who puts himself in the state of another idea by evoking it at will within himself—namely, the artist—apprehends in his breast the foreign will immediately as thing-in-itself and not as Object.

The objectification of an idea in sounds and words, however, is so complete that the will of the objectifying listener is seized by the motion and vibrates with it, while the simple contemplation of the form and shape of an Object does not exert the same effect on the aesthetically disposed Subject.

AESTHETICS

In accordance with these observations, we have to distinguish *two main kinds of aesthetic state*:

1. aesthetic contemplation, and
2. aesthetic empathy or aesthetic sympathy.

4.

In the state of *deep* aesthetic contemplation it is for the will as if its usual motion had suddenly ceased and it had become *motionless*. It is caught entirely in the deception that it is *resting* completely, that all curiosity, all compulsion, all pressure has been taken from it and that it remains a being purely cognising. It is as if it were bathing in an element of miraculous clarity, so light, so inexpressibly well does it feel.

Only objects completely at rest can put us into this genuine state of deep contemplation. Because they have no external motion, we certainly do not bring them into any relation to time. Immediately *we* become timeless because the motion of our will has disappeared entirely from our consciousness and we are completely absorbed in the resting Object. We are living, as it were, in eternity. By means of deception we have the consciousness of absolute rest and are unspeakably blissful. If we are disturbed in this state of deepest contemplation, then we awaken in the strangest way; for our consciousness does not begin, as after sleep; rather, it is merely filled again by *motion*. We step out of eternity, back into time.

Restful nature most easily puts us into a state of deep contemplation, especially the view of the smooth Mediterranean Sea out of which coastlines or small islands arise, in dreamlike stillness, steeped in the blue haze of the distance or the glow of the setting sun.

No other painter has depicted the genuine expression of that deep contemplative state in the facial features and the eyes so superlatively, with so faithful and arresting an effect, as Raphael in the two cherubim at the feet of his Sistine Madonna. We must literally tear our gaze free of them, for they captivate us entirely.

If, in contrast, the Objects are more or less moved, then the contemplation is also less deep, because we bring the Objects into a relation to time and thereby notice within ourselves the elapsing of the present. Thus, the spell of the painless state is cast over us to a lesser degree.

In the state of aesthetic *empathy* our will, as I said above, vibrates with the moved will of the Object. Thus we hearken to the song of a bird, or to other animals' expressions of feeling; or we accompany passionate whispers, expressions of fury and ire, complaints of sorrow, of melancholy, the exultation of joy—in all of which we have no direct interest—with stronger or weaker vibrations of our own will. We do not vibrate as strongly as the persons acting, for if this occurs, as happens often enough, then we turn from aesthetically disposed listeners into active individuals and fall out of the aesthetic into the usual relation. In the state of aesthetic empathy our will is vibrated only gently by the original motion, like a cord lying next to one already struck.

To these two main kinds of aesthetic state a double motion is closely connected: *aesthetic enthusiasm*. Its first part is either aesthetic contemplation or aesthetic sympathy; its second part, in contrast, is either joy, exultation, or courage, hope, yearning, or a very passionate arousal of the will.

This double motion seldom arises out of contemplation and is therefore also the weakest motion. One would like to drift like the clouds across every country, or sway buoyantly like a bird to and fro upon the air:

> Tweet, tweet, tweet goes the little bird's song!
> Come along, come along! –
> Could I, little bird, fly with you,
> Over the mountains we'd fly, we two,
> Through clear blue skies, a voyage begun
> To bathe in the warmth of the beaming sun.
> Narrow's the earth, the heavens are wide
> Poor's the earth, where sorrows preside
> The heavens are wide, where joy resides! –
> Now the little bird's taken to wing,
> Entwining the air with the sweetness she sings.
> God keep, little bird, you near to His heart!
> On the shore must I sit, I cannot take part.
>
> (Folksong)

Or the longing arises within us to be always contemplative, to be able to linger forever in the bliss of contemplation.

In contrast, this double motion very often arises as the combination of a state with aesthetic sympathy. The efficacy of the nerves is sensed distinctly as cold waves; they force, as it were, the will back on itself, concentrate it; the will is then struck by an igniting spark and it flares up into a fervid blaze: this is the inspiration to bold deeds. In this way speeches, war songs, drumming, military music have their effect.

5.

As every man has the capacity to be put into the aesthetic state, so *every* object can be contemplated *aesthetically*. Nevertheless, the one object shall be more, the other less inviting of such contemplation. For many people, for example, it is impossible to contemplate a snake calmly. In the presence of this animal they feel an insurmountable revulsion and do not hold their ground, even when they have no reason to fear it.

6.

Every man is capable of aesthetic contemplation and every object can be contemplated aesthetically, but not every object is *beautiful*. Now, what does it mean to say that an object is beautiful? We have to distinguish:

1. the subjectively beautiful;
2. the foundation of the beautiful in the thing-in-itself;
3. the beautiful Object.

The subjectively beautiful, which can also be called the formally beautiful, is based on à priori forms and functions of the Subject or, as the case may be, on conjunctions synthesised by reason on the basis of à priori forms, and I classify it into the beautiful:

1. of (mathematical) space;
2. of causality;
3. of matter (of substance);
4. of time.

The formally beautiful of *space* expresses itself in the shape of Objects and in the relation in which the parts of an Object stand to the whole, and specifically in the *regularity* of the shape and in its *symmetry*.

The regular shape is firstly an entirety of *lines*. Beautiful lines are the straight line, the curved line, the straight curved line (wavy line) and the straight wound line (spiral).

The beautiful of shape then reveals itself in the *pure figures* of geometry and their parts, therefore especially in the equilateral triangle, the square, the rectangle, hexagon, in the circle, semicircle and in the ellipse.

The beautiful of shape further reveals itself in the *bodies* of stereometry, which are based on the pure figures of geometry; it reveals itself especially in the pyramid, the cube, the rectangular prism, the sphere, the cone and the cylinder (column).

Finally, *symmetry* reveals itself in the harmonic arrangement of the parts of a whole, i.e., in the correct relation of height to breadth and depth, at the right distance and in the precise repetition of the parts at the corresponding places.

The formally beautiful of *causality* unveils itself as *grace* in even, external motion, or in the fluent transition of one motion into a faster or slower motion and particularly in the appropriateness of the motion to the intended aim.

The formally beautiful of matter or, as the case may be, of *substance*, emerges firstly in colours and in the composition of the same, in the *harmony of colours*. It reveals itself most clearly in the three primary colours: yellow, red and blue, and in the three pure mixtures of these: orange, green and violet, (which six colours are the fixed points of the long series of colour nuances) as well as in the poles of white and black. It reveals itself even more pleasantly when those six colours inhere in clear liquids.

It then also reveals itself in the *purity of sound*, in the euphony of the voice.

Finally, the formally beautiful of time reveals itself in the *regular succession* of similar or distinct moments, i.e., in the regular measure of time. A brief combination of such moments is the *bar* and a combination of bars is the *rhythm*.

In continuing this treatise, I will yet have to touch often on the subjectively beautiful and will then pursue its additional bifurcations. Here I was concerned only to show its main branches.

7.

Now, the *foundation of the beautiful* is that which inheres in the *thing-in-itself*, which *corresponds to the subjectively beautiful*, or which compels the Subject to objectify it as beautiful.

From this the explanation of the *beautiful Object* flows of its own accord. It is the product of the thing-in-itself and of the subjectively beautiful, or the beautiful Object is the *phenomenal appearance* of the foundation of the beautiful reposing in the thing-in-itself.

The relation is the same as that of the thing-in-itself to the Object in presentation generally. The Subject does not first of all produce something in the thing-in-itself, does not in any way extend or constrain its essence; rather, it merely objectifies faithfully and accurately, in accordance with its own forms, the thing-in-itself. However, just as the sweetness of sugar or the red colour of common madder—although they refer to very particular qualities in the thing-in-itself—cannot be attributed to the thing-in-itself, so the beauty of an Object has its basis in the thing-in-itself but the thing-in-itself cannot itself be called beautiful. *Only the Object* can be beautiful, because only in it can the foundation of the beautiful (the thing-in-itself) and the subjectively beautiful (the Subject) be wed.

AESTHETICS

What is beautiful would therefore exist without the mind of man as little as the world of presentation in general without the Subject. The beautiful Object stands and falls with the subjectively beautiful in the *mind* of man, as the Object stands and falls with the Subject. "Beautiful" is a predicate which, like the predicate "material" ("substantial"), applies only to the Object.

In contrast, it is equally correct that the foundation of the beautiful exists independently of the subjectively beautiful; just as the thing-in-itself, the foundation of phenomenal appearance, exists independently of the Subject. But just as here the Object falls away, so there the *beautiful Object*.

Now, if, as we recall, the thing-in-itself, independently of the Subject, is immaterial, is only force, is will; what then is the foundation of the beautiful independently of the subjectively beautiful?

To this question there is but one answer: It is *harmonious motion*.

We have seen in the Analytics that motion is not to be separated from the individual will, that it is the only predicate of the will with which the will stands and falls. Because this is the case, I have up to this point sometimes spoken of motion alone; for in doing so it was always self-evident that at the foundation of this motion lay the individual will to life, the idea. Motion plain and simple is striving, is inner motion, which is expressed in the Object as shape and form (objectified sphere of force of the will, which is filled by the will caught in ceaseless motion), as well as in external motion, which is evident in the higher ideas as motion of the limbs, play of the expressions, life of the eyes, language and song.

All striving, all motion in the world is to be traced back to the first motion, to the disintegration of the simple unity into multiplicity. Because this first motion was the deed of a *simple unity*, it was necessarily uniform and harmonious, and since all other motions were and are only continuations of that first motion, so every striving of a thing-in-itself must in its utmost depths be harmonious or, keeping on the safe side, ought in its utmost depths to be harmonious.

In celestial mechanics and in inorganic nature this is also plainly evident. When, in these domains, a unitary striving or a striving which results from other steadily effective strivings can reveal itself purely or essentially unimpeded, then we have always to do with harmonious or, when objectified, with beautiful shapes or beautiful external motions. Thus celestial bodies move in ellipses or parabolas around the sun; crystals, when they can shoot up unhindered, are absolutely beautiful; snowflakes are six-sided regular stars of the most varied forms; a glass plate stroked with the bow of a violin orders the grains of sand on top of it into splendid figures; falling or thrown bodies have a beautiful motion.

It is certainly significant that, according to the Orphic philosophy, the Dionysian child played with cones, spheres and cubes; for Dionysus was the world-builder, the God who put the unity asunder into multiplicity, and in this way the regular shape of the universe and its harmonious motion were symbolically adumbrated. The Pythagorean philosophy is also based on the agreement of the universe with the subjectively beautiful of space and of time.

But already in the inorganic realm, where the striving of the will is unitary and extraordinarily simple, it is the case that in the struggle of the individuals with each other (partly in the struggle for existence) the harmonious inner motion can only seldom be expressed. In the organic realm, where the struggle for existence reigns absolutely and with much greater intensity, almost no striving can reveal itself purely. Now one part, now the other is preferentially stimulated, influenced, and the consequence in most cases is an unharmonious motion of the whole. This is compounded by the fact that already at conception every individual receives a more or less weakened motion; for the inner motion of organisms is no longer a unitary one, but rather the resultant of many, and since the organs are contained VIRTUALITER in the fertilised egg, but one organ can be stronger or weaker at the expense of another, many individuals will therefore come into the world already with a disturbed harmonious motion.

However, it is precisely in the organic realm that we find the majority of beautiful Objects as well as the most beautiful Objects. This is due to the fact that, partly by natural, partly by artificial means, harmful influences can be kept from the organism precisely when it is most susceptible and in the most important phase of its formation. In particular, on the higher rungs of the animal kingdom the new individual, for a longer or shorter period, is entirely sequestered from the struggle for existence because its parents are conducting the struggle on its behalf. There is also the fact that almost everything in the inorganic realm grates and strikes against everything else, while organisms can develop in yielding elements (water and air).

Thus, wherever the arising of organisms did not coincide with a weakening of motion and later harmful influences became less noticeable, we always see beautiful individuals. Most plants grow as if according to an artistic blueprint, and animals, with few exceptions, are regularly constructed. In contrast, only seldom do we find very beautiful people, because nowhere is the struggle for existence more bitterly conducted than in a State, and occupations and ways of life seldom allow the harmonious formation of the whole.

Here, too, the creative drive of the animals must be mentioned. In the *products* of the creative drive, which so astonish us and at which we marvel, it is only the *entire* harmonious motion remaining in the genuine will (here, instinct) at which we marvel. Thus the bee constructs regular hexagonal cells; even the brute savage, not with the mind but on the basis of a dæmonic impetus, gives to his hut the basic form of the circle or the square or the hexagon.

We are thus led back to the *subjectively beautiful*. As we know, the mind of man, in which alone the subjectively beautiful exists, is only divided motion. It is a part of the earlier whole motion, which was harmonious through and through. We can therefore say that the subjectively beautiful is nothing other than harmonious, one-sidedly formed motion which has been developed in a particular direction and has become the standard and mirror for all motion in the world. This motion has been brought into a sanctuary, as it were, which the things-in-themselves flood in upon from all sides but which they cannot infiltrate. Here this motion sits enthroned in assured tranquillity and makes its sovereign determinations about what is and what is not agreeable to it, i.e., what is and what is not beautiful.

8.

If we consider the beautiful Objects in nature somewhat more closely, then in the inorganic realm, for the reasons earlier adduced, we only seldom encounter beautiful solid bodies. The "well-founded" earth is to be viewed as a dreadfully ossified struggle. Only on exceptional occasions does one find in nature pure and completely formed crystals. They show clearly that in forming they have been pressed, shoved, struck, and their strivings constrained in yet other ways.

Particularly beautiful is the motion of thrown, round bodies.

Individual mountains and mountain ranges are distinguished by their pure contours.

Water is almost always beautiful. Particularly beautiful is the sea, at rest and in motion, its principal charm lying in its colour, which moves between the deepest blue and the brightest emerald green. The beautiful form of waterfalls must also be mentioned, their flowing most of all.

Very beautiful is the air and many of the phenomena in it: the blue vault of the heavens; the manifold forms of the clouds; the colours of the sky and of the clouds at sundown; the alpine glow and the blue haze of the distance; the procession of the clouds; the rainbow; the northern lights.

In organic nature we encounter first the various regular cells of plants; then individual trees, such as palms, pines, and firs; then those plants which, in the position of the leaves and branches, exhibit very distinct symmetrical relations; then many leaves and blossoms. Almost every blossom is beautiful owing to the arrangement of its petals, its regular form and its colours. So too are all fruits which have been able to develop undisturbed.

In the animal kingdom the Objects are beautiful firstly owing to their symmetrical construction. The animal, divided in the middle, forms almost always two equal halves. The face has two eyes which lie equidistant from the centre line. The nose is in the middle, the mouth likewise, and so on. The legs, fins, wings are always present in pairs.

Some shapes or parts of the body are also outstandingly beautiful, such as individual horses, stags, dogs, such as the neck of the swan, and the like.

Furthermore, attention must be drawn to the colours of the hide, of the plumage, the shells, the eyes, and to the graceful motion of many animals as well as to the pure forms of bird eggs.

Beautiful above all, however, are beautiful human beings. Upon seeing an absolutely beautiful human being, delight bursts open in our hearts like a rosebud. They have their effect through the flow of the lines, the colour of the skin, of the hair and of the eyes, the purity of the form, the grace of the movements and the melodiousness of the voice.

9.

If we summarise, then the *Subject* is the judge and determines according to its forms what is beautiful, what not. The question now is: Must every person find a beautiful Object beautiful? Without doubt! Even if the Subject is the sovereign judge of the beautiful, it remains subject to the necessity of its nature and *must* objectify as *beautiful every* foundation of the beautiful in the thing-in-itself: it cannot do otherwise. The only prerequisite is that the will of the judging Subject find itself in the aesthetic state, therefore that it confront the Object with complete *disinterest*. If the will changes this relation, if, for example, upon judging a woman's forms the sexual instinct positions itself behind the cognising Subject, then a generally valid judgment is no longer possible. If, in contrast, the will maintains itself in the purity of the aesthetic relation, then the Subject can only err when it is deficiently organised. Such people however have no say in these matters.

What alone it here comes down to is the training of the *sense of beauty* (a modification of the faculty of judgment), which incorruptibly, in accordance with the laws of the subjectively beautiful, delivers its verdict. This sense, like the faculty of judgment, appears in countless gradations and, like this faculty, can be perfected over time, the alterations being inherited. This sense can appear one-sided as the sense of form, sense of colour, musical sense of hearing;

but, whatever this sense in a more perfect constitution declares to be beautiful is beautiful, even when a multitude of individuals with weak senses of beauty or with partial hearts rebels against this judgment. As a man I can rank the Rhein ahead of Lake Como; as a purely aesthetic judge, in contrast, I *must* give the latter precedence.

The genuine sense of beauty *never* errs. It must place the circle above the triangle, the rectangle above the square, the Mediterranean above the North Sea, the beautiful man above the beautiful woman, it cannot judge otherwise; for it judges according to *clear* and *immutable* laws.

10.

We have seen that the foundation of the beautiful is in the thing-in-itself, independent of the Subject, is the inner harmonious motion which must not be called beautiful but only harmonious, uniform. Only an *Object* can be beautiful. If, now, we apprehend ourselves immediately in self-consciousness as thing-in-itself, or if we apprehend the will of another person as caught in harmonious motion, which here appears as a quite idiosyncratic combined effect of the will and mind, then we can most certainly speak of a harmonious will or, if in accordance with spoken convention we lump will and mind together as *soul*, of a harmonious soul. However, instead of this, one usually sees the expression "beautiful soul". This expression is false. Nevertheless, since it has established itself in the idiom, we want to preserve it. One denotes with the term "beautiful soul" that idea called man whose will stands to his mind in a very particular relation, specifically in such a relation that it always moves in moderation. If that idea loses its centre of gravity through dejection or passion, then it soon finds its focus again and not fitfully but fluently.

11.

What is *ugly* I can very easily define. Ugly is everything that does *not* correspond to the laws of the subjectively beautiful. An ugly Object, like a beautiful one, like every Object in general, can be contemplated aesthetically.

12.

The *sublime* is usually placed alongside the beautiful as something similar, related to it, which is incorrect. It is a particular *state* of man, and one ought therefore to speak always of the *sublime state* of man. This state is a double motion. Firstly, the will vacillates between fear of death and contempt of death, with decisive preponderance of the latter, and if the latter is victorious, then the will enters a state of aesthetic contemplation. The individual is repelled by an Object, pushed back on himself, then radiates with admiration.

It is characteristic of the sublime state that in the majority of cases it always generates itself anew, i.e., recapitulates its constituent motions, or in other words, we can keep ourselves in the state of aesthetic contemplation only with difficulty. Again and again we leave this state, sinking back into the struggle between fear of death and contempt of death, and again and again we return, for a longer or shorter period, to the contemplative state.

The *Object* which elevates us above ourselves is *never* sublime. Yet, if one keeps this in mind and merely describes certain Objects as sublime because they easily put us in a sublime mood, then there is no objection to be made against calling them so.

From this point of view the Objects are very correctly subdivided into:

1. the dynamically sublime, and
2. the mathematically sublime.

Dynamically sublime are all natural phenomena which threaten the core of man, his will to *life*. In the desert, in wastelands, which can offer no nourishment, on the shores of the raging sea, before immense waterfalls, during storms and the like, man is easily put into the sublime state because he stares death in the eyes but knows himself to be mostly or completely safe. He recognises distinctly the danger in which he finds himself; yet his safety deceives him into thinking that he would defy that danger if it threatened him. From which convictions he draws this pretended power is irrelevant—whether he believes in his immortality, whether he knows himself to be in the hands of a benevolent god, whether he scorns life and yearns for death, or whether in him no reasoning at all takes place and he elevates himself unconsciously above the danger.

It is easy to see that most men are sublimely disposed only through deception. To many it must first be proven laboriously that there is not, even in the remotest connection, a conceivable danger and yet not even then have they the power to transition for a very brief period into the contemplative state, but persist in a state of anxiety and urge a departure. How few are they who are capable of surrendering entirely to the enjoyment of a mighty storm! They do it like an avaricious gambler who incessantly contemplates the most improbable outcome. Likewise, only very rarely will a man on the open sea take in a storm in a genuinely sublime mood. If, in contrast, the storm has finally passed, then the man will piece together the details which, in the most consuming fear, he glanced only briefly and, contented, rise above himself after the fact.

Mathematically sublime are those Objects which reduce us to a nothingness, which show us our insignificance in the face of the world entire and draw our attention to the brevity and transience of our lives, in contrast to the so-called eternity of the world, or, as Cabanis says, to the *éternelle jeunesse de la nature*. Out of this state of humiliation, of fear, indeed of despair, we rise above ourselves, according to our education, through the most varied considerations and become contemplative. The idealist of the Kantian school takes his bearings from the thought: Time and space are *within* me, the universe is only so immeasurably large inside my head, the thing-in-itself without extension, and the elapsing of phenomena in time is a deception; the pantheist thinks: I myself am this immense universe and immortal: HAE OMNES CREATURAE IN TOTUM EGO SUM ET PRAETER ME ALIUD ENS NON EST; the devout Christian thinks: All the hairs on my head are counted, I repose in a faithful fatherly hand.

13.

The sublime state rests on the imagined quality of the will called firmness or dauntlessness and arises through self-deception. If, however, a will is really undaunted and firm, then sublimity, which is here to be defined simply as *contempt of death*, inheres in the thing-in-itself and one speaks justly of *sublime characters*.

I distinguish three kinds of sublime character:

1. the hero,
2. the wise man,
3. the wise hero.

The hero is in serious situations fully conscious of the fact that his life is really threatened, and although he loves his life, he does not hesitate, when necessary, to let it go. A hero is therefore every soldier under fire who has overcome the fear of death, and every person who puts his life in jeopardy to save another.

The wise man has recognised the worthlessness of life, which Jesus Sirach captures so aptly in the words:

It is a miserably pathetic business the life of all men, from the maternal body onwards, until they are buried in the earth which is mother of us all. There is always worry, fear, hope and finally death;

and this recognition has *ignited* his will. This ignition of the will is a condition SINE QUA NON of the wise man, whom we have in view, because the actual elevation *above life* is the sole criterion of sublimity. The mere recognition that life is worthless cannot yield the sweet fruit of resignation.

The most sublime character is the wise hero. He sees things from the standpoint of the wise man, but unlike the wise man he does not wait, resigned, for death, but rather considers his life a valuable weapon with which to fight for the well-being of mankind. He dies with sword in hand (in the figurative or real sense) for the ideals of humanity, and in every minute of his existence he is ready to sacrifice his blood and treasure for the realisation of those ideals. The wise hero is the purest phenomenon on our earth, the mere sight of him elevates other men because they are caught in the deception that, precisely because they too are men, they would have the same capacity as he to suffer and to die for another. The wise hero is in possession of the sweetest individuality and lives the genuine, blissful life:

> For should great misfortune befall him,
> What of it?

14.

Most closely related to the sublime state is *humour*. Yet, before we define it, we want to immerse ourselves in the essence of the humorist.

We found, above, that the genuine wise man must actually be elevated above life, that his will must have been ignited on the recognition of life's worthlessness. If *only* the recognition is present, and has not transitioned, as it were, into the blood, into the dæmon, or we might say: if the will, as mind, recognises the fact that in life it will never find the satisfaction for which it is searching, but in the next moment embraces life greedily with a thousand arms, then the phenomenon of the true wise man will never appear.

Now, this peculiar relation between will and mind lies at the foundation of the humorist's essence. The humorist cannot survive *for a prolonged period* at the clear summit where the wise man stands.

The usual man is absorbed entirely in life, he does not rack his brain on the world, he asks himself neither: *Whence do I come?*, nor: *Whither do I go?* His earthly objectives he always holds firmly in view. The wise man, on the other hand, lives in a narrow sphere which he has drawn about himself, and has become—it matters not by which path—entirely clear-headed about himself and the world. Each of these men rests firmly on himself. Not so the humorist. He has savoured the wise man's peace; he has felt the bliss of the aesthetic state; he has been a guest at the table of the gods; he has lived in an aether of transparent clarity. And yet he is drawn back into the mire of the world by an irresistible force. He escapes this mire because he can approve only a single striving, the striving for the tranquillity of the grave, and must repudiate all else as folly; but again and again the sirens lure him back into the maelstrom, and he dances and hops in the sultry room, a deep yearning for rest and peace in his heart; for we can call him the child of an angel and of a daughter of man. He belongs to two worlds, for he lacks the power to renounce one of them. In the feasthall of the gods his pure joy is disturbed by a cry from below, and if he throws himself down into the arms of pleasure, his yearning for above sours his pure enjoyment. His dæmon is thus cast to and fro and feels torn. The humorist's basic disposition is unpleasure.

But that within him which does not yield and falter, which stands firm as stone, which he has taken hold of and no longer releases, is the *recognition* that death is to be preferred to life, "that the day of death is better than the day of birth." He is no wise man, even less a wise hero, but it is for that reason he who is fully aware of the greatness of these nobles, of the sublimity of their character, and it is he who empathises wholeheartedly with the blissful feeling which imbues them. He bears them as an ideal within himself and knows that, because he is a man, he can realise within himself that ideal if—yes, if—"the sun stands in favourable relation to the planets."

From these facts, and from the firm knowledge that death is preferable to life, he takes heart, escaping his unpleasure, and rises above himself. He is now free from unpleasure and, this must be noted, now his own state which he has escaped becomes *objective* for him. He measures it against the state of his ideal and sneers at the foolishness of his half-measure: for laughter always arises when we discover a discrepancy, i.e., when we measure something against a mental standard and find it too short or too long. Having entered the ingenious relation to his own state he does not, however, lose sight of the fact that he shall soon fall back into the foolishness at which he has sneered, because he knows well the power of his love for the world, and so only the one eye laughs while the other cries, now the mouth jokes while the heart bleeds and would break, now deepest solemnity is hidden behind the mask of joviality.

Humour is thus a very peculiar and quite idiosyncratic double motion. Its first part is an unpleasurable vacillating to and fro between two worlds, and its second part is no purely contemplative state. In this part, too, the will vacillates between complete freedom from unpleasure and tearful melancholy.

The same is the case when the humorist glances at the world. Against every phenomenen in that world he quietly lays his ideal and none of them is congruent with it. Here he must smile. But he soon recalls how powerfully life lures man in, how unspeakably difficult it is for man to renounce it, since all of us are through and through hungry will to life. He now thinks, speaks, or writes about others with the same delicate mildness with which he judges himself, and with tears in his eyes, smiling, joking with quivering lips, his heart almost bursts with compassion for men:

> All the misery of humanity takes hold of him. – **Goethe**

Since humour can appear in every character, every temperament, it shall therefore always have an individual hue. Remember the sentimental Sterne, the strife-riven Heine, the dry Shakespeare, the warm-hearted Jean Paul and the chivalrous Cervantes.

Clearly the humorist is better suited than any other mortal to becoming a true wise man. If his inalienable recognition is in some way suddenly ignited in the will, then the joke escapes his smiling lips and both eyes become serious. The humorist then steps, like the hero, the wise man, and the wise hero, from the aesthetic domain entirely into the ethical.

15.

The *comical* has multiple points of contact with the beautiful and one with humour.

I divide the comical into:

1. the sensory-comical,
2. the abstract-comical.

In considering the sensory-comical we must distinguish:

1. the subjective standard,
2. the comical Object, and
3. the comical state of the will.

The *subjective standard*, the indispensable prerequisite for the comical in general, is, for the *sensory-comical*, a normal figure with particular motions (of the limbs, features, eyes) or—as the case may be if one is judging only the motions that are detached, as it were, from the Object: words and sounds—an average, normal manner of speaking or singing.

Both norms, although they have a rather broad scope, are not arbitrary. They are a fluid average, which is not gained in a mechanical manner but through a "dynamic effect" from all kinds of men and from the natural varieties of behaviour of the individuals constituting those kinds. Implicit in this fact is the condemnation of every standard gained in a one-sided manner. However, in this fact lies also the great difference which exists between the subjective standard for the sensory-comical and the subjective standard for the beautiful. The former standard has a fluid, the latter a fixed definition. A particular circle that, at one point, deviates however insignificantly from the eternally defined general form, is no longer beautiful. In contrast, the rather wide tolerance for the standards of the comical is balanced by the fact that an Object is comical only when, upon measuring it by those standards, a rather *large* discrepancy is also evident, which of course must fall outside the tolerance range.

What is beautiful or, as the case may be, what is ugly stands in no relation at all to what is comical. An Object can be simultaneously very beautiful and comical; it can be very ugly and yet not comical; finally, it can be ugly *and* comical. Furthermore, it must be remarked that large physical malformations certainly have a comical effect (as evidenced daily by the laughter and mockery it provokes in the uneducated), but in finer natures this comical aspect is immediately smothered by *compassion*.

16.

Now, every Object is comical which does *not* correspond to the subjective standard, i.e., which, held up to it, either falls short of or extends beyond it in such a way that a substantial discrepancy is evident.

Just as the subjective standard of the beautiful, with regard to the fixity of its definition, is essentially different from that of the comical, so the Subject also finds an Object comical in a manner quite different from how it finds it beautiful. An Object is beautiful if it corresponds to the subjectively beautiful; in contrast, an Object is comical if it does *not* correspond to the subjective standard. Accordingly, what is comical, like what is ugly, stands in a negative relation to the relevant standard. For this reason I must also refrain from defining the *subjective* standard. The sensory-comical is best read off from the comical *Objects* themselves.

Like the subjectively beautiful, I divide the sensory-comical into the comical of:

1. space,
2. causality,
3. substance (matter),
4. time.

The comical of *space* reveals itself above all in large deviations of the figure from the normal type of men: therefore, in immeasurably tall, short, spindle-thin and fat individuals; in parts of the body, as in long or flat, misshapenly thick or too thin, pointy noses; in bestial mouths; in too long or too small ears, feet, hands, legs, arms, necks, and so on. The extraordinary daintiness of small hands, feet, and ears is always admired with a smile. One need only think of the extremely comical impression made by the little hands and feet of infants, because we compare them (here entirely inappropriately) with our own hands and feet. The comical of space reveals itself further in towering hairstyles and in those feminine costumes which either give the individual a colossal circumference (crinoline) or are supposed to show individual body parts as unnaturally developed: wasp waste, false bosom, *cul de Paris*. Finally, I mention the making of faces, grimaces, masks, and caricatures.

The comical of *causality* appears in the *difficult transition from effect to cause*, thus in stupidity; in *pointless* or *superfluous movement*: intense gesticulation, stiff flailing of the arms, affected hand movements, a splayed, wooden gait, a wagging backside, clumsy bows, above all clumsy mannerisms, Chinese ceremony, circuitousness, pedantry; in *unfortunate movements*: slipping over, stumbling, unsuccessful jumps; in the *disproportionate application of force to achieve an end*: slamming of open doors as well as pointless noise, immense preparations for a minute result, long overtures, fabulous evasions; in the *application of false means for a desired end*: incorrect use of foreign words, incorrect quotations, incorrect expression in a foreign language and in one's mother tongue, halting speech; in *imitation* which does not suit the essence of the imitator: all affectations, European courtliness, courtly ceremony, titles on the Sandwich Islands, men in women's clothing and women in men's; finally, in the inappropriateness of costume.

The comical of *time* appears in too rapid or too slow a tempo of speech: overhastiness of words, unctuous elongation of words; in stuttering; in mumbling; in the abrupt ejaculation of words; in the droning of melodies.

The comical of *substance* reveals itself in the loud composition of glaring colours in clothing; in voices which grunt or sound nasal, muffled, echoic, or very reedy.

17.

The *comical state* is a double motion whose first part is aesthetic contemplation; for if the individual does not stand in disinterested relation to the comical Object, then its discrepancy from the subjective standard only annoys or upsets him. The second part is a cheerful expansion of the will which, depending on its intensity, moves externally through the gradations from gentle smiling up to convulsive, diaphragm-rupturing laughter. This is also the point of contact of the comical with humour; for here, as there, the perception of a discrepancy stirs merriment within us.

18.

In considering the abstract-comical, we must distinguish:

1. the subjective standard;
2. the incongruence which reveals itself against that standard.

In relation to the abstract-comical, it is the *concept* that plays the main role, although here too it is only ever more or less clearly realised concepts which are compared with each other, therefore presentations, of which the one is the standard the other that which is measured against it.

The abstract-comical is divided into:

1. irony,
2. satire,
3. wit,
4. foolish action,
5. wordplay.

In *irony* a man, as he really is, is taken as the standard. Alongside this standard the mocker, in complete earnest, draws with words a copy which now, be it in shape or in character, deviates fundamentally from the original and does so decisively in *favour* of the original. Every attentive person at once recognises the scorn or, in other words, the discrepancy between original and copy and must laugh. Naturally, they will elicit the greatest sense of irony who either really consider themselves to be better than they are, or who at least want to appear better, lovelier, nobler, abler than they are. The mocker enters into their self-delusion, beautifies or ennobles it in a skilled, apparently harmless manner, until at last an ideal is juxtaposed with a dismal reality: two ideas which, with the exception perhaps of him who is mocked, no man can reconcile.

Opinions, views, hypotheses, prejudices, and the like are also fertile soil for the unfolding of irony. The mocker appears to show an interest in the view of the one whom he intends to mock, develops it in every direction and draws out its consequences, whereby that view becomes mired in logical contradiction and absurdity to the great delight of all present.

In *satire*, the corrupt political or social state of affairs of a nation, a province, a city, even the corrupt state of affairs in a family, is measured against an ideal, be it derived from the good old days or from the life of another people or even from the distant future of men, and then the discrepancy is mercilessly laid bare by the satirist. Here, too, laughter is heard, but it is the furious laughter of scorn.

In *wit*, first of all either two ideas are brought *by means of suitable comparison* under *one* concept, or two ideas already standing under *one* concept are considered. Then the concept is realised, the *same* pronouncement being made about each of the two ideas, whereby, however, the ideas at once separate from each other. The discrepancy is a total one: the standard and that which is measured against it come into contact only at their ends.

In the very witty epitaph of a doctor: "Here, like a hero, he lies, and the slain lie all about him", the idea of a doctor, by means of an apt comparison, is first brought with the idea of a brave army commander under the one concept "hero". Then, however, the same statement is made about both, namely: that they rested amongst those they had slain, which once again separates both ideas completely; for the statement bestows honour on the one, but shame on the other. (Standard: a hero in the narrow sense.)

In the well-known anecdote of the Gascon who wore summer clothing in the depths of winter and, to the king who laughed at him, replied: "If you had put on what I've put on—namely, your entire wardrobe—then you would not laugh," two very different Objects stand ready under one concept: entire wardrobe. Then the same pronouncement is made about both, and immediately the Objects diverge substantially from each other. (Standard: the large wardrobe of a king.)

In *foolish action*, the actor starts from a given concept, such as Don Quixote from the general maxim: A good Christian shall help all the oppressed. He now acts according to this maxim, intentionally or unintentionally, even in such cases as are no longer entirely subject to the rule. Thus, Don Quixote freed galley slaves, who were certainly *oppressed* persons, but not such as a Christian is supposed to help. Here the standard is the reasonable thought: Oppressed persons should be freed from their oppressed situation, but not criminals.

Finally, in *wordplay*, concepts that sound the same or similar (in consummate wordplay *only* those which sound the same) but are of disparate meaning are whimsically confused. Here, the word in its usual meaning is the standard and the word in its more remote meaning is that which is measured against this standard. The discrepancy is a total one.

19.

We had, for the purpose of defining the comical, to place ourselves on the highest vantage point. There we found the *philosophical* standards for the sensory-comical and can rest assured. We do not, however, want to conclude without casting a glance at the false standards already mentioned, which circulate and prevail in ordinary life.

The foundation of what is comical: the standard and what is measured against it, must of course not be undermined. Discrepancy, which can only reveal itself against a particular standard, is a CONDITIO SINE QUA NON of the comical. Now, there is in the *Object* no room for caprice, for the Object is however it appears to be. It is therefore the *standards* alone which can be modified.

Now, for the production of these standards amongst the people, whatever is *usual* is the guide. Whatever seems unusual to a man is called by him comical or funny, without a second thought. Thus one says: You seem so funny to me today, i.e., today you are acting differently from how you usually act. Indeed, often enough I have heard: the wine tastes funny, the chime of the clock sounds funny—expressions which must be supposed merely to allude to a perceived discrepancy.

Thus, a peasant who comes for the first time to a large town will find everything in that place funny, i.e., unusual, and will, if he discovers a large discrepancy while in the aesthetic relation, laugh heartily. A Chinaman will still be found funny in Europe, in San Francisco no longer, for here in Europe he is still breaking into the narrow compass of what is usual, whereas there he falls already within its compass.

Furthermore, one speaks often of funny characters and understands by that expression eccentric people, characters whose deeds and pursuits are simply different from those of the usual man. Such individuals are seldom judged fairly, for the effort is not made to penetrate into their essence, mostly however because we haven't the ability to do so. Thus, the same short standard is applied to all who have left the great military road and wander on their own paths. The petit bourgeois will find ludicrous someone who has a free and noble character; indeed, those dismal spirits never die out who take a wise man or a wise hero for a fool.

The false standards, when they are applied by the individual in the aesthetic relation, of course produce the same comical state as the correct ones. For this reason, more *and* less in the world is ridiculed than ought to be ridiculed.

Clearly, for the most part, it is man alone who can be a comical Object. There are very few comical animals (such as a cab horse used as a riding horse). They mainly become comical only once they have been intentionally brought into human situations (Reynard the Fox) or when one *cannot but* compare them with humans, like the apes.

20.

If we look back from our current standpoint then we find what I said at the beginning thoroughly confirmed, namely, that aesthetics treats only of one particular state of man into which he is put by a specific mode of contemplating ideas. The state, the aesthetic state, showed itself to us as being of two main kinds: contemplation and aesthetic sympathy.

All other states which we come into contact with are composite states, having arisen from the combination of the aesthetic state with the states dealt with in the Physics, which for the sake of brevity I will here call *physical* states. Only in humour did we find a moral state of the will, compassion (for oneself and for others), which we will have to consider more closely in the Ethics. Aesthetic enthusiasm, the sublime and comical states are thus physical-aesthetic double motions and humour is a physical-aesthetic-ethical motion of the will.

The aesthetic state is based not on a *liberation* of the mind from the will, which is absurd and entirely impossible, but on the dæmon's lack of desire, which is always lacking when, in physiological terms, the blood flows calmly. The blood then preferentially actuates the brain, the will becomes immersed, as it were, entirely in one of its organs and—since the organ feels all motions, just not its own—the will is here embraced by the illusion that it is completely at rest. The dæmon's entry into and maintenance in the aesthetic relation is facilitated by Objects which do not provoke it. If in the aesthetic relation it encounters an Object which awakens its desire, then all composure is at once also lost.

If the will is not completely satisfied, then only with great difficulty does it become contemplative, indeed most men will at that point be *unable* to put aside the usual mode of considering things. Take someone who is freezing, who is in pain, or whose stomach is growling and place him before the most beautiful image, into the most glorious natural environment—his mind will be unable to serve as a spotless mirror.

On the other hand, the principle also applies that the more developed the mind, specifically the more cultivated the sense of beauty, then the more frequently the will shall savour aesthetic joy; for the mind is the will's advisor born of the will itself, and the greater the scope of its vision the greater too is the number of powerful *countermotives* which it can lay before the will until, finally, it gives the will a motive which, once fervently apprehended, holds the will entirely captive and smothers in it all other desires—a topic whereof the Ethics shall treat.

21.

We thus arrive at art and the artist. However, before we bestow our attention upon these topics, we want to enter a field where man influences *natural* Objects aesthetically, i.e., in accordance with the laws of the subjectively beautiful, and, as it were, cultivates these Objects aesthetically.

In that field we encounter first the gardener. Initially he ensures, through the warding off of all harmful influences and the enhancement of stimuli, that the plants can develop unhindered and their inner harmonious motion can vigorously unfold. He refines in this way the natural growth. He then refines, through his influence on fertilisation, the blossoms and also the fruits.

He then reshapes the soil surface. Here he creates small hills, there valleys; he divides up the terrain by means of straight or beautifully winding paths and in individual sections describes beds which form regular figures: circles, ellipses, stars.

He also makes use of water, in one moment collecting it in ponds, in another letting it cascade over rockwork, then letting it soar upwards as a fountain.

He then plants the prepared terrain. Here he conjures up lush, beautiful lawns; there he forms avenues, here groves of trees whose foliage exhibits every gradation of green; there well-maintained hedgerows. He fills the beds with flowers and foliage plants in patterns (carpet bedding) and here and there emplaces on the lawns a rare, evergreen tree or a group of larger plants. He also hangs from tree to tree garlands of creepers, on which the eye lingers with delight.

Only very few animals can be beautified. With a few, beautification can be achieved indirectly through refinement, then directly, in narrow limits however, through dressage, as with the horse, whose movements can be made decidedly more graceful.

In contrast, man is the only natural Object which, in various directions, has the capacity for beautification. Man can be aesthetically cultivated.

Through cleanliness and caring of the skin, as well as through temperance, one can, to begin with, give the body a delighting freshness. Then the tasteful arrangement of the hair of both sexes and of men's beards is an important means of beautification; for often a small modification of the hairstyle, the changed situation of a curl, gives the face a different, much more appealing expression.

That said, emphasis is to be placed chiefly on the training of the body and on the beautification of its movements. The former is achieved through diligent gymnastics, jumping, running, riding, fencing, swimming; the latter through dance and cultivation in the narrow sense. Grace is certainly inborn, but it can also be acquired through learning, at least awkward movements can be smoothed out and pointless ones unlearned. Physical exercises give the body, apart from suppleness, often a modified form too, because they strengthen it and effect fullness of the muscles and rounding out of the fleshy parts. Often the face also receives a more winning expression, for one has come to know one's strengths and is confident in them.

An important institution for the aesthetic cultivation of man is the army. Not only is the body of the soldier trained through the means mentioned, but his sense of beauty is also educated by the regular, beautiful movements of the single soldier and of the troop units; for tight drilling and fluent manoeuvring are beautiful.

Man can, furthermore, beautify the sound of his voice ("a soft, gentle and low voice – an excellent thing in a woman" – Shakespeare) and his speech above all; the latter by avoiding all thoughtless blathering, practising fluent speech without falling into rants, and lending his delivery a certain nobility.

Man is further beautified by simple manners.

Clear penmanship also belongs here.

Finally, I mention simple but tasteful and well-sitting clothing which lets the beauty of the body stand out, sometimes even heightens it. The colour of clothing is also important, especially for women. We say: This colour suits a woman, it becomes her.

22.

Art is the *transfigured* reflection of the world, and he who brings this reflection about is called an artist.

The requirements for the artist are: firstly, the capacity to transition easily into the aesthetic state; secondly, the drive to make reproductions or to create; thirdly, a developed sense of beauty; fourthly, a vivid imagination, an acute faculty of judgment, and a good memory, i.e., the auxiliary faculties of reason must be highly developed.

Thus equipped, he apprehends the ideas as phenomena (Objects), and the idea of man too, according to their innermost essence, as thing-in-itself, and forms their *ideals*.

The ideas (the *individual* wills to life) are caught in a constant flux of becoming. Motion is life, and since we cannot even think of the will without motion, so—however far we may lose ourselves in the past of the world, or to whatever extent we may anticipate its future—we always have the flux of becoming. In this flux the individuals struggle against each other incessantly, submerge and rise again to the surface, as the same individuals or unnoticeably modified. These modifications can be inherited in organic beings, can bury themselves ever deeper into the essence of the idea and impress upon the idea a particular character. The lower the idea stands on the ladder, i.e., the simpler its essence, then the more constant will it be; however, the more highly organised it is, then the less it can assert its individuality in the struggle and the more it must yield to the most varied influences.

Nowhere is the jostling and friction greater than in the State of man. Here there is always severe want, and the death of one man is the life of another. No matter where we look, the most shameless egoism and utter recklessness grin back at us. Here the order of the day is to be vigilant and to thrust, right and left, with hands braced on one's hips so that one is not torn to the ground and crushed under foot. And so it comes to be that no man is comparable to another, and each has a particular character.

Nevertheless, everything in nature is only individual will to life, and although every man has an idiosyncratic character, the general idea of man yet expresses itself in each. But it is a grave error—an error which swathes the faculty of judgment in a veil and plunges it into a fanciful dream-life—to assume that hidden behind similar individuals there reposes a unity and that this unity is the true, the genuine idea. To do so would be to mistake shadows for real things. The kind or the species is a conceptual unity, to which in actual reality a multiplicity of more-or-less similar real individuals corresponds—nothing more. If by means of natural science we go back and arbitrarily interrupt the flux of becoming, then we can arrive at a primordial form in which all currently living individuals of one kind pre-existed VIRTUALITER. But this primitive form was smashed to pieces, it is no more and none of the individuals now living resembles it.

Now, the artist's ideal is certainly a single form, but not the primitive form arrived at by science which an imaginative natural researcher, on the basis of palaeontology, may well be capable of creating for a species, more or less precisely; rather, it is a form that floats in the midst of the *living* individuals of a given kind. The artist observes the individuals closely, apprehends in them what is essential and characteristic, and lets what is inessential recede—in short: judges, synthesises, and allows what has been synthesised to be retained by the imagination. This all occurs by means of a "dynamic effect", not through a mechanical superposition of individuals in order to obtain some average, and in the process of synthesising the sense of beauty is already active. In this way the artist gains a half finished ideal, which, if he is an ideal artist, he then remodels entirely during the process of reproduction and according to the laws of the subjectively beautiful, submerging it fully in the cleansing flood of the formally beautiful, from which he then removes it transfigured and fresh as dew.

Here, now, is the point where art separates into two large branches—into:

1. ideal art,
2. realistic art.

The cognising Subject must accommodate itself, in its usual life, to the external world, i.e., it *must* objectify what is proffered it, and in particular must do so precisely and without the merest arbitrary modification: it can do nothing else. It cannot *see* an Object which is murky green as pure green; it cannot *see* an irregular figure as regular; it cannot *see* a stiff movement as graceful; it must *hear* the performance of a speaking, singing, music-making man as it sounds; it cannot *hear* concatenations of dissimilar time intervals following irregularly upon each other as sequences of rhythmic articulations; it must also objectify the outbursts of passion as they *are*, however horrifying they may be. In short: The Subject must reflect the external world as it is, ugly as well as beautiful, repellent as well as attractive Objects; clattering, squeaking, and melodious sounds alike.

Not so the artist. His mind is not the thrall of the external world but creates a *new* world: a world of grace, of pure forms, of pure colours; he reveals the inner world of man in states which are modest and combines sounds and melodious words into sequences which are commanded by rhythm. In short: He leads us into that marvellous paradise which is formed according to the laws of the subjectively beautiful alone.

Now, if the artist forms only beautiful single Objects, or groups of such Objects in harmonious arrangement about a centre-point; if he reveals to us the *beautiful soul*, then he serves ideal art and is an ideal artist.

But art would not reflect the entire world, which is of course its task, if it only reproduced what is beautiful. It is supposed to unveil the essential nature of each living thing in the bewitching manner idiosyncratic to it, i.e., art is supposed to present to man, sugar-coated and thoroughly sweetened, the bitter fruit of the tree of knowledge, which he accepts from the hand of religion and philosophy only seldom and reluctantly, so that he savours it and his eyes are then opened—or, as the poet says:

> *Così all'egro fanciul porgiamo aspersi*
> *Di soavi licor gli orli del vaso:*
> *Succhi amari ingannato intanto ei beve;*
> *E dall' inganno suo vita riceve.*
>
> **Tasso**.
>
> So we, if children young diseased we find,
> Anoint with sweets the vessel's foremost parts
> To make them taste the potions sharp we give;
> They drink deceived, and so deceived, they live.

Where the sober concept and arid doctrine fail, the captivating image and sweet melody succeed. Now, if the artist shows the world as it is: the ghastly struggle of its individuals for existence; the guile, malice, and wickedness of one man, the mildness, meekness, and sublimity of another; the agony of one, the pleasure of another, the restlessness of all; the various characters and their shining through into corporeality, in this visage reflected the insatiable desire for life, in that visage renunciation—then he is a realistic artist and serves realistic art.

Each of these genres of art is fully justified. Whereas the creations of ideal art put us into the aesthetic mood with incomparably more ease than the real Objects and let us enjoy the blissfulness of rest to which, amidst the bland doings of the world, we yearn ever more deeply to return; the works of realistic art put us into the moved aesthetic state, we become aware of what we are and, shocked, we shrink back. Whatever kind of artistic domain we may enter—we always see, in the blue haze of the distance, the heights of the ethical domain which awaken yearning within us, and in this regard the close relationship of art to morals is manifest.

The aesthete demands only one thing from the realistic artist, namely, that he *idealise* and not be a pure naturalist, i.e., he should *transfigure* reality, not copy it with photographic fidelity. If he does the latter, then his works are stimulating merely by chance, because reality, as is often the case with landscapes, is by chance already a complete ideal; usually such works will be dull and repellent. Here he should temper, there enhance, here soften, there intensify, without obliterating the character of what he depicts. Specifically, he should capture an event at its most interesting moment, the expression of a face when it shows its character most distinctly, and should present no disintegrating groups.

23.

Next to ideal and realistic art one can place a third kind: *fantastical* art. In its figures is reflected not the world, but only parts of the world, which the artist either leaves as they are or arbitrarily modifies, and which he then combines into a whole.

Such figures can be of extraordinary beauty; usually, however, they have only a cultural-historical value and, conceived as whole Objects, are mostly ugly and repellent.

Fantastical art is rooted in the rich soil of religion and must be viewed as the mother of the two other types of art; for in the youth of humanity, where the individual still lay wholly in the grip of nature and trembled before the omnipotence of the whole which defied his grasp, man struggled to shape the powers thought to lie beyond his senses and thereby to bring them nearer his feeling. He wanted to be able to see his gods and, trembling before them, to sacrifice to them what he most loved in order to propitiate them. Now, since for the shaping of idols there was nought at his disposal but the intuitive world, he therefore had to compose within its forms; but, on the other hand, because he was not allowed to place the gods on a level with himself, there remained for him no other way out but to augment these forms to colossal proportions and, moreover, to compose the whole such that no being in nature corresponded to it. Thus arose those idols with many heads, countless eyes, many arms (which allude at once to omniscience and omnipotence), the winged bulls and lions, the sphinxes, and the like. Later, when religion had become purer and more transparent, the artists furnished beautiful people with wings (Amor, Nike, etc.). The Christian artists composed the most beautiful fantastical figures (wonderfully sweet children with wings), but also the ugliest (devils with horns, the legs of horses and goats, wings of a bat, and glass eyes as large as thalers).

Here belong also those figures which blossomed not out of religion but are rooted in legends and fairytales, such as lindworms, centaurs, mermaids, goblins, and the like.

24.

Art encompasses five distinct arts:

1. the art of construction (architecture),
2. the art of sculpture,
3. painting,
4. the art of poetry,
5. the art of sound (music),

which one tends to call the fine arts, as distinct from the practical arts, which appear in the wake of the former.

The three first arts have only to do with visible Objects, and their creations are thus spatial and material, but free from time. In contrast, poetry and music (the former describes and depicts Objects only in passing) concern themselves immediately with the thing-in-itself, the sound-artist understanding in his own breast all of man's states, the poet understanding all of man's states and all of the qualities of man's will, more or less clearly; for genius has precisely the capacity to generate temporarily within itself qualities of the will which it could not otherwise experience, and to put itself in every state. What is found in this way, however, is set down in substantial Objects, in words and sounds, and thus the works of poets and sound-artists are free of space and matter, but within time. (Substance, which is the vessel, is eclipsed by the content.)

25.

Architecture is the most subjective of all arts, i.e., the one most independent of Objects; for it does not reproduce Objects but creates them with complete freedom. The architect does not represent the chemical ideas but only composes within them; they are mere material in which he reveals purely the formally beautiful of space. A beautiful building is nothing other than the formally beautiful of space become visible in a particular direction.

The ideas of the material, as has already been said, are a secondary concern. They are only significant insofar as one material more than another—through its colour, its lustre, etc.—can correspond to the formally beautiful of matter, a fact which is certainly important. A temple built out of white marble will be essentially more beautiful than another, of the same form, built out of red sandstone. If, however, one emphasises the essential nature of material, gravity and impenetrability, and places the aim of beautiful constructive art in putting the play of these forces on display; if, in other words, one makes column and load the principal concern and lets the form retreat, then one is revering a grave error.

The art of construction thus reveals almost exclusively the subjectively beautiful of space by representing and juxtaposing the beautiful figures and bodies already mentioned above, or their parts.

All regular figures and bodies are beautiful, but their beauty has degrees.

In considering the floor plan, the circle is the most complete figure. After the circle comes the rectangle composed of two squares; this is followed by rectangles having other relations of length to breadth, the square, and so forth.

In considering the elevation, the vertical straight line predominates, and cylinders, columns, cubes arise. If the building is defined by inclined straight lines, then cones and pyramids arise.

If we turn our attention finally to the roof, then we find the higher or lower gabled roof, the cupola, and so on, and on the inside the horizontal, gabled, barrel-vault, ogival, and dome ceiling.

All relations and articulations of a beautiful work of construction are dominated with inexorable strictness by *symmetry* and the formally beautiful of *causality*, the latter of which appears as the economy with which an architectural work meets its purpose. Every part should correspond to its purpose in the simplest manner, nothing should be overloaded or uselessly convoluted. Just how disruptive an effect a violation of the beautiful of causality has can be seen clearly from the Solomonic column.

Within the laws of the subjectively beautiful, the architect has the freest room to play when elaborating façades. One can call these the blossoms of a work of construction.

The main construction styles, as is well known, are the Greek, the Roman, the Moorish, the Gothic, and the Renaissance styles. The Greek style is of the noblest simplicity and reveals the subjectively beautiful of the art of construction most superbly. One calls it the classic or ideal style.

In the wake of the beautiful art of construction come: the practical art of construction, the art of ship construction, the art of machine construction, the technical art of construction (bridging structures, viaducts, aqueducts, and so on), the trade of the carpenter and of the potter (kilns). Gemcutting must also be mentioned.

26.

With *sculpture*, it is no longer a matter of realising the formally beautiful with complete freedom, but of the representation of ideas in pure forms. The artist either sculpts them as ideals, or he merely idealises them.

The subjectively beautiful of *space* reveals itself in the domain of sculpture in the clean flow of the lines, in the proportional structure of the body and in the rounding off of the fleshy parts; the subjectively beautiful of *matter* in the colour and purity of the material; the subjectively beautiful of *causality* as grace. Every motion, every pose must stand in the simplest relation to intention, and the act of the will must express itself purely and clearly therein. All stiffness, woodenness, stiltedness—however obscurely it may appear—is odious.

The sculptor's chief Object is man. In the representation of this Object, however, he is essentially constrained.

Firstly, the inner life of man can express itself in his external aspect only incompletely: it comes to the surface heavily veiled. It reflects itself, insofar as it is here considered, most imprecisely in the shape, more distinctly in the pose, and most clearly in the countenance, particularly in the eyes.

In the representation of this external aspect the sculptor is constrained yet further. In the sculpture, the warm tones of the flesh are found to be lacking, which even the most beautiful material is incapable of replacing. The sensitive Greeks perceived this deficiency only too well and they sought to overcome it by sculpting the work of art out of various materials: the fleshy parts out of ivory, the robes out of gold. Indeed, they went so far as to colour the hair and to insert coloured eyes. However, the deficiency cannot be eliminated at all, and a plastic work sculpted from beautiful material of a single colour always earns preference. To ornament the sculpture through painting is entirely inappropriate, since the contrast between the rigid image and the pulsating reality would be too great. In viewing a painting, the observer knows he has only to do with illusory bodies, and so he cannot become disillusioned with the work. In the plastic arts, however, he would first succumb to the illusion of the true-to-life statue, which itself would then also disillusion him, and all composure in the Subject would be lost.

Secondly, the sculptor can show the Object in only *one* pose. Now, if this pose is the expression of an intense motion, then there is an imminent danger (since the motion is as if petrified, whereas the natural man never assumes one and the same pose for long) that it will not long dispose the viewer to contemplation. For this reason, the artist usually sculpts man in the state of rest, in which state the individual can be thought to persist for a considerable duration, and for that reason the contrast with life does not have an unsettling effect.

For the same reason, a passionate motion in the facial features is not advisable. The passionate states, however often they may arise, are still always transitory. It is recommended for this reason that the facial features be charged only with the expressions that *augur* the outburst, not the outburst itself; the tensions must, however, be expressed very distinctly and, as it were, tellingly.

Finally, the sculptor is still constrained by the brittleness of the material and the difficulty of sculpting easily surveyable groups. The Farnese Bull is, as a group, a misguided work of art. For this reason, the artist will usually sculpt individuals or groups of at most two or three people.

He can move more freely in relief work, where the plastic arts cross over into the domain of painting, so to speak. In reliefs, motion can also be more passionate, since the eye does not long linger on single features.

In contrast, the sculptor can completely represent the shape, the outlines of the corporeality.

The ideal of the human form is not singular. Each race will have a different one. But the human ideal of the Greeks will assert itself through all time as the noblest and most beautiful. The Greeks were a beautiful breed of human, and it is to be assumed that single individuals were so outstandingly beautiful that the artist had only to recognise this beauty and imitate it. Additionally, there also prevailed a form of public and private life that permitted corporeality to blossom to its utmost. From earliest youth onwards, the body of the Greek noble was exercised in gymnastics; the joints were made supple and capable of displaying the greatest expressions of power effortlessly and gracefully. Through social institutions, the aristocratic Greeks were relieved of all harsh labours which forced the body to develop one-sidedly, while on the other hand the passions, which can have such a destructive influence on the organism, expressed themselves in the Golden Age of that people only modestly, through natural disposition and social convention. Will and mind stood, in the leading individuals of this blessed people, in the most favourable relation to one another.

Thus arose those imperishable exemplars of the noblest human corporeality which, although they are for the most part available to us only in copies, delight our hearts and elevate us so easily into aesthetic contemplation. Just as before the ancient Greeks there was no people which expressed the idea of man in its shape as purely as they, so there shall also never appear a second people in the development of the human race which, in itself and its cultural life, would carry the prerequisites for such achievements. With the Greeks everything came together: beautiful Objects in abundance; a consummate sense of beauty; youth of the people; dissolution of the entire ego in harmonious, noble sensuality; a cheerful nature; free, public life; a mild religion; and mild but strictly presiding conventions.

If we now enter more closely into the particulars of this ideal, then firstly the face exhibits a noble oval. The forehead is moderately high and smoothly domed. The eyes glance peacefully and clearly. The nose is the direct continuation of the forehead, its top is a little rounded and one sees on the nostrils that they will move in agitation. The mouth is not too small and is formed from gracefully swollen lips. The chin protrudes nobly. The splendidly domed cranium is covered with full curly hair.

The neck, not too short, rests freely on a broad chest, and in the same way the rest of the body flows onwards in radiant beauty as the slender abdomen, narrow waist, strong thighs, full calves, down to the well-formed feet.

Now, into this general ideal the artist brought youth and age, or the particular character of the god or hero, here adding something, there taking something away.

The female body was formed in a similar way. The chest is narrower, the shoulders fall off at a greater incline, the waist is broader and the entire shape is more tender, less powerful, more yielding than that of the man.

If the figure is entirely or partly clothed, then in this aspect the artist is given ample opportunity to represent the subjectively beautiful of space in the flowing of the garments, in the the way the folds fall, and so on.

27.

Hellenic plastic arts and *ideal* sculptural art are interchangeable concepts.

Now, in realistic sculptural art it is not a matter of representing ideal figures in which the individual idiosyncrasies are extinguished, but of emphasising and idealising the individuality. Specifically, great important men who outshone their contemporaries should be preserved in effigy for subsequent generations. The Object is the thing-in-itself that has passed through the subjective forms, and the thing-in-itself expresses itself faithfully in the Object insofar as it is perceptible. In realistic plastic arts, the artist must therefore adhere primarily to the given phenomenon, but he has sufficient leeway to transfigure it. The individual shows himself in many dispositions which modify his features. These the artist considers, and he chooses that expression which is the most beautiful. One then tends to say: The artist has apprehended the individual in his most beautiful moment. Furthermore, he can, without impairing the similarity, soften an ugly feature here, let a beautiful one stand out there.

The most beautiful works of realistic plastic art arose from the soil of the Christian religion in the thirteenth century. They are works representing good, devout, saintly people who are entirely saturated with faith in the gospel's redeeming power, their faces impressed with the yearning for the eternal, painless kingdom of God. Their entire frame is broken and full of humility, the head gracefully inclined, the transfigured facial features express clearly that here the desire for earthly life has been utterly extinguished, and from the eyes—as far as the plastic arts can show it at all—shine chasteness and love and that peace which is higher than all reason.

In the wake of sculpture follow the arts of gold- and silversmithing, stonemasonry, wood carving, and the trades which produce the manifold objects made out of bronze and other metals, out of fired clay, glass, porcelain, volcanic rock, and the like. The art of stone engraving must also be mentioned.

28.

Painting, like sculptural art, has as its purpose the representation of ideas as phenomena. However, it achieves more than sculptural art and is a more complete art, firstly, because by means of colour it can better and more faithfully reproduce reality in general and the inner life of the idea in particular, which is reflected so wonderfully in the eyes and the play of the facial features; secondly, because, being hindered by no difficulty in the material, it draws into the domain of its representation the entirety of nature as well as the works of architecture and the plastic arts. Painting's lack of complete corporeality is adequately compensated by illusion.

According to the ideas with which it is primarily concerned, painting is landscape painting, animal painting, portraiture, genre painting, or historical painting, branches which are more closely considered by the specialist subfields of aesthetics.

The subjectively beautiful of sculpture pertains to painting too; however, because representation through painting is more complete, new laws also obtain. The beautiful of *space* demands a correct perspective; that of *causality* the effective grouping of persons around a real or ideal centre-point, the clear expression of the action in its most significant moment and the telling nature of the relation in which the acting people stand to each other—in short, a considered composition; the beautiful of *matter* demands consummate complexions, flesh tones which are lifelike in their warmth, harmonious colour composition, pure efficacy of light, and correctly shaded distances (midground, background) in the landscape.

Even if Greek sculpture has established the ideal of the human form, painting autonomously formed and still forms the pure beautiful corporeality in those domains where the mind has free play: in the domains of legend, of mythology and of religion. Like a red thread, *ideal* historical painting runs through the history of this artform, and I remind the reader of Raphael's Galatea, of his Madonnas and of Titian's images of Venus.

Connected to ideal historical painting is *ideal landscape painting*. The ideal landscape shows nature in its highest transfiguration: the sky without clouds or with clear clouds of delicate form with golden linings and which arouse yearning in the viewer:

> It is as if the sky wanted to open its arms to the world;

the sea in glassy blues; the mountain ranges of beautifully contoured lines resting in the haze of the distance; the trees in the foreground, the most beautiful of their kind or glorious figures of fancy, dream in quiet repose; beneath them lies a couple in love or a shepherd with his flock or a merry group. Pan sleeps and everything is blissful, bathed in light, and breathes peace and contentment. Such are the landscapes of the unforgettable Claude Lorrain.

But the ideal direction of painting is heavily outweighed by the realistic. Because the painter can work easily, he likes to seek out the individuality and immerse himself in its particularity. He shows nature in glowing tropical splendour and in icy torpor, in storm and sunshine; he shows animals and men individually and in groups, at rest and in passionate motion; he depicts the quiet happiness of the family and their destroyed peace as well as the atrocities of battle and the most important events in the cultural life of humanity. He even deals with comical appearances and with what is ugly up to the limit beyond which it would have a disgusting effect. Wherever he can he idealises his figures and laves them in the purifying bath of the subjectively beautiful.

We have already seen in relation to sculpture how, in the Golden Age of the Christian faith, sculptors sought to express in face and form the blissful inwardness of the pious man. And they succeeded, within the limits of their art, utterly. The sacred painters of the Middle Ages now approached the same idea and revealed it in its most glorious perfection. In the eyes of these arresting figures glows a superlunary fire, and on their lips one reads the most beautiful prayer: "Thy will be done!" They illustrate the saviour's profound words: "Behold, the kingdom of God is within you."

The most ingenious painters of every age sought in particular to apprehend Christ himself, the God-man, entirely according to his idea and to give him an objective form. They sought to represent him and to reveal his character in all the significant moments of his sublime life. Amongst the many relevant images, Titian's *The Tribute Money*, Leonardo's study of Christ for *The Last Supper*, and Correggio's *The Veil of Veronica* must be emphasised. They show the wise hero's spiritual superiority, his chaste holiness, his consummate humility, and his overwhelming steadfastness in all his suffering. They are the most precious pearls of the visual arts. Held against these, what is the *Zeus of Otricoli*, the *Venus de Milo*? Just as the overcoming of life is higher than the desire for life, and ethics higher than physics, so the former creations are higher than these latter from the best age of the Greeks when they were full with the joys of life.

In the wake of painting, we find the art of mosaic, the art of copper engraving, xylography, lithography, ornamentation, drafting (for tapestries, fabrics, embroidery).

Architecture and the visual arts are mutually supportive, for at root they are concerned with arranging the habitations of gods and men according to the laws of what is beautiful.

We cannot leave painting and the plastic arts without having thought of pantomime, ballet, and tableaux vivants. In them, these arts are united with real life; the artists compose in living substance, as it were, and in it they represent what is beautiful completely.

29.

In turning now to *poetry*, we bear in mind that we no longer have to do, in the main, with Objects, but with the thing-in-itself immediately.

No matter when or how often we immerse ourselves in our inner being, we shall constantly feel ourselves in a particular state. In the Physics we investigated the principal states of man, from the barely noticeable normal state up to passionate hatred, and at the start of this Aesthetics have come to know even more of them. Every state is caused by a particular inner motion, either by a simple or by a double motion.

These motions, apprehended with self-consciousness, are what is given to us most immediately and lead us to the bare core of our essence. For by initially paying attention to what moves us in general, to what we inexhaustibly want, we arrive at what we are, namely, insatiable will to life, and by taking note of those states into which we most easily transition and by assembling the motives which most easily move us, we become aware of the channels into which our will primarily flows and call these very channels character traits, the sum of which constitutes our idiosyncratic character, our dæmon.

Now, it belongs to the nature of man that his expansive motions initially force their way beyond the sphere of individuality, i.e., man has the striving to communicate and to proclaim the state of his will. Thus arise the sounds which are nothing other than the inner motions become audible, they are propagations of the inner vibrations in a foreign substance.

When concepts, along with the developed and trained higher faculties of the mind, entered human life, feeling took command of them and made natural sounds into bearers of those concepts. Thus arose language, which is the most complete medium in which man expresses himself and reveals the states of his will.

In words and in their particular timbre man therefore shows his inner being, and they are therefore the material of the poetic art, which concerns itself almost exclusively with the highest idea, with man; for it makes use of the other ideas only in order to give the feelings of man a background against which they stand out more distinctly, and even the most effusive description of nature is nothing other than the expression of the sensation of man's moved heart.

I said that it is the expansive motions in particular which want to be communicated. And in fact the motions that go from the periphery to the centre are usually not accompanied by sounds and words. Only in the greatest grief does the natural man sob, only at the height of fear does he scream. We have at the same time, by means of civilisation, become ready and ample speakers; most men are talkative, listen to each other with pleasure and are happy when they can communicate their hatred, their grief, their worries, and the like—in short, when they can pour their hearts out.

30.

Poetry is the highest art because on one hand it unveils the entire thing-in-itself, its states and its qualities, and on the other it also reflects the Object by describing it and compelling the listener to represent it with his imagination. It therefore encompasses, in the true sense, the entire world, nature, and reflects it in concepts.

From this the first rule of the subjectively beautiful for poetry arises. The concepts are epitomes and the majority of them are epitomes of the same or very similar Objects. The narrower the sphere of a concept of the latter kind is, the more easily is it realised, i.e., the more easily does the mind find an intuitive representative for it, and the narrower, in turn, such a concept becomes through a nearer definition, the more *intuitive* shall the representative also become. The transition from the concept of a horse to the presentation of a horse is easily effected, although one man shall present to himself a black horse, the other a white, one an old, the other a young, one a slow, the other a spirited horse, and so on. If the poet now says: a spirited black horse, then he compels the reader or the listener to a particular presentation that no longer leaves much scope for modification. The subjectively beautiful of *causality* therefore demands above all a *poetic language*, i.e., concepts which make the transition to the image easy.

Furthermore, the beautiful of causality emerges in combinations of concepts, i.e., in sentences, as *clarity* and *comprehensibility*. The longer the period is, the more intermediate links it contains, the less beautiful is the style. What is clearly thought or purely sensed is also clearly and purely spoken and written. No *style empesé*, but concise diction, a "chaste style".

If the poet reflects merely dispositions, then the beautiful of causality demands *noble, pregnant reproduction of these* and *a correct relation of the effect to the cause*. If the poet complains for no reason, or if he grasps for the gold of the sun in order to adorn his beloved with it, then what is beautiful is lost without a trace, for what is beautiful is always modest.

If, in contrast, the poet shows us acts of the will, then the beautiful of causality appears as a *strict law of motivation*, which can never be infringed with impunity. It is as impossible that someone could act without sufficient motive as that a stone could remain suspended in the air, and it is equally impossible that he should act contrary to his character without a compelling motive. Every action therefore demands a precise justification, and the more comprehensible the motive for the action is, the more beautiful it is. If chance in the narrowest sense enters the game, then it must not come out of the blue but must already have shown itself in the distance; for in real life one is soon reconciled with surprising happenstance, but in art every improbability is upsetting, because one falsely imputes intention to it, and every deus ex machina is odious.

Finally, the beautiful of causality also shows itself in *forced development*. The usual flow of life is all too often uninteresting, our dispositions are distributed over hours, effects often do not show themselves until days, months later. The poet concentrates everything and with one drop of rose oil gives the scent of a thousand roses, so to speak. The events follow more quickly upon each other, the effects are brought closer to the causes, and the context thereby becomes clearer, i.e., more beautiful.

In poetry, the beautiful of *time* is called *metre*. The concepts are simple syllables or compounds of syllables of unequal length and varied emphasis. Now, if the words are combined without consideration of this quantity and quality, then the whole does not readily flow but is to be compared to a current with ice floes bumping into and grating against each other. It is not necessary that the speech be thoroughly measured—even in prose an elegant flow is possible when the masses are at least rhythmically organised—but of course the beautiful of time reveals itself completely in verse. Every metre is beautiful, the one more, the other less, and the Sapphic stanza, e.g.,

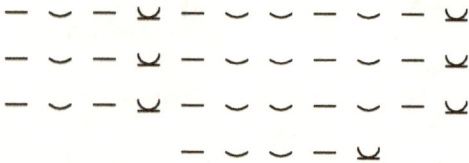

is pleasing as a mere scheme.

As I already explained above, the formally beautiful of *substance* also appears in poetry (and in music) because the communication of feelings is only possible through substantial Objects, i.e., words and sounds. It shows itself here in the changes of the vowels (avoidance of harsh consonant clusters, melodic vocalisation) and particularly in the rhyme, which often has a magical effect; in the spoken word it reveals itself in the melodiousness of the voice.

31.

It is clear that the subjectively beautiful here discussed cannot explain the difference between ideal and realistic poetry; for poetry has as its main purpose the revelation of the thing-in-itself, and the thing-in-itself is independent of the subjectively beautiful. The subjectively beautiful, in its various directions, addresses itself only to the utterances of the inner man.

AESTHETICS

Ideal poetry is based on the *beautiful soul*, which is the genuine ideal of poetry; for it is essential to the ideal that it is an average, and the beautiful soul is equidistant from the sublime character, who has extinguished all human yearning within himself and is no longer rooted in this world, and from the pure man of nature, who has not yet cultivated his individuality into personality.

If, for this reason, we follow the usual division of poetry into lyric, epic, and dramatic poetry, then we will set for ideal lyric poetry the aim of revealing in an unblemished form the dispositions of the beautiful soul, which avoids all extremes, of praising and extolling its acts, and of praising in song its pure relation to the godhead. The beautiful soul is not in itself cold, although it certainly is in comparison with the passionate individuality; for the latter is an intensely moved flame, the former a peaceful clear light. Additionally, it lies in the essence of the beautiful soul, as I have already emphasised, that it is certainly capable of passionate arousal, but in a manner which provides the soothing certainty that the return to equilibrium shall soon take place. Its sensation may therefore be spirited.

The realistic lyricist, in contrast, will be more inclined to let himself go and glide about on the undulations of the most varied sensations.

Since epic poetry in its greater works presents to us the characters, dispositions, and acts of many persons, the field for the epic must be more broadly marked out. One can give the epic only the task of characterising the multitude of characters in a manner free of crudeness on one hand, and free of pronounced individualism on the other. In this regard the hymns of Homer shall forever remain exemplary. His heroes are not exceedingly noble and not ignoble; they pursue real aims, consistently borne by a youthfully vigorous worldview; they fear the gods without quivering; they honour their leaders without the mentality of slaves; and they unfold their individuality within the bounds of social convention.

Realistic epic poetry, in contrast, presents all characters without exception: wise men and mad, evil men and good, the just and the unjust, natures passionate and passive, and the realistic epicist does justice to each individuality.

Man is reflected most completely in drama, in which the players themselves talk and act and unveil their most deeply hidden character traits. Not as one is supposed to think, feel, and act, but as one actually thinks, feels, and acts in the world—that is what the good drama should show: the triumph of the villain and the fall of the just man, the friction between individuals, their need, their torment and their alleged happiness; the course of universal fate, which is created from the acts of all individuals, and the course of individual fate, which is formed on one hand by chance on the other by the drives of the dæmon. Shakespeare will, for all time, remain the greatest realistic dramatist.

The ideal dramatist, in contrast, selects for himself those persons who are not too distant from the ideal of the beautiful soul. He shows them to us at rest and in motion, culpable and innocent, but always transfigured, not lifeless or insensibly fast, not eccentric and extravagant. Amongst the more ancient dramatists, Sophocles in particular presented us such men. Amongst the younger ideal dramatists only our great Goethe can be mentioned. One cannot read *Torquato Tasso* and *Iphigenia in Tauris* without feeling the deepest contentment. The princess and Iphigenia are the true and genuine archetypes of the beautiful soul. And how Goethe knew, within the limits of ideal poetry, to distinguish the other characters so clearly from each other! Where the one or the other, such as Tasso or Orest, wanted to stride, there Goethe held the magical meshwork of beauty over the flame and the flame receded.

It is clear that the laws of the subjectively beautiful are valid for the realistic as well as for the ideal poet; they are binding upon both and cannot be infringed.

In the wake of poetry we find the arts of oratory and acting, which infuse the works of poetic art with heightened life and fundamentally strengthen their impression.

32.

As we have seen, the art of poetry shows us the idea of man, on one hand, as thing-in-itself completely; on the other, it shows us the idea of man as Object by compelling the Subject, through appropriate description, to sketch an image of the idea. I therefore said that poetic art reflects the entire idea, both its inner and outer aspects. Furthermore, poetic art draws into its domain all the other ideas by means of depiction, and I therefore said that poetic art reflects all of nature and must be called the highest artform. Now, *music* has to do with man only, all other ideas are foreign to it, and specifically it deals only with the inner aspect of man and, of that, only with the *states* of the will. It is therefore an essentially less complete art than poetry. But since its material is sound and not the sounding word, it speaks a language comprehensible to all and is that artform which puts us most easily into the aesthetic state, for which reason it must be called the *most powerful* artform.

We recognised above that sounds are nothing more than the inner motions of man become audible or propagations of the inner vibrations in a foreign substance. Yet it must certainly be noted that the sound is not identical with the motion of the soul but is an Object, just as the colour of an Object is not identical with the constitution of the thing-in-itself that causes it.

AESTHETICS

Now, the soul-bewitching magic of human song consists in the fact that the sounds put the will of the listener into the same state from which the sound itself arose, but in such a way that we mourn and yet do not mourn, are jubilant and yet not jubilant, hate and yet do not hate, love and yet do not love, and this cannot be explained any other way than that the sounds take from us our own motion only *in part* and give us theirs in exchange. We metamorphose, as it were, only on the surface of our motion, just as the sea in a heavy storm remains calm in its depths. The same effect is exerted on us by the sounds of instruments when the artist has breathed into them his soul, the state of his will, so to speak, for otherwise their effect is more a mechanical one and does not engage the listener.

33.

The sound-artist's material is therefore sound. Sound rings out and fades away. Accordingly, it has a duration, and one differentiates whole, half, quarter, eighth sounds, and so on. The formally beautiful of *time* now reveals itself in *rhythm*, which encompasses the bar, the accent, the pause, and the tempo of combined sounds. The bar is the regular return of a portion of time in which one sound, or multiple sounds which taken together have the duration of the one sound, move. In order to mark the regular return distinctly, one makes use of accent, i.e., the first sound of a measure is always emphasised. The entire motion of combined sounds can be slow, quick, prolonged, sluggish, fiery, and so on and is called tempo.

The powerful effect of rhythm alone is convincingly evidenced by the beat of a drum.

The formally beautiful of *substance* shows itself in the pure tone of the sound, in the timbre, and in the harmony.

The heights and depths of the sounds are rooted in the number of their oscillations. Middle C makes twice as many oscillations as the C of the small octave, the second $9/8$, the third $5/4$, the fourth $4/8$, the fifth $3/2$, the sixth $6/8$, the seventh $15/8$ as many, or expressed in simple numbers,

c	d	e	f	g	a	b	c̲	makes
24	27	30	32	36	40	45	48	

oscillations in the same time. Now, if sound also rests on motion or, as the case may be, on time, then its oscillations do not enter consciousness, they are objectified as a unity which only through its duration comes to be subject to time and consequently belongs to rhythm. The tone as such and its purity fall under the formally beautiful of substance.

Harmony is the simultaneous ringing out of multiple sounds, i.e., the sounds surrender, as it were, their individuality and there arises, as in chemical compounds, a new individuality, a higher unity. Consonance is present when the harmony is completely pure. If the individual sounds are not entirely dissolved in the harmony, but if the one or the other is still in conflict with it, then dissonance arises. Consonance and dissonance are opposed like satisfaction and longing, states which should indeed also be depicted through music and must necessarily alternate in their appearance, since a series of consonant chords would not be bearable.

The formally beautiful of substance even appears in *major* and *minor*.

34.

Apart from ideal and realistic kinds, music can only be divided into instrumental and vocal music since, from the philosophical standpoint, it reveals only the states of men and is therefore in itself indivisible. Whether I hear a simple song or a polyphonic tune, a duet, a trio, a sonata, a cantata, a mass, a motet, a great hymn, a requiem, an oratorio, or a symphony, always the music tells me of the weal and woe, the grief, the love, the yearning, the joy, the doubt, the peace of man.

Ideal or classical music deals primarily with the states of the beautiful soul: the measured joy, the constrained jubilation, the modest passion. Because all of these motions of the will take place without haste, the ideal sound-artist can completely showcase the formally beautiful. His compositions will be transparent, clear, simple, full of nobility and mostly in a major key, which is powerful and healthy.

The realistic sound-artist, in contrast, depicts all the states of man: fear, doubt, powerful fatigue, immodest jubilation, precipitous transitions from pleasure to unpleasure, boundless passion, disjointed feeling. In order to be able to bring this about completely, he must extend the limits of the formally beautiful considerably, yet the genius realist composer, like Beethoven, will as often as he can bring them closer together again. He will not often destroy the rhythm through overlong pauses, through too many syncopations, by sustaining sounds excessively, by continually preying on the tempo; he will not aim at cheap effects through frequent contrasts, letting the entire storm of the orchestra suddenly fall into the tones of a harp, create physical pain by lingering on a few sounds in the highest regions; he will furthermore not ceaselessly obscure the clarity of the harmony through the accumulation of seventh and ninth chords, nor repeatedly delay the dissolution of the dissonances, but will let what is beautiful float, peacefully and transfiguring, over the most turbluent sea of sensation.

In opera, music enters quite decisively into the service of poetry, for the sounds illuminate, as it were, the actors' hearts, unveil for us the wellspring from which the actions flow, and let the motions of the soul influence us more powerfully than mere words are able.

35.

If we cast a glance back at art, then we see first of all that it easily puts man into the aesthetic state, the unspeakably happy and blissful state. It lets him savour the bread and wine of the purest sensory awareness and awakens in him the yearning for a life full of undisturbed rest. And the ties which bind him to this world of restlessness, care, and torment are loosened.

It then awakens in him love of moderation and hatred of passion's unrestraint, for what he sees and hears, what gladdens him so greatly in image, word, and sound is, all of it, nought but measure and harmony. The formally beautiful is developed ever more within him until it flourishes as the most complete sense of beauty.

Eventually, it enlightens him about the true essence of ideas. It leads him into them with a mellifluous voice along smooth, flower-strewn paths and lets fall before his eyes the veil which obscures their very heart. Smiling, it holds him back when he wants to fly in horror from that hell and leads him up to the brink of the abyss, whispering to him: It is the abyss of *your* soul, you poor child of man—did you not know?

And he knows it henceforth. Certainly, the flood of everyday life will again inundate that awareness and the desire for life will once more rear its head defiantly, but the awareness has left indelible traces in his heart; like wounds they burn and leave him no more rest. Ardently he yearns for another life, but where is he supposed to find it? Art cannot give it to him. It can only put him from time to time into the aesthetic state, in which there is no possibility of lingering. It is here that ethics takes charge of him.

36.

The mental activity of the man who stands in the aesthetic relation to ideas can be called aesthetic cognition, and since this is the mother not only of art but of science too, so it is best called *objective* or *ingenious* cognition.

Art prepares the human heart for redemption, but science alone can redeem it, for science alone has the word which allays all pains, because the philosopher, in cognising objectively, apprehends the *coherence* of *all* ideas and the *fate* of the world, the world-course, which is continuously begotten out of the efficacy of those ideas.

Ethics

Expecting that a person do something to which he is prompted by no interest at all is like expecting that a piece of wood move towards me without a thread pulling it.

Schopenhauer

Simplex sigillum veri: the naked truth must be so simple and comprehensible that it can be taught to all in its true form without diluting it with myths and fables.

Schopenhauer

1.

Ethics is *eudaemonics* or the *theory of happiness*—an explanation which has been battered for centuries without collapsing. The task of ethics is: To investigate happiness, i.e., the state of satisfaction of the human heart in all its phases, to apprehend it in its most perfect form, and to place it on a firm foundation, i.e., to specify the means by which man can attain *complete peace of heart*, the highest happiness.

2.

There is nothing in the world but individual will, which has one principal striving: To live and to maintain itself in existence. This striving appears in man as egoism, which is the veil of his character, i.e., of the manner in which he wants to live and to maintain himself in existence.

Character is innate. Man enters life with very definite qualities of will, i.e., the channels into which his will in its development shall primarily flow are already prefigured. Alongside these channels, all other qualities of the will pertaining to the general idea of man are present in embryo, having the capacity to unfold themselves.

A particular man is the combination of a particular dæmon with a particular mind, for although there is but one principle, individual will, the individuals yet differ from each other in their motion. In man the motion is not manifested as a simple but rather as a resultant motion, and we are therefore required to speak of a combination of principal factors of motion. But this combination is essentially inseparable, and so the motion is only one after all; for what does *this* particular character and *this* particular mind express other than *this* particular motion of the will?

3.

The egoism of man is manifested not only as a drive to self-preservation, but also as a *drive to happiness*, i.e., man wants not only to remain in life in accordance with his character, but he wants also, in every moment of life, the full satisfaction of his wishes, of his inclinations, of his yearnings, in which he places his utmost happiness. Wish – instant satisfaction – new wish – instant satisfaction; these are the links in the chain of a life as *natural egoism* wants it.

A life such as this, which were a ceaseless tumbling from yearning to enjoyment, is nowhere encountered and is practically impossible. No idea is completely independent and autonomous; to be sure, it has its effect unrelentingly and wants to assert its individuality, be it a chemical force or a man;

but just as unrelentingly, the rest of the world has its effect on the idea and constrains it. If we remove a large part of these influences and remain only with those which are exercised by man upon man, then we already gain a picture of the utmost struggle, the consequence of which is that amongst a hundred wishes only one is satisfied and it is almost always that wish whose satisfaction is least desired; for *every* man wants the full satisfaction of his particular yearning, and because that satisfaction is contested he must struggle for it, and for that reason no life-course is ever to be encountered which consisted in a smooth succession of fulfilled wishes, not even where the individual is vested with unrestrained authority over millions. For precisely in this position, indeed in the individual himself, there lie immovable constraints, against which the will invariably surges up only to be thrown back, unsatisfied, upon itself.

4.

Now, since man's natural egoism cannot have such a life as it most dearly wants, it seeks to attain enjoyment (satisfied yearning) *as often as possible*, or, since it can also find itself in situations which are no longer a matter of enjoyment at all but of pain—situations which, depending on the type of struggle, are more common—it seeks the *least* pain. If man therefore stands before two enjoyments, he wants them both; if, however, he must choose between them, then he wants the greater. And if he stands before two evils, then he wants neither of them; if, however, he must choose, then he chooses the lesser.

Confronted with evils or enjoyments in the present, man therefore acts on the presupposition that his mind can correctly weigh up the alternatives. However, since he, owing to his higher cognitive faculty, is not restricted to the present alone but can imagine the consequences that actions shall have in the future, the choice he confronts entails twelve other cases, namely between:

1) an enjoyment in the present, a greater enjoyment in the future
2) an enjoyment in the present, a lesser enjoyment in the future
3) an enjoyment in the present, an equal enjoyment in the future
4) an enjoyment in the present, a greater suffering in the future
5) an enjoyment in the present, a lesser suffering in the future
6) an enjoyment in the present, an equal suffering in the future
7) a suffering in the present, a greater suffering in the future
8) a suffering in the present, a lesser suffering in the future
9) a suffering in the present, an equal suffering in the future
10) a suffering in the present, a greater enjoyment in the future

11) a suffering in the present, a lesser enjoyment in the future
12) a suffering in the present, an equal enjoyment in the future

In cases 2, 3, 5, 6, 8, 9, 11, 12, i.e., in 8 cases, no struggle will eventuate, for the will must:

1) in cases 2 and 3, prefer an enjoyment in the present to a lesser or equal enjoyment in the future;
2) in cases 5 and 6, seize an enjoyment in the present, if in exchange for that enjoyment a lesser or equal suffering shall also befall it in the future;
3) in cases 8 and 9, prefer a lesser or equal suffering in the future to a suffering in the present;
4) in cases 11 and 12, forgo an enjoyment in the future, if in exchange for that enjoyment a greater or equal suffering shall befall it in the present.

The will would have to act in this way if it were *sure* that it would in the future encounter the suffering or, as the case may be, the enjoyment. But since no man can know what form the future will take, whether he will encounter the enjoyment or the suffering, or, what's more, whether he will even be alive at the time when the enjoyment is supposed to be bestowed on him or the suffering to befall him; so in practical life the necessity of acting in the manner specified is significantly more compelling.

In contrast, in cases 1, 4, 7, and 10 the will shall waver intensely. Now, if it assumes the complete uncertainty of the future, then it will very often choose the present, richer in enjoyment or freer of pain, as the case may be. For who:

1) in cases 1 and 10, can guarantee it the greater enjoyment which it purchases, in case 1, by relinquishing enjoyment in the present and, in case 10, enduring suffering in the present?
2) can claim that, in case 4, the will does not after all escape the suffering that it, through enjoyment in the present, is supposed some day to incur, and that, in case 7, it has also really escaped a greater suffering in the future by having borne a suffering in the present?

If, however, the will is in some way certain of the future—and there are indeed actions whose consequences affect man quite certainly in the future—then it will be subject to an intense struggle, but finally, if it is soberminded, decide for the future in all four cases. Then the will must

1) in cases 1 and 4, forgo an enjoyment in the present in order, in case 1, to purchase for itself a greater enjoyment in the future and in or-

der, in case 4, to escape a greater suffering in the future.
2) in cases 7 and 10, endure a suffering in the present in order, in case 7, to escape a greater suffering in the future, and, in case 10, to achieve a greater enjoyment in the future.

However, already at this juncture I want to point out that because the power of the present significantly outweighs that of the future, *assured* enjoyments in the future draw the individual to themselves and *assured* evils in the future can effectively influence the individual only when they *significantly* surpass in magnitude the enjoyment in the present or, as the case may be, the suffering that is to be endured in the present. The individual must see his advantage clearly and distinctly, otherwise he will not fail to fall under the spell of the present.

It follows from all this that man has a perfect *capacity for deliberation* or a *perfect ability to decide between alternatives* and, under certain circumstances, must act *contrary* to his character, namely, if an action were opposed to his well-being considered as a whole, i.e., to his general well-being.

5.

It is the *mind* which ascertains this general well-being in each individual case, or even once and for all; for although it is the will itself which thinks, as it is the will which digests, grabs, walks, procreates, and so on, we may yet, for the reason specified above, consider the cognitive faculty as distinct from the will. In doing so, we always remain conscious of the fact that we have to do with an inseparable combination and, fundamentally, with a single principle, as we also remain conscious of the fact that, as we have seen in the Physics, an *antagonism* between will and mind can *never* arise. Only figuratively can it be said that the mind counsels the will or quarrels with it, and the like; for it is always the will itself which, by means of one of its organs, counsels itself, quarrels with itself. But to speak, even figuratively, of reason's *compelling* of and its possible dominion over the will is completely inadmissible; for even if we had really to do with a fusing together of two autonomous principles, the mind would yet never enter into a relation to the will like that of a lord to his servant, but could at best only be the will's powerless advisor.

As we know, the mind, although it enters into life with certain dispositions, is highly capable of training. The auxiliary faculties of reason, upon which alone the degree of intelligence depends, can, according to how they are treated, atrophy, such that stupidity arises, or they can be brought to unfold to that extent called genius. Development of the mind is the sole task of nurturing, if we disregard physical training; for character can only be influenced by means of the mind and, namely, in such a way that the pupil is clearly and unambiguously shown the disadvantages and advantages which are the consequences of his actions; or, in other words, in such a way that he is enabled to recognise distinctly where his *true well-being* lies.

Good nurturing strengthens the faculties of judgment and memory and either wakes the fancy or bridles it. At the same time it lets the mind absorb a greater or smaller sum of cognitions which are based on experience and are at any moment confirmed by experience. All other cognitions with which it familiarises him it stamps with uncertainty.

This good nurturing is accompanied by bad, in school and family, which fills man's head with chimeras, superstitions, and prejudices, and thereby renders him incapable of taking a clear-eyed look at the world. Later experience will certainly examine his head and rid it of many imagined and false notions, but often it will also strengthen these very notions and allow them to show themselves in earnest only when the individual has the misfortune of stumbling into milieux where his every absurd notion receives fruitful care.

Now, according as the mind of a man is more or less cultivated or corrupted, is a developed or stunted mind, the will shall be more or less enabled to recognise its genuine well-being in general and to judge in every particular case which action best corresponds to its interest, and to take decisions accordingly.

6.

Man's *character* is innate but not unmodifiable; its modifiability, however, moves within very narrow limits, since the temperament cannot undergo a modification at all and individual qualities of the will can undergo one only insofar as a prominent quality of the will can be pressed back once again into a mere germ, or another awoken and unfolded, through the early impression of doctrines and through example, or through the blows of fate, through great unhappiness and severe suffering—which all depends on cognition, since only through the mind can they influence the will.

Were the human will not cognisant, it would be simply unmodifiable, like the nature of chemical force, or to put it a better way, the unrelenting influences of the climate, of the struggle for existence over millennia would be needed in order to bring about a slight modification, as has been demonstrated in plants and animals. But by means of its mind the human will is exposed to influences which penetrate much deeper into it than these just mentioned, influences which choke it and shake it to its very core. Indeed, as we shall later see, cognitions can so kindle the will that it melts and must be viewed as a totally different one insofar as its deeds are now entirely different.

It is then as if a thornbush suddenly bore figs, and yet no miracle has taken place.

7.

In every moment of his life, however, a man is the combination of a particular dæmon and of a particular mind, in short, he exhibits a quite particular individuality, like every thing in nature. Each of his actions is the product of this momentarily fixed character and of a sufficient motive, and must occur of the same necessity whereof a stone falls to the earth. If multiple motives—let them stand vividly before him in the present or lie in the past and future—have an effect on him simultaneously, then a struggle takes place from which the strongest motive emerges victorious. Then the deed occurs just as if *only* one sufficient motive had been present from the first.

8.

It is a result of the foregoing considerations that the deeds of man do not constantly arise in the same manner. Either the will follows only its inclination in the present, without considering the future, without attending to its *knowledge* in the broadest sense, or it decides in accordance with its general well-being. In the latter case, man acts either in agreement with the nature of his will or against it.

Now if, under the spell of the present, he acts in accordance with his inclination but against his better *knowledge*, then after the deed, according to its significance, he will feel intense or gentle *pangs of conscience*, i.e., the same voice within him which, *before* the deed and with a view to his general well-being, advised him to forsake the present enjoyment, becomes *after* the deed loud once more and reproaches him with his impetuousness. It says to him: You *knew* that forbearance lay in your genuine interest and have done the deed anyway.

Pangs of conscience escalate into *anxiety of conscience*, either out of fear that a punishable act will be discovered, or out of fear of a particular punishment after death.

Different from a pang of conscience, but very closely related to it, is *regret*; for regret arises only out of knowledge *gained after the fact*. If I have acted in haste, i.e., if my conscience had no time to warn me, or if I acted under the influence of a motive which I held to be genuine but which afterwards proved to be false, or if at some later juncture, my cognisance of matters having been rectified, I place my well-being in something entirely different from that in which I placed it at the time of the deed, then I am regretting deeds which can

ETHICS

in no way burden my conscience; for the voice which now speaks to me in my regret was, *before* the deed, silent.

Pangs of conscience, anxiety of conscience, and regret are ethical states of the will and, specifically, states of unpleasure.

Hallucination also belongs amongst these states. Tortured by pangs of conscience, the dæmon (objectively expressed: the blood) is so violently agitated that it compels the mind to concern itself always with just one object, whereby, and owing to the elevated activation of the brain's life, the impressions of the external world are suppressed and now, for example, the murder victim emerges from the darkness, distinct and purely objective, and places himself before the horrified dæmon.

9.

Now, it might seem that man has the LIBERUM ARBITRIUM INDIFFERENTIAE, i.e., that his will is *free* because, as we have seen, he can carry out deeds which are *not* at all in accordance with his character, but rather are entirely at odds with his nature. But this is not the case. The will is never free and everything in the world happens of necessity.

In the moment he is confronted with a motive, every man has a particular character, which, if the motive is sufficient, *must* act. The motive appears of necessity (for every motive is always the link in a causal chain, which is under the control of necessity), and the character must of necessity obey it, for the character is a particular one and the motive is sufficient.

I now posit the case: The motive is sufficient for my *character*, but insufficient for my *entire ego*, because my *mind* deploys my general well-being as a countermotive, and this latter is stronger than the former. Have I now acted freely because I did not yield to a motive sufficient for my character? Not at all! For my mind is by nature a particular mind and its training in some direction or other happened of necessity, because I belong to *this* family, was born in *this* city, had *these* teachers, kept *this* society, had *these* particular experiences, and so on. The fact that this mind, which has become of necessity, can in the moment of temptation give me a countermotive which is stronger than all others in no way breaks the chain of necessity. Even a cat acts against its character under the influence of a countermotive when, in the presence of the cook, it does not nibble at the food, and yet no-one has to this day attributed free will to an animal.

At this juncture I suggest, furthermore, that the will, through the recognition of its true well-being, can be brought so far as to deny its innermost kernel and to want life no longer, i.e., to place itself in complete contradiction with itself. But, if it does this, is it acting freely? No! For then the recognition has arisen within it of *necessity* and it must of necessity heed that recognition. It cannot do otherwise, as little as water can flow uphill.

Hence, if we see a person not acting in accordance with his familiar character, then we are nevertheless standing before an action which had to take place just as necessarily as that of another person who merely followed his inclination; for in the first case the action arose from a particular will and a particular mind capable of deliberation, both of which had their combined effect of necessity. There is no greater fallacy than to infer from the mind's deliberative capacity the freedom of the will.

In the world we have always to do only with necessary motions of the individual will, be they simple or resultant motions. The will in man is not free because it is combined with a mind capable of deliberation, but rather it has for this reason only a different motion from the animal. And it is here that the focal point of the entire investigation also lies. The plant has a motion different from a gas or a liquid or a solid body, the animal has one different from the plant, man has one different from animals. The last of these differences arises because in man the animal's one-sided faculty of reason has developed further into a complete one. By means of this new tool, born of the will, man surveys the past and looks to the future. Now, in any given case, his well-being can move him to forgo an enjoyment or endure a suffering, i.e., compel him to deeds which are not in accordance with his will. The will has not become free, but it has made an extraordinarily great gain; it has acquired a new motion, a motion whose great significance we will come to recognise fully further below.

Man is therefore *never* free, though he carries within himself a principle which can enable him to act *contrary* to his character; for this principle has become of necessity, belongs of necessity to his essence, since it is a part of the motion inhering in him and has its effect of necessity.

10.

Hitherto we have spoken of the actions of man in general and have found:

1) that the will of man is not free;
2) that all of his actions happen of necessity;
3) that, on the basis of his drive for happiness and by means of his mind, he can form for himself a notion of his general well-being;
4) that this notion of well-being, under certain circumstances, can induce him to act *contrary* to his character.

These results stand, as it were, in the vestibule of the ethics. We now enter the temple proper, i.e., we have to consider the actions of the man who moves within particular social conditions and forms, and to examine his happiness.

ETHICS

The first condition that we encounter is the *state of nature*. In the Ethics we have simply to define this state as the negation of the State, or as that form of man's life which preceded the State.

If we now consider man independently of the State, free of its coercive force, i.e., merely as a part of nature like every other individual will, then he is subject to no other coercive force than that of nature. He is a self-contained individuality which, like very other individual, be it chemical force, plant, or animal, wants life in a very particular way and strives unrelentingly to maintain itself in existence. In this striving, however, it is constrained by all other individuals, which have the same striving.

Thus arises the struggle for existence, from which the strongest or most cunning individual emerges victorious. Every man engages in this struggle in order to maintain himself in existence. This is his entire striving and no voice, neither from on high nor from the deep nor within him, constrains him in the means that he can put to use. Everything is granted to his egoism, all actions which in the State we call murder, robbery, theft, mendacity, deception, rape, and so on; for what other power does he confront in the state of nature but individual wills like himself, which want, like him, to maintain themselves in existence?

In this struggle he neither commits injustice nor has he a right to anything; only power decides, or cunning. He has neither a right to himself nor to any possessions whatever, nor has he a right to other beings or their possessions. He simply *exists*, and he seeks to maintain himself in existence. If he can do this only through murder and robbery, then he murders and robs, doing no injustice, and if he cannot defend himself or his possessions, then he will be robbed and annihilated, without an injustice being done to him. For who should prevent him? Who should prevent the others? A powerful, earthly judge? In the state of nature there is no judge. A consciousness of God? In the state of nature man has no consciousness of God, as little as animals do.

Justice and injustice are concepts which in the state of nature are without any significance whatever; only in the State do they have a meaning, to which we now wish to turn our attention.

11.

Man's every action, the highest as well as the lowest, is *egoistic*, for it flows out of a *particular individuality*, a particular *ego* upon sufficient motive, and can in no way be avoided. This is not the place to enter into the reasons for the variability of characters; we have simply to accept it as a fact. Now, it is as impossible for the merciful man to let his neighbour go wanting as it is for the hard-hearted man to spring to the aid of the poor man. Each of these men acts in accordance with his character, his nature, his ego, his happiness, therefore egoistically; for if the merciful man did not dry the tears of others, would he be happy? And if the hard-hearted man alleviated the suffering of others, would he be satisfied?

In what follows, the incontrovertible truth that every action is egoistic shall become obvious. I have mentioned it here since, from this point onwards, we cannot do without it.

In the state of nature, the strongest and most cunning man is *usually* the victor, the weak or dumb man *usually* the vanquished. However, cases can occur in which the strongest is overcome and the most cunning outfoxed—for who guards the strong man while he *sleeps*? Or when he is old or sick? Or how shall he triumph when he is attacked by the weak in concert? These easily-shifted relations of power in the state of nature had to lead every man, the weak as well as the strong, to recognise that a mutual curtailment of power lay in the interest of all.

My task here is not to investigate how the transition from the state of nature to the State took place, whether by purely *dæmonic* impetus or through the *rational* choice of the lesser of two evils. In the Ethics we assume that the State is a work of reason and rests on a *contract* concluded by men reluctantly: out of need, to guard against an evil greater than the curtailment of their individual power.

The fundamental character of the genuine State, even in its most incomplete form, is that it gives its citizens *more* than it takes from them, that it affords them, all in all, an *advantage* which outweighs their sacrifice; for had the advantage been as great as their sacrifice and no greater, then the State would never have arisen.

Thus men, guided by the recognition that a secure life in the state of nature is impossible, that an insecure life is an evil grounded in the constitution of nature and cannot be destroyed in the usual way, came together and said: "We are all violent men; each is enclosed in his egoism and considers himself to be the sole reality in the world; where we can harm others to our advantage, we do it; but our well-being is not thereby promoted. We must sleep, we must absent ourselves from our huts because otherwise we will starve, we can become sick, and our strength wanes in old age. Our power is therefore great in one moment, small in the next, and all the advantages which we gain for ourselves when our power is great dissolve in a minute when it is small. Never do we become glad of our possessions, because they are not secure. Of what help to us then is the satisfaction of our desires if, all in all, we thereby only lose out? We each therefore want henceforth to leave the possessions of the others undisputed." And only now did the concept of *theft* arise, which was not at all possible in the state of nature, for the concept of theft stands and falls with *guaranteed* possession.

They said furthermore: "We are all violent men; if a man puts himself between us and our advantage, then we only brood over how we can annihilate him, and are out for his blood. But our strength or cunning is not always the same. Today we can be the victors and tomorrow the vanquished. We can thus never become glad of our lives, because we hang constantly in mortal peril. We want therefore to sacrifice an additional part of our power, so that our well-being as a whole grows, and we declare: Henceforth shall the life of each man be secured by us." And only now did the concept of murder arise, for it signifies the annihilation of *guaranteed* life.

In this way men constrained themselves by means of the primitive laws:

1) none may steal;
2) none may murder.

A contract was thus concluded, the social contract, and now each man who was party to it had *obligations* and *rights* which he was unable to have in the *pure* state of nature, for they stand and fall with a contract. Each man now had the *obligation* to leave untouched the life and possessions of all others, and in exchange he had a *right* to his possessions and his life. This right was infringed when he was robbed and his life threatened, and *injustice* was thereby done him, which in the state of nature was quite impossible.

The immediate consequence of these laws was that every individual laid his ceded power in the hand of a judge and so a coercive power was created which was greater than the individual's. Each man could now be *compelled* to do right, for the transgression of law was followed by *punishment*, which is nothing other than a countermotive to a forbidden possible action. By enforcing the law, its efficacy is merely maintained.

If in the State an individual's possessions or his life are threatened, if an injustice should befall him which the State, in the moment of danger, cannot keep from him, then the individual, with respect to the transgressor of law, enters the state of *self-defence*. The transgressor has of his own volition placed himself in the state of nature, and the attacked individual is allowed to follow him there. And this individual now, as in the state of nature, has every means at his disposal, he can repel his attacker with violence or cunning, with lies and deception, and even kill him, without doing injustice, whenever his own life is threatened.

The State is therefore that institution which protects the individuality of the individual, be it ever so far extended (wife, child, possessions), and in exchange demands of him that he leave untouched the individuality of all others. Therefore, in the first instance, the State demands of each citizen as his first obligation: *subjection to the law*, obedience. It then demands of its citizens that they afford it the means to exercise its protective office, be it against transgressors of the law or against foreign enemies, that is, it demands the sacrifice of blood and treasure or, expressed in general terms, it demands as the second obligation: *protection of the State*.

12.

Through the primitive laws of the State the knowledge of man is increased. He now knows that he must refrain from certain actions if he does not want to gamble with his general well-being, and in moments of temptation his mind holds up to him the threatened punishment as a countermotive.

If we now consider first of all the general *well-being* of man in the State—we here conceive of the State in its *primitive form*, as an institution of pure coercion with the aforementioned laws—then it cannot be doubted that it is much greater than in the state of nature; for man is now removed from the constant worry about his possessions and his life. Both are guaranteed to him by a power which can actually fulfil its duty:

> And over every house and every throne
> Hangs the contract like a cherub watching.
>
> **Schiller**

But how do things stand with man's *happiness*?

Here is now the place to enter somewhat more closely into the question of happiness in general. The will, as we know, is caught in ceaseless motion, because it wills life continually. If it ceased for even a moment to will life, then it would be dead. This fundamental willing is objectified in the life of the blood, which is independent of our volition, this being a willing composed of sensibility, irritability, and action of the blood. The dæmon, the genuine will to life, is initially pleased to have life at all, and if we do not direct our attention towards it, then it enters only weakly into consciousness. But, as we have seen, man subsequently wants an elevated life; he wants, with the aid of the mind, an enhanced feeling of life, and thus the will to life becomes a *desire* for life, a desire for a particular way of life. Now, every desire is fundamentally a lack of something, for as long as its object is not possessed the desire endures. It is for this reason a vivid feeling of unpleasure. If, however, the desire is satisfied, then the satisfaction expresses itself likewise as an elevated feeling of life, and specifically as enjoyment, i.e., as a vivid feeling of pleasure. In this way an equalisation takes place.

Every vivid feeling of pleasure must therefore be purchased with a vivid feeling of unpleasure, and with every purchase of this kind the will ultimately gains nothing. Indeed, since the desire persists much longer than the feeling of its satisfaction, the will—every time it disturbs its peace in order, by means of desire, to procure a joy for itself—is also deceived.

Man is therefore happy in the normal state, which we defined more closely in the Physics, and in the more excited states of pleasure. The distinguishing mark of happiness is therefore always satisfaction of the heart. We are happy when the smooth surface of the heart is not moved, and we are also happy during the stilling of desire.

From this definition of happiness, the definition of unhappiness flows of its own accord. We are unhappy in the states of unpleasure. Certainly it might seem that we cannot be unhappy in desire, that in the vigorous motion towards our goal there already lies a great enjoyment. But this is not the case; for if we already feel pleasure in desire, then, as the merchant would say, we are devaluing its satisfaction, and this fluctuating between desire and its forefelt stilling puts us in a mixed state which keeps us from feeling the unadulterated lack of what we desire. If satisfaction is then achieved, it is also essentially weaker.

We are also unhappy, indeed very unhappy, when, with regard to our general well-being, we inhibit and suppress a desire or bear an evil, in short, when we must act *contrary* to our character.

We can now confront the question again: Is man happier in the State than in the state of nature? Yet we cannot answer this question in the Ethics, for to do so would require above all that the course of humanity's development lay clearly before us. We shall deal with the question in the Politics and content ourselves here with the simple investigation of whether, *in relation to the above laws of State*, man is happy.

And it is glaringly obvious that this cannot be the case. In accordance with his character man would of course like the *benefits* of the lawful condition for himself; the *burdens*, however, he loathes and bears them with great unwillingness. He finds himself compelled by a stronger motive, just as he did in the state of nature when he avoided the stronger opponent; he feels himself bound and not satisfied at all. If someone offends against him, then he would like to exact his revenge out of all proportion; if, in contrast, it is he who offends, then he would like to place himself under the protection of the authorities. Furthermore, he wants on one hand to have a judge who awards him his due right in disputes, he likewise wants to know his possessions and his life protected from the desire of a foreign power; but on the other hand, he clutches his money when he is expected to pay the judge, and he resists with all his might the call to take up arms in defence of his fatherland. He therefore broods constantly over how he can evade the law without being punished, how he can shrug the burdens off his own shoulders and onto another's and, by so doing, enjoy the advantages of community. His general well-being has grown by means of the laws, but before the laws he feels unhappy.

13.

The State, in the form here conceived, binds the individual no more than he has bound himself through the social contract. It demands of him only that he help to protect the community and not injure his fellow citizens. It punishes him when he steals from or murders a citizen, but it does not punish him if, without infringing the law, he sucks a citizen dry, makes him destitute, and lets him starve.

However, it lay in the necessary course of humanity's development that man, emerging from the state of nature, would be constrained yet further, his natural egoism bound even more than the State was capable of binding it. The coercive force to which this task fell was *religion*.

When the animal-man had developed into man on the lowest rung by means of the higher faculties of mind joining what had passed with what was present and this, in turn, with what was to come, the individual saw himself as helpless in the hand of a hostile power which was able at any moment to annihilate his possessions and his life. Man recognised that neither he nor the State was in a position to effect anything at all against this omnipotence and, inconsolable and feeling completely powerless, he fell down in the dust before it. Thus arose in the brutish primitive men the first relation to an incomprehensible supramundane power which could reveal itself in nature as terrible, destructive, desolating, and they formed for themselves gods. They were unable to act in any other way, for on one hand the superior power was not to be denied out of existence, on the other hand their intelligence was so weak that they were in no way able to grasp nature in its true coherence.

Here is not the place to trace the course of religion's development. We will approach it more closely in the Politics, but for now we place ourselves all at once at its end, namely on the soil of the *Christian religion*, which every insightful person must acknowledge as the best and most complete. It teaches of an all-wise, all-bountiful, almighty and all-knowing extramundane God and announces His *will*. It confirms first of all the laws of the State, by commanding man in the name of God: Thou shallt be subject to authority. It then says: Thou shallt not only not infringe the law, therefore not steal, commit adultery, rape, murder; but thou shallt also love thy neighbour as thyself.

ETHICS

Outrageous demand! The cold, crude egoist, whose slogan is: PEREAT MUNDUS, DUM EGO SALVUS SIM, is supposed to love his neighbour as himself—as himself! Oh, he knows quite well what that means; he is familiar with the severity of the sacrifice that he is supposed to make. He is supposed to forget himself for the sake of despised creatures to which he can concede no right at all to exist. He cannot reconcile himself with this impertinence and writhes like a worm. He rebels against this commandment with his whole, immediately apprehended individuality and implores the priests not to demand the impossible of him. But they must always repeat: Thou shallt love thy neighbour as thyself.

We assume here, only temporarily of course, that *all* men stand on the foundations of Christianity. They believe in God, in the immortality of the soul, and in judgment after death. Every infringement of the laws of State, like every transgression of God's commandments, is a *sin* and no-one escapes the all-knowing God. And every sin is punished, and every just action is rewarded. They believe in a kingdom of heaven, the abode of the blessed, and in a hell, the abode of the damned.

14.

The Christian religion, however, does not stop at the commandment of neighbourly love. It firstly intensifies this commandment by demanding of man that he love his neighbours *without exception*, even his *enemies*:

For if ye love them which love you, what reward have ye? (Matt 5:46)

And if ye salute your brethren only, what do ye more than others? (Matt 5:47)

Love your enemies, bless them that curse you, do good to them that hate you. (Matt 5:44)

It then demands poverty and, in every permitted enjoyment, temperance. It does not demand repression of the procreative drive, but promises the highest reward for *virginity*: immediate entry into the kingdom of God.

It is clear that by these commandments the natural egoism of the man of faith is entirely bound. Religion has taken charge of that entire portion left unconstrained by the State and has constrained it. Now the voice of conscience is much more bothersome. Man can take next to no action without conscience speaking in advance. He must now refrain from all actions which might flow from his character if he does not want to endanger his general well-being; for nothing escapes the eye of God. Men he can deceive, the authorities he can deceive, but before God his artifice is at its end:

> In the corrupted currents of this world
> Offence's gilded hand may shove by justice;
> And oft 'tis seen the wicked prize itself
> Buys out the law. But 'tis not so above.
> There is no shuffling, there the action lies
> In his true nature
>
> **Shakespeare**

And no escape is possible either. Death must come, and then begins either an eternal life of bliss, or one of torment. An eternal life! What, against eternity, is the brief period of life? Blissful for eternity, suffering for eternity! And the kingdom of heaven is believed in and hell is believed in: that is where the emphasis lies.

The genuine well-being of man cannot therefore be on this earth. It lies in an eternal life full of bliss after death, and even if the innermost essence of the clever man revolts against the commandments of religion, they are nevertheless followed: the hard-hearted man helps his neighbour, the parsimonious man gives to the poor, for some day it shall all be repaid a hundred- and a thousandfold.

If therefore the natural egoist lives according to the commandments of religion, then there can be no doubt that his well-being, considered on the whole, has grown; for he believes in the immortality of his soul and has to think of eternal life. But is he happy? Not at all! He quarrels with God: "Why can I not become blissful without having my drives subdued? Why can I not be happy here *and* there? Why must I purchase the blissful life beyond the grave so dearly?" To be sure, he apprehends the lesser evil, he purchases for himself the greater well-being, but he does so with a resentful and lacerated heart. He is unhappy on earth, in order that he might be happy after death.

15.

If, from this vantage point, we look back upon religion and the State and consider those actions which, contrary to man's character, were compelled by the stronger motives posited, then we see that they bear the seal of *legality* but have no *moral* worth.

Now, the question is: What is a *moral action*? That it must accord with the primitive laws of the State and the commandments of religion, or, in other words, that it must, in accordance with the laws of the State and of God, be legal, has never been disputed. All moralists are agreed that it must correspond to the one or other part of the proposition:

NEMINEM LAEDE; IMO OMNES, QUANTUM POTES, JUVA.

This is an irrefutable criterion. It is, however, self-evidently inadequate, and it must be joined by others in order that one be able to recognise a moral action.

The absence of all *egoistic* motivation can *never* be the second criterion of a moral action. All actions are egoistic, and an exception is completely inconceivable, for I act either in accordance with my inclination or against my character; in the first case I act absolutely egoistically and in the latter no differently, in that I must have an interest if I want to compel my character, because otherwise I could as little move myself as a stone at rest could move itself. Thus, not because an action is egoistic, not because the hope of recompense (to which self-satisfaction also belongs) or the fear of punishment (to which the dissatisfaction of my heart also belongs) drives me to that action does it have no moral value—these facts can never nullify its ethical significance.

An action has moral value when:

1) as already remarked, it corresponds to the laws of the State or to the commandments of religion, i.e., is *legal*;
2) it is taken *gladly*, i.e., when, in the man who acts it evokes the state of deep satisfaction, of pure happiness.

Accordingly, it is clear that they all act morally whose character is honest and merciful, for from such a character the moral actions flow of their own accord and give the individual the satisfaction which is felt by every person who is able to act in accordance with his character. But how do things stand with those who have no innately good will? Are they incapable of any moral action and can they in the most favourable instance only act *legally*? No! Their deeds, too, can have moral value; but their will must experience a transient or enduring metamorphosis, it must be *ignited* by cognition, cognition must kindle it, plant in it the right seed.

16.

I remind the reader that we still find ourselves on the soil of the State *and* of Christianity.

All the actions of man flow of necessity from his idea and it is all the same whether they are in accordance with or contrary to his character while being consistent with his general well-being. They are always the product of his idea and of a sufficient motive. No-one at all can act contrary to his character without gaining some advantage from doing so: it is plainly impossible. However, each man can suppress his nature if he gains an advantage from doing so, and then the action is as necessary as any other. It only has a more complicated origin, since reason sifts through the motives, weighs them, and the will follows the strongest of them.

Now, let us take first an uneducated citizen who reluctantly fulfils his duty to the State out of fear of punishment. This must come as no surprise, for he does not clearly recognise the essence of the State. He has never contemplated its essential nature and never yet has anyone made the effort to enlighten him about it. On the contrary, from youth onwards he has heard complaints about the burden of the State and then himself experienced how grievous it is to make severe sacrifices to an institution into the uses of which no insight can be gained. He nevertheless obeys, because he feels too weak to contend with the authorities.

We now posit that this man's cognition be in some way or other refined. He feels within himself the anxiety of man in the state of nature, he evokes the horrors of incipient anarchy or of a war with a foreign power on home soil; he sees the fruits of his yearlong diligence annihilated in a moment, sees the violation of his wife, the mortal peril of his children, his parents, his siblings, in short, of the most beloved things he has. He recognises, furthermore, the worth of the people to which he belongs and the regard which it enjoys amongst other peoples; he feels pride and sincerely wishes that his people never lose this regard, that he never, in foreign lands, be treated with disdain when he mentions his fatherland. Finally, he also contemplates with relish how all the cultural progress of humanity depends on the rivalry of national individualities, and how a very particular mission within this competition has fallen to his people. At the same time, he recognises very clearly that all of this is only achieved or, as the case may be, avoided when *each* citizen fulfils his duty wholeheartedly.

This newfound recognition works continuously upon his will. Natural egoism will certainly raise its voice and say: It would be better if you let the others struggle and *yet* still shared in the fruits with them. But the recognition never rests and points again and again to the fact that everything can only be achieved when *each* citizen does his duty. In this struggle with itself the will can be *ignited* and give birth to *patriotism*. The recognition, which was, as it were, floating on the surface like a small piece of wood, can become heavy and sink to the very bottom of the will. Now the sacrifices demanded are *gladly* made and the one who acts is filled with great satisfaction. Furthermore, he feels he acts in accordance with the law, in short, he acts *morally*.

We now want to consider a man who, only out of fear of punishment, reluctantly gives to each his own. In a favourable hour he recognises very distinctly how the constraints which the State imposes on the individual are absolutely necessary; how it would certainly be more pleasant to be able to enrich oneself at the expense of others; that, however, if each man wanted this, a regression to the state of nature would take place; at the same time he evokes for himself in vivid detail the war of every man against every man and the advantages that the law so abundantly affords him. He also lingers with delight on the notion of a totality of which each member, however great or small, acts *honestly*. Despite all of the objections of natural egoism, the will can be ignited by this recognition and the virtue of *justice* can take root in him. The maxim: I will always act honestly and righteously, sinks, as it were, into his heart and every action is henceforth accompanied by the feeling of pure satisfaction. Furthermore, he feels himself to be in accordance with the law, i.e., he acts *morally*.

Finally, let us imagine a faithful Christian who alleviates where he can the hardship of his neighbour, yet not out of innate mercifulness, but out of fear of hell and for the sake of reward in the kingdom of heaven.

Some misfortune or other: a severe illness, a great loss, a bitter injustice which has befallen him, has thrown him back onto himself entirely and, since he can find consolation nowhere else, he seeks it with God. He contemplates his own past and sees with pain (which is mixed with astonishment, since he has never before felt such an inner composure and the everyday social conditions have therefore never appeared to him in such a clear light) that his life has been nothing but a chain of hardship and affliction, anguish and torment, great sufferings and fleeting joys. Furthermore, he lets the lives of his acquaintances drift past his mind; he gathers up all that he had experienced in the noise of day and soon after lost sight of in the confusion of things, and is astonished by the way they cluster: what an abundance of unhappiness on one side, what meagre joys on the other!

It is a wretchedly miserable thing, the life of all men; from the maternal body onwards until they are buried in the earth, which is mother of us all.

There is always care, fear, hope and finally death; for him who sits in the highest honour as well as for him who is humblest on the earth. For him who wears silk and crown as well as for him who has on a coarse tunic; there is always wrath, zeal, obnoxiousness, strife and mortal peril, envy and quarreling.

Wisdom of Sirach (Ch. 40)

And now he envisions the hour of death, which must come sooner or later. He does not think of hell; rather, in complete contrast to the earthly life filled with agony which he has just been pondering, eternal life in God's loving care and protection floats up before him. He imagines it to be free of care, free of sorrow, hardship, strife, envy, quarreling, free of unpleasure and physical pain, free of motion, free of birth and death, and then: full of bliss. He remembers the unspeakably happy state of his heart when he was entirely absorbed in aesthetic contemplation and now, in viewing God and the splendour of His kingdom, which must certainly render what is most beautiful in this world hateful and unclean, he imagines such a state uninterrupted. *Eternal, blissful contemplation!*

Whereupon a powerful yearning, an intense craving such as he has never yet felt, can take hold of him and his will can be ignited. His heart has taken hold of the thought and lets it go no more: the *thought* has become the *way of thinking*. Henceforth his craving is directed at one thing: eternal life and the peace of eternal life. And to the extent that this craving becomes more fervid, he dies away from the world more and more. All the motives that would be able to stimulate his character are vanquished by the one motive: to be blissful after death, and the thorn|bush actually bears apricots, without signs and wonders. It is as if the deeds flowed out of a *good* will and bore the mark of morality. Man acts in accordance with the commandments of God, in whom he firmly *believes*, and on earth he already has the kingdom of heaven; for what else is the kingdom of heaven but peace of heart?

> Behold, the kingdom of God is within you.

17.

The *transformation* of the will through *cognition* is a fact which philosophy must not overlook; indeed, it is the most important and most significant phenomenon in this world. It is, however, infrequent. It takes place with individuals in silence and sometimes noisily with many people at the same time, *always* of necessity.

Cognition is a precondition, and namely the clear recognition of a *guaranteed, great advantage* which outweighs all other advantages. This we must hold onto firmly as a fundamental truth of ethics. The holiest action is only apparently selfless; like the meanest and most wicked, it is egoistic, for no man can act against his ego, his self—it is simply impossible.

However, a distinction has to be made, since philosophy can hold *illegal*, *legal*, and *moral* actions strictly apart from each other even though they are all equally egoistic, and I say for this reason that all *illegal* (forbidden by law) and all *legal* (carried out reluctantly, out of fear of punishment) actions flow from *natural* egoism and all *moral* actions (whether they arise from an *innately good* or from an *ignited* will) from *refined egoism*. All human actions of interest to the ethicist are thus classified. Their *necessarily egoistic* character is preserved and yet an essential difference is posited. One can also say: Egoism is the common root of two stems: of natural (crude) egoism and of refined egoism, and every action belongs to one of these stems.

18.

The greater, the surer the advantage is, the faster the will ignites upon a clear recognition of it; indeed, it is certain that the will *must* be ignited when the advantage heavily outweighs all others and is *not doubted* by the affected individual. In this regard it is all the same whether the advantage is really greater and surer, or whether it only exists as such in the imagination. Everyone else may condemn and ridicule it, as long as the affected individual does not doubt it and is convinced of its greatness.

History testifies incontrovertibly to the will's *moral* ignition. On one hand, the Greeks' true and genuine patriotism at the time of the Persian wars will not be doubted; nor, on the other hand, will it be doubted that life must have appeared particularly valuable for them of all peoples; for what was this blessed people lacking? It was the sole branch of humanity which had a beautiful, happy youth; for all others, life proceeded as it does for those individuals who, through one circumstance or another, remain unconscious of their youth and only upon their death beds get over the happiness which has been denied them. And precisely because the Greeks knew to value life in their country, they had to exercise their duty as citizens in passionate patriotism; for they were a small people when they were attacked by the colossal superpower of the Persians, each man had to be convinced that only when *every* man put his life on the line would victory be possible, and each man knew what fate defeat would bring: being frogmarched into slavery. There the will *had* to be ignited, there every mouth *had* to declare: Sooner death!

How differently, by the way, are the conditions today. Certainly a conquered civilisation still loses much; but the disadvantage is significantly smaller than it used to be and most individuals come nowhere near to recognising it. Herein the corrosive poison of cosmopolitanism is at work, which, in the current conditions, may be infused into a people only with the utmost prudence and when it shall have a favourable effect. "All men are brothers; we do not struggle against our brothers; the world is our fatherland"; so cry out the callowest minds, not knowing the history even of their own country, let alone the arduous course of humanity's development according to one great immutable law which reveals itself in the diversest configurations. And hence genuine enduring patriotism, which must not be confounded with belligerence or with volatile patriotic intoxication, is now so seldom encountered.

Genuine unwavering faith also brought about sudden transformations. Recall the elevating manifestations of the first three centuries of Christianity.

People who, on the day before their transformation, had still a thoroughly profane disposition, who caroused and lived extravagantly, they thought all at once of nothing other than the salvation of their immortal souls and under the most atrocious ordeals gladly expired. Had a miracle occurred? Not at all! They had clearly recognised where their salvation lay, they had recognised that years of torment are nothing against an eternity of torments; that the happiest earthly life is nothing against eternal bliss. And people came to believe in the immortality of the soul and in judgment after death, as taught by the Church. Whereupon man *had* to be reborn, whereupon the will had to be ignited, just as a stone has to fall to the earth. Just as he had previously to live extravagantly and to strive anxiously to keep every pain at bay, so he had now to give his possessions to the poor and go forth and confess: "I am a Christian", for overnight he had simply come to know an irresistibly strong motive:

Whosoever therefore shall confess me before men, him will I confess also before my Father which is in heaven. (Matt 10:32)

Blessed are they which are persecuted for righteousness' sake: for theirs is the kingdom of heaven. (Matt 5:10)

So imbued was the atmosphere with this new doctrine that it even provoked a spiritual epidemic. Whole masses pressed in around the forum of the Roman governors and craved a death full of torment. As Tertullian recounts, a praetor called out to such a crowd: "If you want to die, you wretches, you can use ropes or precipices." He knew not that the kingdom of heaven was at stake and that this kingdom, as promised, was most easily gained through the martyr's death.

If we now turn away from the martyrs and consider the simpler manifestations, then we encounter pure, genuine neighbourly love radiating towards us on all sides from men out of whose character it was *un*able to flow. They were all as if transfigured, but—of this we must take note—of *necessity, in a manner entirely natural.*

19.

The moral ignition of the will is a fact which I attempted in the foregoing to explain purely immanently. It is a fact like the transformation of a chemical idea from the normal into the charged state, like the transformation of man from the normal state into an emotional one. I want to call it *moral enthusiasm*. It is a double motion, like aesthetic enthusiasm but essentially different from it. Initially it is not, like aesthetic enthusiasm, a coherent motion, for its parts lie distant from each other in time. The first part is an intense fluctuation of the will between pleasure and unpleasure, brought about by inspired cognising; whereas the first part of aesthetic enthusiasm is the painless aesthetic state. Its second part, in contrast, is no intense outflowing of the will, but *pure peace of heart*. This peace of heart is capable of intensification, which is very peculiar. Namely, under the continued influence of clear cognition (therefore not through the unpleasure of a desire), it can intensify into:

1) moral courage,
2) moral joy,
3) moral love.

An individual in the state of moral enthusiasm—be it a transient or enduring state, be it arisen on the soil of the State, purely or with the aid of faith, or through faith alone—has only the one aim in view, namely, where his real or supposed advantage lies, and for everything else he is as good as dead. Thus the noble man, whose will has been ignited by the mission of his fatherland, rebuffs his wife and child with the words: "Beg if you are hungry". Thus the just man would rather collapse on the road and starve in silence than let wickedness stain his pure, bright soul. Thus the saint leaves his mother, his sisters, and brothers—indeed, he renounces them—and says: "Who is my mother and who are my brothers?" For all those ties which keep him bound to the world are torn asunder, and only his eternal life captivates his whole being.

20.

We have seen that an action is *moral* when it accords with the laws of the State and of Christianity and when it happens gladly, and in doing so we have drawn no distinction based on whether it arises from an originally good, or an ignited will. Furthermore, we have seen that the will can be ignited only by the clear recognition of a *great advantage*. This is very important and must be noted.

From what we have hitherto seen it becomes apparent that a genuine Christian whose will has been ignited on the saviour's doctrine—therefore, a saint—is the *happiest* man conceivable, for his will is like a lake's smooth surface, the serenity of which runs so deep that the strongest storm cannot trouble it. He has that complete inner peace which nothing more in this whole world—even were it the greatest misfortune in man's eyes—can upset or disturb. In this regard we want also to remark that, to be sure, the transformation can only happen by means of the clearest recognition of that great advantage; that, however, once the transformation is complete, the hope of the kingdom of heaven after death can disappear entirely, as the testimony of "deified" men (as the mystics say) clearly proves. The reason is obvious. They stand in such inner joyfulness, peace, and invulnerability to temptation that they become indifferent to everything: life, death, and life after death. They are certain that the state in which they find themselves cannot fade, and the kingdom of heaven that is within them contains completely within itself the kingdom of heaven to come. They live filled with inexpressible bliss in the *present* alone, i.e., in the feeling of constant inner *immovability*, even if this is only an illusion—or in other words: The fleeting state of the deepest aesthetic contemplation has for the saint become *permanent*, it endures, because nothing in the world is capable of *moving* the *innermost core* of the individual. And just as in aesthetic contemplation the Subject as well as the Object are raised out of time, so the saint also lives timelessly; he is indescribably well in this apparent peace, this enduring inner immovability, even if the external man must still move, feel, and suffer. And this life he would not leave:

> even if he might thereby have an angel's life.
>
> **The Franckforter**

Here ecstasy or *intellectual bliss* should also find its place. It is essentially different from the even, calm peace of the saint. It arises from the intense desire to see God's kingdom already in the world. The will, brought through asceticism and solitude into the most awful agitation, concentrates its entire power in a single organ. It withdraws itself from the peripheral nervous system and flees, as it were, into the brain. The nervous life is thereby driven to the highest level possible, the impressions of the senses are completely overcome, and the mind now depicts in empty space, as it does in sleep, that which the will has longed so intensely to behold. But during such a vision the eyes of the rapturous man are open and his consciousness is clearer and brighter than ever. In his rapture he must feel the highest bliss conceivable, for which reason this state has very fittingly also been called intellectual bliss; but how dearly it is purchased! The unpleasure that precedes it and the terrible lassitude that follows make it the most extravagant enjoyment.

21.

Immanent philosophy must recognise the state of the saint as the happiest, but can it conclude the Ethics once it has shed light on the greatest happiness of man and has shown how even a *bad* will, despite lacking the LIBERUM ARBITRIUM, can partake of it too? Not at all. For if the genuine saint also:

> stands in a freedom, thus has lost the fear of torment or *of hell and the hope of reward or of the kingdom of heaven;*
>
> **The Franckforter**

then his will was able to be ignited only *on this* hope of reward or of the kingdom of heaven, because it is a fundamental proposition of immanent ethics, confirmed time and again by experience, that man, *without discerning some advantage*, can as little act against his character as water, without appropriate pressure, can flow uphill.

Faith is therefore a CONDITIO SINE QUA NON of the most blissful state, yet immanent philosophy was allowed to place itself on the soil of Christianity only transiently in order to develop its ethics, to stake out the territory of ethics, so to speak. The result of our investigations hitherto is therefore that we have found the happiest state of man, but we have done so based on a presupposition which we cannot admit, and the Ethics cannot be concluded until we have investigated whether this blissful state can also emanate from an immanent basis in cognition or whether it is simply inaccessible to anyone who cannot *have faith*. That is: We stand before the most important problem of ethics. This problem is customarily expressed in our asking after the *scientific foundation of morals*, i.e., whether morality too can be established without dogmas, without the assumption of a revealed divine will. Was St John justified when he wrote:

Who is he that overcometh the world, but he that *believeth* that Jesus is the Son of God? (1 John 5:5)

22.

Immanent philosophy, which can acknowledge no other sources than nature (which lies open before the eyes of all) and our inner being, disposes of the assumption of a hidden simple unity in, above, or behind the world. It knows only innumerable ideas, i.e., individual wills to life which, in their totality, form a self-contained collective unity.

From our current standpoint we therefore acknowledge initially no other *authority* than that of the *State* established by man. This authority has appeared because the will, gifted with reason, after correctly recognising the essence of two evils, *must* choose the lesser. The will cannot act differently; for if we see a man choose the greater of two evils, then either we have erred in our judgment, because we could not immerse ourselves in the individuality of the man making the choice, or *he* has not recognised that the chosen evil was the greater. In the latter case, had the man had our mind, which wonders at the choice, then he could not have chosen as he did. This law is as resolute as the one that says every effect must have a cause.

The insightful man cannot want the State to be annihilated. Whoever wants this sincerely, he wants only a temporary abrogation of the laws, namely, for as long as he needs it to procure for himself a more favourable situation. Once he has acquired this, he wants the protection of the laws with the same ardour with which he previously wanted their suspension.

For the natural egoists, therefore, the State is a necessary evil which they must embrace because it is the lesser of two. If they overthrew it, then they would have the greater in hand for doing so.

The State demands only upholding of the social contract, strict fulfilment of the obligations entered into, namely, respect for the laws and maintenance of the State. We may assume that almost no man fulfils these duties gladly; for even the man with a good heart will not always treat honestly with his fellow man and will usually pay the State ungladly, as well as fulfil his military duty unwillingly if he is not drawn to the soldier's life by insurmountable inclination. We want, however, to concede with caution that there are men who by their very natures are of steadfast integrity and who love their fatherland sincerely and from the heart. They gladly give to each his own and gladly make sacrifices to the State, sacrifices which the State for its maintenance must demand of them. Their peace—their happiness—is therefore not upset by all these actions. We set them aside and concern ourselves now with those who subject themselves to the laws of the State only out of fear of punishment and with the greatest reluctance. They have no peace within themselves and are unhappy before the laws. Their character draws them in one direction, coercive power draws them in another. They are thus tugged to and fro and endure agonies. If they fall on the side of coercive power, then they make sacrifices begrudgingly; if, on the other hand, they follow their inclination because the threatened evil is rendered powerless through reflection (probability of not being discovered), then, having done the deed, they fear discovery and are not pleased with their gains. If the crime is discovered and if punishment finds them, then conscience torments them in a manner unbearable, and the freedom-wanting heart rages against coercion and the endless chain of privations—unhappily and without success.

We now go further and consider that many such people who are obedient only out of fear of punishment are ignited by the clear recognition of their advantage. We shall for now disregard the fact that the recognised advantage of integrity, as might become salient from considerations such as those set out above, can have next to *no* effect. St Paul expresses this very beautifully:

Because the law worketh wrath: for where no law is, there is no transgression. Therefore [*righteousness*] is of *faith* ... (Rom 4:15-16)

We further disregard the fact that nowadays the recognised advantage of having the State's protection can likewise only very seldom ignite the will, and we simply assume the ignition does come about.

In this way we have, with regard to the laws, happy men in the State: men who are just by natural disposition and men who are just through illuminated will. Indeed, we want to go so far as to assume there were *only* righteous people in our State. In this State, therefore, all citizens live in accordance with the laws and do not grow unhappy through the demands of the political authority. Each man is given his own, but no more. Complete integrity reigns in all commerce; no-one deceives; all are honest. If, however, a hungry pauper comes to them and demands a scrap of bread, then they slam their doors in his face, except those who are merciful; for if the merciful gave nothing, then they would certainly be acting contrary to their character and would be unhappy.

We thus have in our State a *limited morality*; for all actions that are in accordance with the laws *and* occur gladly have moral worth and are not merely legal. The merciful man does not, however, act morally when he raises up the needy, as little as the hard-hearted man acts illegally when he lets the poor starve at his door; for there exists no *law* commanding charity and it is *one* of the preconditions of a *moral* action that it accord with the law. Of course, neither can the merciful man act illegally when he supports the needy. His action has no particular character at all but bears only the general egoistic one. He merely follows his reformed egoism, offends no law and is happy.

Against this examination of the matter our inner being rebels, and we feel that it must be false. Yet from our current standpoint this is in no way the case. This feeling is the effect either of mercifulness or of a spectre from our years of apprenticeship; for no matter how emancipated from all prejudice we consider ourselves to be, we all more or less still bear the chains of faith, of treasured recollections, and of affectionate words from venerated mouths. From our current standpoint, however, *only* cold reason may speak and it must speak as we have just heard. Later, a different solution may present itself—for now, it is impossible. For us, the authority of *religion* does *not* exist, and no other authority has yet taken its place. Would it not be an obvious folly if the hard-hearted man constrained himself for the benefit of the poor man, i.e., acted against his character, without sufficient motive? In fact, would it even be possible at all? And how ought a merciful deed to be moral without the will of an almighty God commanding works of neighbourly love?

For this reason we would also strike out on an erroneous path if we wanted to make mercifulness, or that state into which foreign suffering puts the merciful will: compassion, the foundation of morals. For how could we presume to decree: merciful deeds, deeds born of compassion are moral deeds? Their very independence of a commanding authority would prevent their being so. Would not every person have the right to overturn our independent decree? And what would we respond to the hard-hearted or cruel man if, with all the defiance of his rebellious individuality, he asked us: "How could you, without the assumption of an omnipotent God, say that I act immorally? I claim with the same right that merciful acts are immoral." Be honest! Could you answer him without placing yourself on the soil of the Christian or any other religion at all, which commands neighbourly love in the name of an *acknowledged power*?

We must for the time being therefore remain with the view that, in the State we have conceived, merciful deeds can *not* be moral, because no power commands them and actions only have moral value when they happen gladly *and* accord with a law.

The citizens of that State which we have conceived are, as has been assumed, all just, i.e., they never come into conflict with themselves when the State imposes a demand on them which they are obligated by treaty to meet. They obey gladly and it is for that reason impossible for the laws to make them unhappy.

We now go further and say: good. If we consider the life of these citizens only in its relation to the State and the fundamental laws of the State, then that life is a happy one. But life is not merely a chain of fulfilled obligations to the State: of thefts forgone, murders forgone, of tax payments and service at time of war; the other relationships of life predominate decisively therein. And so we ask: Are our just men also happy in other respects?

This question is very important, and until it has been answered we cannot advance another step in the Ethics. Our next task therefore consists in rendering a judgment on the value of human life itself.

23.

I am perfectly aware that all those who have contemplated the value of existence only once but *purely objectively* are no longer in need of the philosopher's judgment; for either they have arrived at the conviction that all human progress is only apparent, or at the other conviction that the human race in fact is always moving through better states towards even better ones. In both cases, however, they have become painfully aware of the fact that human life in its *current* forms is an essentially unhappy one.

I would also be unable to find my way to examining life as it now is. Others have done this and have done it so masterfully that for every insightful man the matter is closed. Only those who have no overview of life in all its forms or those whose judgment is forged by a compulsion for life still too intense can cry out: It is a pleasure to live and every man must count himself happy that he breathes and moves! One should not enter into a discussion with such people, bearing the words of Scotus Erigena in mind:

ADVERSUS STULTITIAM PUGNARE NIL EST LABORIOSIUS. NULLA ENIM AUCTORITATE VINCI FATETUR, NULLA RATIONE SUADETUR.

They have not yet suffered enough and their cognition lies in a sorry state. They will—if not in what is left of their individual life, then certainly in their progeny—some day awaken, and their awakening will be terrible.

Not, therefore, with life as it presently flows on in the freest and best State will we now concern ourselves, for that life has been condemned; rather, we assume the standpoint of the rational *optimists* just mentioned, who look to the future and bestow on all of humanity a happy life some day, because the real development towards ever more perfect states cannot be denied. We will thus have to conceptualise an *ideal State* and judge life in it. We leave entirely to one side the question of whether such a State could ever lie in the development of things; but it is clear that we may conceptualise it, because we are endeavouring to view life in a favourable light.

We place ourselves in the very midst of this ideal State, not concerning ourselves with how it came to be.

It encompasses "all that bears a human visage", it encompasses humanity entire. There are no more wars and no revolutions. Political power no longer resides with particular classes, but rather humanity is one people which lives according to laws which everyone has had a hand in composing. Social misery has been extinguished. Labour is organised and oppresses no-one any more. The spirit of invention has seen all heavy labour imposed on machines, the operation of which robs the citizens of only a few hours in the day. When he wakes up, every man can say: the day is mine.

> ... the whips and scorns of time,
> Th' oppressor's wrong, the proud man's contumely,
> ..., the law's delay,
> The insolence of office, and the spurns
> That patient merit of th' unworthy takes
>
> **Shakespeare**

All this has been eradicated.

Poverty has fled from the earth where for millennia it wrought appalling misfortune. Every man lives without concern for the necessities of life. Habitations are healthy and comfortable. One man can no longer exploit the other, for limits are placed upon the stronger man and the weaker is protected by the totality.

We therefore assume that the unfortunate political and social conditions, the contemplation of which led so many to the conviction that life is not worth the effort, have all been arranged for the well-being of every man. Little work, much amusement—these are life's distinctive features in our ideal State.

At the same time we assume that men in the course of time—through suffering, cognition, and the gradual removal of all *bad* motives—have become modest and harmonious beings, in short, that we now have to do only with *beautiful souls*. Should there really still be something or other in our State which could arouse passion or else pangs of the soul, then the individual thus aroused would soon regain his balance and harmonious motion would be restored. The great misfortune which passionate characters cannot escape:

> The heartache and the thousand natural shocks
> That flesh is heir to –
>
> **Shakespeare**

all this, too, is gone from the world.

Even the most hysterical worshipper of the will to life will have to concede—bearing in mind that man cannot be entirely free of labour, since he must eat, live, and clothe himself—that neither a better social order nor beings who bore within themselves the conditions for a better life are possible; for we have given all men a noble individuality and removed from life everything which cannot be seen as fundamentally joined therewith.

There remain therefore only four evils from which no human power can divorce life: the pangs of childbirth, as well as sickness, age, and the death of every individual. Man in the most perfect State must be born in pain; he must make his way through a smaller or greater number of sicknesses; he must, if

> in the vigour of youth
> the Norns reap
>
> **Uhland**

him not, become old, i.e., become physically infirm and mentally dull; finally, he must die.

The lesser evils joined with existence we reckon to be nothing; but we do want to mention a few of them. We have first sleep, which steals a third of life (if life is a joy, then sleep is self-evidently an evil); then the first childhood, which only serves to acquaint man with the ideas and their coherence as far as is necessary in order that he be able to find his way in the world (if life is a joy, then the first childhood is naturally an evil); then work, which in the Old

Testament is rightly deemed the consequence of a divine curse; finally, various evils which Pope Innocent III compiled as follows:

Impure procreation, revolting nourishment in the mother's body, wickedness of the material from which man develops, hideous stench, discharge of saliva, urine, and vomit.

Let these evils not be deemed too minor. Whoever has achieved a certain level of refinement of the nerves rightly takes offence to many of them. Even Byron was unable to watch the Countess Guiccioli eat, the reason for which lay much deeper than lies the English spleen.

As I have said, we pass over these evils and remain at those few main evils mentioned. But even of these we set three aside. We assume that the birth of man shall in future proceed without pain; that science shall succeed in preserving man from every illness; finally, that such sheltered men shall in old age be spry and hale when their lives are promptly terminated by a gentle, painless death (euthanasia).

Only death cannot be removed, and thus we have before us a short life without suffering. Is it a happy life? Let us examine it closely.

The citizens of our ideal State are men of gentle character and cultivated intelligence. They have been impressed, so to speak, with a kind of finished knowledge, free of perversion and error and, no matter how they reflect on it, they always find it confirmed. There are no longer any effects whose causes are mysterious. Science has actually attained its peak, and every citizen is sated with its fruits. The sense of beauty has unfolded powerfully in everyone. Even if we must not assume that everyone is an artist, they do have the capacity to enter easily into the aesthetic relation.

All cares are taken from them, for work has been organised in a superlative manner and every man is his own master.

Are they happy? They would be if they did not sense a horrible barrenness and emptiness in themselves. They have escaped need, they are really without cares and suffering, but for that reason boredom has taken hold of them. They have paradise on earth, but the air of that paradise is suffocating:

One must have something left to wish for in order not to be unhappy out of sheer happiness. The body wants to breathe and the spirit to strive.

Gracian

If they should indeed still have enough energy to bear such a life to its natural end, then they certainly haven't the courage to make their way through it once more as rejuvenated beings. Need is a terrible evil, but boredom is the most terrible of all. It is better to exist in need than in boredom, and the fact that complete annihilation is preferable even to boredom certainly requires no demonstration. And thus, for good measure, we would claim to have shown indirectly too that life in the best State is not worth our time. Life in general is a "wretchedly miserable thing": it has always been wretched and miserable and will always be wretched and miserable, and *it is better not to be than to be.*

24.

However, it could now be said: We admit everything, only not that life in this ideal State is really boring. You have characterised the citizen *falsely* and your conclusions from his character and his relationships are therefore false.

I cannot remove this doubt through a direct proof, although through an indirect one I certainly can.

I will not take as a basis the generally acknowledged empirical proposition that people who have fortunately escaped need are at a loss for what to do with their existence; for there one can justly object that, for lack of intelligence or education, they knew not what to concern themselves with. Even less shall I call to my aid the poet's words:

> All in the world can be borne in some way,
> Just not a succession of beautiful days;

Goethe

although it expresses an invincible truth. I take as a basis merely the fact that even if there never has been an ideal State on this earth, many such citizens as I described above have already lived. They were free of need and led a comfortably industrious life. They had a noble character and a highly developed mind, i.e., they had thoughts of their own and did not accept others' thoughts unproven.

Over the imagined citizens of an ideal State all of these individuals had the great advantage that their environment was much more fertile and interesting. Wherever they looked they found distinctive individualities, a plenitude of forceful characters. Society had not yet been levelled out and even nature found itself under man's dominion only to the smallest degree. These individuals lived under the charm of opposites; they were seldom unaware of their comfortable and exempted position, for wherever they might look it stood out against the other forms of life like a bright image against a dark background. Science, furthermore, had not yet arrived at the summit of perfection; there were still riddles aplenty, effects enough in the search for whose causes brains could be racked. And whoever has already felt what joy there is in searching after truth, in pursuing its trail, will concede that those individuals were actually at an advantage; for was not Lessing correct when he declared:

> If God held sealed in his right hand all truth and in his left that unique, inner, spirited drive for truth, albeit subject to the condition that I should always and eternally err, and said to me: Choose!, I would with humility fall upon his left hand.

And nevertheless all of these outstanding individuals, who form a chain reaching from the primitive ages of the human race up to our own day, condemned life as essentially luckless and placed non-being above being. I will not tarry in naming them all and repeating their aptest pronouncements. I will name just two of them, who stand nearer us than Buddha and Salamo, and whom all educated people know, the greatest poet and the greatest natural philosopher of the Germans: Goethe and Humboldt.

Need I relate the happy circumstances of their lives, praise their minds and their characters? I would only wish that all men might possess such a sublime individuality and find themselves in such a favourable situation as these men did. And what did Goethe say?

> We all suffer from life.
>
> I have always been praised as a man specially favoured by fortune; and I do not want to complain, nor would I inveigh against the course of my life. However, at bottom it has been nothing but effort and work, and I can certainly say that in my seventy-five years I have not had even four weeks of genuine comfort. It was the eternal rolling of a stone that had always to be raised again.
>
> *(Conversations with Eckermann)*

And what does Humboldt say?

> I am not cut out to be a paterfamilias. Moreover, I consider marriage a sin, procreation a *crime*.
>
> I am also convinced that he is a fool, even more a sinner, who willingly sets the yoke of marriage upon himself. A fool because he thereby discards his freedom without commensurate redress; a sinner because he gives life to children without being able to give them the certainty of happiness. I despise humanity in all its strata; I foresee that *our progeny* shall be *far unhappier* than we. Should I not be a sinner if, despite this foresight, I planned to reproduce, i.e., to beget *unhappy beings*?
>
> The whole of life is the greatest nonsense. And when one has been striving and researching eighty years, then one must ultimately admit to oneself that through all that striving and researching nothing has been gained. If we only knew at the very least why we are in this world. But to the thinker everything is and remains puzzling, and to be born a *halfwit* is still the *greatest happiness*.
>
> *(Memoirs)*

"If we only knew at the very least why we are in this world!" Thus, in the whole rich life of this gifted man there was nothing, nothing that he would have been able to conceive as an aim of life. Not joy in creation, not the delicious moments of inspired cognisance: Nothing!

And in our ideal State the citizens are meant to be happy?

25.

We can now bring the Ethics to a close.

We first of all overturn our ideal State. It was a fantasy and will never appear in the phenomenal world.

However, what cannot be denied is the real development of the human species and that a time will come when an *ideal State* will be established, although not the one conceived by us. It will be my task in the Politics to demonstrate how all of the chains of development, from the beginning of history onwards, point to that State as their goal. In the Ethics we must claim it without proof. In that same State, society will in fact be levelled out and every citizen will experience the blessings of a high mental culture. All of humanity will live more painlessly than it does now, than it ever has.

It follows from this that there is a *necessary motion of humanity executing itself* with *irresistible force*, which no power is capable of delaying or diverting. It is a motion which thrusts the willing and the non-willing inexorably onwards along that trajectory which leads to the ideal State, and that State must appear in the phenomenal world. This real, unmodifiable motion is a part of the world-course which is continually created out of the motions of all individual, dynamically coherent ideas, and it here reveals itself as the necessary *fate of humanity*. It is *just as strong*, just as superior to every individual essence in strength and power—because it contains the efficacy of every particular individual essence within itself—*as the will of an individual unity* in, above, or behind the world, and if immanent philosophy puts it in the place of this simple unity, then it fills out that place completely. However, whereas the simple unity must be *believed* in and was and will be constantly exposed to controversy and doubt, the essence of *fate*, by virtue of general causality's extension to community, is clearly *cognised* by man and can therefore never be disputed.

Now, if it was a commandment of God for man to be just and merciful, then the fate of humanity demands of every man with *equal authority* the strictest justness and philanthropy; for even if the motion towards the ideal State will execute itself despite the dishonesty and hard-heartedness of many, it yet demands loudly and distinctly of every man justness and philanthropy, so that it can execute itself *more quickly*.

ETHICS

Now that difficulty is also resolved which, above, we had to abandon abruptly and against which our inner being rebelled, namely, that a merciful deed, in a State without religion, can have no moral worth; for now that deed also bears the stamp of morality because it accords with the demands of fate and is gladly done.

The State is the form in which the conceived motion takes place, in which the fate of humanity unfolds itself. It has for some time now extended almost everywhere its fundamental form, as we earlier ascertained and made use of it. It has developed itself further from a self-sustaining coercive institution which prevents theft and murder, into a broad form for the *progress of humanity towards the best community conceivable*. To approach its citizens and institutions and to remodel them until they have become suitable for the ideal community, i.e., until the ideal community has become real—that is the sense underlying the demanded virtues of patriotism, justice, and philanthropy. In other words: The inexorable fate of humanity demands of each citizen *commitment to the universal*, nothing less than *love for the State*, which was already taught by the great Heraclitus in words which etch themselves deeply upon one's heart. Each man, holding before his eyes the ideal State as a paradigm, is supposed to lay a vigorous hand on what is presently real and help it to reshape itself.

The commandment therefore exists, and it has emanated from a power which, by means of its terrible might, upholds the commandment with respect to every individual and always will uphold it, unwaveringly. The only question is: How does the individual position himself with respect to the commandment?

Recall here the apostle Paul's profound pronouncement, already cited above:

Because the law worketh wrath; for where no law is, there is no transgression. Therefore [righteousness] is of *faith* ... (Rom 4:15-16)

Immanent philosophy modifies the last sentence as follows:

Therefore commitment to the universal must come through *knowledge*.

He who is disposed by nature to be merciful and just is in an easier position before the commandment than the natural egoist. In accordance with his character, he gladly gives to each man his own, or better, he gladly *leaves* to each man his own, and if his neighbour has his back to the wall then he will support him to the best of his ability. But one sees immediately that *this* behaviour cannot be in complete correspondence with the demands of fate. To leave to each man his own, not to deceive him, is not *enough*. To give to his fellow man in need, when his own path leads directly past him, is not *enough*.

As a just man I am supposed to exercise my influence so that he receives *everything which is his due as a citizen of the State*; I am supposed to exercise my influence so that *every* citizen partakes of *all the benefits of the State*; and as a philanthropist, I am supposed to exercise my influence with all other merciful men so that *poverty* disappears from the State *entirely*.

However, in the man disposed by nature to be just and merciful, this mode of thinking can arise only under the stimulus of cognition, of *knowledge*, as a flower bud can only open under the stimulus of light. Or, in other words, the originally good will as well as the bad will can only be ignited—i.e., commit itself wholeheartedly to the universal, align itself *gladly* with the trajectory of humanity's motion—when cognition promises it a *great advantage* from doing so.

Is this possible?

The natural egoist, whose motto is: PEREAT MUNDUS, DUM EGO SALVUS SIM, when confronted with the commandment, recoils entirely into himself and assumes a position hostile to the real motion. He thinks only of his *personal* advantage, and if he can attain that advantage (without, however, coming into conflict with the laws) at the expense of the peace and well-being of the many, then the complaints and pains of the many in no way trouble him. He lets the gold pieces glide through his fingers, and for the tears of those whom he has robbed his senses are as good as dead.

Furthermore, the man naturally disposed to justice and mercy will, to be sure, gladly leave to each his own and here and there alleviate the needs of his fellow men; but adjust himself to the motion of humanity to such an extent that he *sacrifices all his possessions, abandons his wife and child, and spills his blood for the well-being of humanity*—this he will *not* do.

Christianity threatened its professors with hell and promised them the kingdom of heaven, but immanent ethics knows no judgment after death, no reward, no punishment of an immortal soul. In contrast, it knows the hell of the present State and the heavenly kingdom of the ideal State, and in pointing to both it has a firm footing in physics.

Immanent ethics thus takes hold of each person at that point where he is rooted in humanity and in life and calls to him: *You live on in your children*, in your children you celebrate your rebirth, and what affects *them* will affect *you* in them. But as long as the ideal State has not become real, so long do men's situations and positions in life alter. The rich man becomes poor and the poor man rich; the mighty man becomes small and the small man mighty; the strong man becomes weak and the weak man strong. In such an order of things you are the anvil today, tomorrow the hammer, the hammer today, tomorrow the anvil. You therefore act *against* your general well-being when you strive to uphold this order of things. This is the threat of immanent ethics; its promise, however, is the ideal State, i.e., an order of things in which everything which is not fundamentally joined to life is divorced from it: *misery* and *need*. Immanent ethics whispers to the poor son of man: No longer shall there be fear or screaming, no longer shall there be tears or tired eyes because of misery and need.

This knowledge of the man who is rooted in life—for this is a precondition: he must be unbroken will to life, must live and want to maintain himself in life even beyond death—this knowledge of man, I say:

1) that he lives on in his children, or, to express the same generally, that he is rooted in humanity, can maintain himself only in humanity and through humanity;
2) that the current order of things necessitates the changing of situations (in Hamburg they say: The moneybag and the beggar's sack do not hang a century in front of the same door);
3) that in the ideal State the best conceivable life is guaranteed *to all*;
4) finally, that the motion of humanity, despite the influence of the non-willing and the counter-striving, has the ideal State as its goal and will reach this goal;

this knowledge, this recognition which presses itself upon every thinking man, can ignite the will: gradually or in an instant. He then enters completely *into* the motion of the totality, he then swims with the current. He now struggles courageously, joyfully, and lovingly *within* the State and—as long as the motion of humanity is still in the main generated principally from the combined effect of large, national individualities, of large individual States working with and against each other—he also struggles *with* his State (and, as the case may be, those allied with it) *against* other States *for* the ideal State. He is now aglow with genuine patriotism, genuine justice, genuine love for humanity; he stands *in* the motion of fate, he acts in accordance with fate's commandment and does so gladly, i.e., his actions are eminently moral and his reward is: peace with himself, pure bright happiness. If need be, he now sacrifices willingly and in moral enthusiasm his individual life; for out of that *better* condition of humanity for which he struggled there would arise for him a new, a better individual life in his children.

26.

But even if the fundamental disposition of the hero is a profound peace, therefore pure happiness, then only seldom is his breast aglow with it, almost only in great moments; for life is for every man a hard struggle, and whoever is still rooted firmly in the world—though his eyes be quite intoxicated with the light of the ideal State—will *never* be free from need, pain, and heartache. No hero has the Christian saint's pure *enduring* peace of heart. Ought that peace really to be unattainable without faith?

The motion of humanity towards the ideal State is a fact; it takes but a moment's reflection to recognise that as little in the life of the whole as in the life of the individual can things come to a *standstill*. The motion must be a restless one up to the point where life can no longer be spoken of at all. Thus, if humanity finds itself in the ideal State, then there can be no rest. But whither shall it then move? There is but one motion left to it: the motion towards *complete annihilation*, the motion out of *being into non-being*. And humanity (all individual men who will then be living) will carry out this motion in irresistible yearning for the rest of absolute death.

The motion of humanity towards the ideal State will therefore be followed by that other motion, from being into non-being, or in other words: The motion of humanity as such is the motion out of being into non-being. If, however, we keep both motions separated, then as from the first motion there came the commandment of complete surrender to the universal, so from the latter there comes the commandment of *virginity*, which in the Christian religion, to be sure, is not demanded, but is recommended as the *highest* and *most perfect virtue*; for even if the motion is to execute itself despite the animal sex-drive and despite lust, it still approaches the individual with the earnest demand *to be chaste*, so that it can arrive *more quickly* at its objective.

From this demand the just and the unjust, the merciful and the hard-hearted, heroes and criminals recoil, and with the exception of the few who, as Christ said, were born eunuchs from their mother's womb, no man can gladly fulfil this demand without having experienced a *complete transformation* of his will. All transformations, all ignitions of the will which we have hitherto considered were modifications of a will which continued to want *life*, and the hero, like the Christian saint, only sacrificed his life—i.e., he scorned death—because he obtained a better *life* in exchange. Now, however, the will is supposed not merely to scorn death but to *love* it, for *chasteness is love of death*. An outrageous demand! The will to life wants to live and exist, to exist and live. It wants to live for all time, and since it can only remain in existence by means of procreation, it therefore concentrates its fundamental willing in the sex-drive, which is the most complete affirmation of the will to life and far excels in intensity and strength all other drives and desires.

Now, how is man supposed to fulfil this demand, how is he supposed to be able to overcome the sex-drive, which appears to every honest observer of nature as downright invincible? Only fear of a *great punishment*, in combination with an *advantage outweighing all advantages*, can give man the strength to vanquish it, i.e., the will must be ignited by a clear and entirely certain recognition. It is the recognition, already mentioned above, that *it is better not to be than to be*, or the recognition that life is hell, and the sweet still night of absolute death is the annihilation of hell.

And the man who has clearly and unambiguously recognised that all life is suffering; that, in whatever form it may arise, it is essentially unhappy and painful (*even in the ideal State*), so that, like the Christchild in the arms of the Sistine Madonna, he can only gaze upon the world with eyes aghast; and who then ponders the profound rest, the inexpressible happiness in aesthetic contemplation and, in contrast to the waking state, the happiness (which he feels through reflection) of stateless sleep, the exaltation of which into eternity is all that absolute death is; such a man must ignite his will on the proffered advantage—he cannot do otherwise. On one hand, the thought of being reborn, i.e., of having to proceed restlessly along the thorny and stony road of existence in unhappy children, is for him the most terrible and desperate thought he can have; on the other hand, the thought of being able to interrupt the long, long chain of development in which, always with bleeding feet, he had to forge ahead, shoved, harrowed, tormented and pining for rest, is the sweetest and most invigorating. And once he is on the right path, then with every step his sex-drive disturbs him less and less, with every step his heart feels lighter, until his inner being stands at last in the same *joyousness*, *blissful merriment*, and *complete immobility* as the genuine Christian saint. He feels himself to be in accordance with humanity's motion from being into non-being, from the agony of life into absolute death, gladly he joins this motion of the whole, he acts in a manner eminently moral, and his reward is that undisturbed peace of heart, that "calmness of temper", that peace which is higher than all reason. And all of this can take place without faith in a unity in, above, or behind the world; without fear of a hell or hope for a heavenly kingdom after death; without mystical intellectual intuition; without the inconceivable workings of grace; without being at odds with nature and our consciousness of our own self: those sole sources from which we may draw certainty; but merely in consequence of an unprejudiced, pure, cold recognition by our faculty of reason, "that supreme power of man".

27.

We would thus have found the happiness of the saint, which we had to designate the greatest and highest happiness, independently of any religion. At the same time we have found the *immanent* foundation of morals. It is the *real motion of humanity* cognised by the Subject, a motion which demands the practice of the virtues: patriotism, justice, love of man (philanthropy, charity), and chasteness.

An important consequence follows from this, namely, that the motion of humanity is as little a *moral* one as the things-in-themselves are beautiful. From the standpoint of nature *no* man acts *morally*; he who loves his neighbour acts no more meritoriously than he who hates, torments and pesters him. Humanity has but one *course*, which he who acts morally *hastens*. From the standpoint of the Subject, in contrast, every action is moral which, consciously or unconsciously, is in accordance with the fundamental motion of humanity and which happens gladly. The injunction to act morally draws its power from the fact that it assures the individual either of transient peace of soul and a better life in the world, or of enduring peace of soul in this life and complete annihilation in death, assures him therefore of the advantage of being redeemed earlier than the totality. And this latter advantage so greatly outweighs all earthly advantages that it draws the individual who recognises it irresistibly, as iron is drawn to a magnet, onto that path where it lies.

In those people who have an innately merciful will, the transformation takes place most easily; for they are wills whom the course of the world has already weakened, whose natural egoism the course of the world has already transformed into reformed egoism. The suffering of their neighbours provokes in them the ethical, extraordinarily significant state of compassion, the fruits of which are genuinely moral deeds. In the state of compassion we sense a positive suffering within ourselves; it is a deep feeling of unpleasure which lacerates our heart and which we can only abolish by *relieving of his suffering* our suffering neighbour.

28.

The will's igniting itself on the recognition that humanity is moving out of being into non-being and on that other recognition, that it is better not to be than to be, or even on the latter alone—which, independently of the former, can be obtained by taking a clear-eyed look at the world—is the philosophical *denial of the individual will to life*. The will thus ignited wants, until death and uninterrupted, the happy state of peace of heart and, in death, complete annihilation, complete redemption of itself. It wants to be struck forever from the book of life, it wants with its extinguished motion to lose life and with life to lose the innermost core of its being completely. This particular idea wants to be annihilated, this particular type, this particular form wants forever to be destroyed.

Immanent philosophy knows no miracles and can give no account of events in some uncognisable other world which were consequences of actions in this one. For this reason there is for immanent philosophy only *one* completely sure denial of the will to life: denial through *virginity*. As we have seen in the Physics, man finds in death absolute annihilation; yet the annihilation is only apparent if he lives on in children; for in these children he has already been resurrected from death, in them he has once again seized life and affirmed it for an indeterminable period of time. Every man feels this instinctively. The invincible repulsion of the sexes after copulation in the animal kingdom appears in man as a profound sadness. In him a quiet voice complains like Proserpina:

> How all at once these joys,
> This unconcealed bliss
> Is cut through
> By appalling pains,
> By iron hands of Hell! - -
> What have I perpetrated,
> In my indulgence?

And mockingly the world cries:

> You are ours!
> Fasting hadst thou to return;
> And the bitten apple makes you ours!
>
> **Goethe**

For this reason immanent philosophy can also not attach the least importance or significance to the *hour of death*. In that hour man no longer has a decision to make about whether he wants life once again, or wants to be dead forever. Regret about bad deeds, which so often appears on our deathbed because our cognition changes suddenly and we see clearly and unambiguously how useless all earthly striving was—everything on which the heart hung must be left behind—is the most foolish self-torture. The dying man ought to forget everything in view of the fact that he has suffered enough in this life and has already served his sentence in living, and ought only to address his progeny, admonishing them insistently to abandon life, to which suffering is essential. And in the hope that his words have fallen on fertile soil, that he shall soon be redeemed in his children, he may *calmly* sigh out his life.

In contrast, immanent philosophy attaches the utmost importance to the hour in which a new life is supposed to be kindled; for in that hour the decision whether he wants to live on or be completely annihilated in death lies wholly within man's power. It is not life's struggle with death on the deathbed, in which death is victorious; but death's struggle with life in copulation, in which life is victorious, that is replete with meaning. When the individual, amidst the intensest passion, sinks his teeth into existence and holds it in an iron embrace—when he is in the *frenzy of lust*—redemption is trifled away. In his foolish, boisterous jubilation, the poor dupe fails to notice that the *most precious of all treasures* has been wrested from him. For that brief moment of bliss he must pay the price not of endless, but perhaps of long, long suffering, of the intense agony of existence, and the Parcae rejoice:

> You are ours!

while his guardian spirit hides its face.

29.

Although the denial of the will therefore severs the individual's life-thread in death only when that denial is accomplished on the basis of complete chasteness, it can still take hold of such men as already live on in their children. However, it then brings about only the happiness of the individual for what remains of his own life. Yet the imperfect consequences of the will's denial in such cases should not and will not upset the individual. He will attempt to awaken in his children true cognition and to lead them with a gentle hand onto the path of redemption. He will also draw complete consolation from the certainty that *individual* redemption is accompanied by *universal* redemption, that the ideal State will sooner or later encompass humanity entire, which will then make the "great sacrifice", as the Indians say. Indeed, he will thence be inspired to commit himself wholeheartedly to the universal, so that the ideal State is realised as soon as possible.

30.

Those who confidently await redemption through death do indeed stand uprooted in the world and have only the one demand: to step *soon* out of their profound peace of heart into complete annihilation, but their original character is not dead. It has only retreated into the background; and even if it can no longer induce the individual to perform deeds that would be in accordance with it, then it will still give a special hue to what remains of the life of him who denies the will to life.

For this reason, those who are certain of individual redemption will not all have the same appearance. Nothing would be more confused than to assume they should. He who was proud and reticent will not become merry and sociable; while he whose loving essence spread soothing warmth wherever it arrived will not become shy and sombre; nor will he who was melancholy become boisterously merry.

Likewise, activity and occupation will not be the same for everyone. One man will cut himself off from the world completely, escape into solitude and, like the religious penitents, mortify himself because he proceeds from the recognition that only a will which is constantly humiliated can be maintained in renunciation; another will keep his old profession; a third will continue as he formerly did, stopping the tears of the unfortunate with word and deed; a fourth will struggle for his people or for humanity entire, will so employ his life, which is utterly worthless to him, that the motion towards the ideal State, in which alone everyone can be redeemed, becomes a hastened one.

Whoever in denying the will withdraws *entirely into himself* earns the complete admiration of the children of this world; for he is a *"child of the light"* wandering on the right path. Only the ignorant or the bad would venture to sling mud at him. But higher still must and should that man be prized who, *immovable in his inner being*, lets the external man move intensely and suffer in order to help his benighted brothers: getting to his feet again—tireless, stumbling, bleeding—never letting fall from his hand the banner of redemption, until in the struggle for humanity he collapses and the magnificent, gentle light in his eyes is extinguished. He is the purest phenomenon on this earth: an illuminated man, a redeemer, a victor, a martyr, a wise hero.

Such men will be in accord with each other only insofar as they are dead to all baseness and are unreceptive to everything which can move natural egoism, insofar as they despise life and love death. And they will all have one distinguishing mark: *beneficence*. "They envy not, they vaunteth not themselves, they are not puffed up, they beareth all things, they endureth all things", they do not condemn and do not stone men to death, they are always forgiving and only amiably will they commend the path on which they have found such delightful rest and the most glorious peace.

Finally, I mention here that peculiar state which can precede the denial of the will: *hatred of oneself*. It is a transitional state, comparable to a sultry spring night on which the flowerbuds open.

31.

In conclusion I want to say a few words about the religion of redemption.

Christ, by promising the kingdom of heaven only to those who are not merely just and merciful but also bear injustices and agonies without bitterness:

But I say unto you, that ye resist not evil: but whosoever shall smite thee on thy right cheek, turn to him the other also (Matt 5:39);

demanded from man almost complete self-denial. However, by also promising those who suppress their sex-drive a very special reward, he called on man to surrender his individuality completely, to kill his *natural* egoism *entirely*.

Why did he impose these severe demands? The answer lies precisely in the promise of the kingdom of heaven; for only he who has lost his original individuality, in whom Adam is dead and Christ resurrected, can become truly happy and attain inner peace.

Because this is a truth which can *never* be overthrown, indeed because it is the highest truth, even philosophy can put no other truth in its place. And for this reason the core of Christianity is an indestructible one and contains the blossoms of all human wisdom. Because the immutable motion of humanity is the soil in which Christianity is rooted, its *ethics* rests on an indestructible basis and can only perish when humanity itself perishes.

Now, even if immanent philosophy is obligated simply to confirm the demands of the beneficent saviour, then obviously, on the other hand, it cannot acknowledge the dogmatic foundation of those demands. It is as impossible for the educated man of our time to believe in Church dogmas as it was impossible for the faithful Christian of the Middle Ages to exchange his redeemer for the Gods of Greece and Rome or the wrathful God of the Jews. Now, so that the indestructible core of the Christian doctrine is not discarded with the faith and so that the possibility of man's partaking of the *true peace of heart* is not thereby foreclosed, it is philosophy's task to establish the truth of salvation in accordance with nature.

This Ethics is the first attempt to achieve this task in the *purely immanent domain*, by *purely immanent means*. It was only possible once the transcendent domain had been completely separated from the immanent and once it had been demonstrated that both domains do not lie next to each other or the one within the other, but that the perishing of the one was the arising of the other. The immanent *succeeded* the transcendent and it alone persists. The simple, premundane unity has perished in multiplicity and this multiplicity was made by the primordial leap out of a simple unity into a firmly self-contained collective unity having a single motion which, as regards humanity, is the motion out of being into absolute death.

32.

Mohammedanism and Christianity—the former the best of all bad religions, the latter the best of all ethical religions—with regard to the rewards they promise in the afterlife for morality of disposition, are related to immanent philosophy like King Lear's two eldest daughters to his youngest,

Cordelia. Whereas Mohammedanism promises the virtuous man a life full of intoxication and lust, therefore an elevated life of the blood, and Christianity promises him a state of eternal contemplation and intellectual bliss, therefore a life of the blood which has faded from consciousness; immanent ethics can proffer only *sleep*, "*the chief nourisher in life's feast*". But just as the physically exhausted man spurns everything and wants only sleep, so too the man weary of life wants only death, absolute annihilation in death, and from the philosopher's hand he gratefully receives the certainty that *no* new state awaits him, neither of bliss nor of torment, but that with the annihilation of his innermost being all states vanish of their own accord.

Politics

In the life of humanity everything is in common,
everything is but one development; the individual belongs
to the whole, but also the whole to the individual.

Varnhagen

Whoever is acquainted with and acknowledges nature's
law also in history can make prophecy; whoever does not
knows not what shall happen tomorrow and would be a
minister of state.

Börne

He who of three thousand years
knows not how account to give,
lies in the grip of naïve fears,
from day to day must live.

Goethe

1.

Politics treats of the motion of humanity entire, which results from the strivings of *all* individuals. As we had to propose without proof in the Ethics, this motion, when contemplated from a low standpoint, is the motion towards the ideal State; but when considered from the highest standpoint, it is the motion out of life into absolute death, since it is impossible to stand still in the ideal State.

This motion can have no moral aspect; for morals rest on the Subject, and only actions of the *individual, in relation to* the motion of the totality, can be *moral*.

This motion executes itself merely through irresistible power and, defined in general terms, it is humanity's omnipotent fate which smites and shatters like glass all that opposes it, though it were an army of millions; but from that point onwards where it issues in the State it is called *civilisation*.

The general *form* of civilisation is therefore the *State*; its particular forms: *economic, political*, and *intellectual*, I call *historical* forms. The principal law according to which it executes itself is the *law of suffering*, which effects the *weakening of the will* and the *strengthening of the mind*. It differentiates itself into various individual laws which I call *historical laws*.

2.

Our task is now first and foremost: To demonstrate the course of civilisation in the principal events passed down to us by history and, from the turmoil of phenomena, to read off the forms in and laws according to which humanity has developed into our own age; then to investigate the currents in our period of history, and finally to envisage that locus towards which all those developmental chains we are considering point. We will in general but especially in the latter task avoid losing ourselves in minutiae; for it would be downright foolhardy to want to ascertain in minute detail and with precision what form the future shall take.

3.

In the Ethics we briefly traced the State back to a contract which put an end to the state of nature. We were allowed to do this because in the Ethics we were concerned above all only with the fundamental law of the State. However, we are now obliged to investigate more precisely the relations out of which the State arose.

The assumption that the human race has a single origin in no way contradicts the results of natural science, while on the other hand it gives to philosophical politics an excellent foundation in every regard. Moreover, there flows unforced from this assumption the proposition, convincing and full of impelling truth for everyone, that all men are brothers; a truth to gain which one needn't believe in an intangible unity hidden behind individuals, a unity which in some favourable moment or other is supposed to be cognisable through intellectual intuition only.

Primitive man can have distanced himself only very gradually from the animal from which he arose. The gulf between them cannot initially have been wide. What occasioned it was the breaking open, as it were, of the seeds in which the auxiliary faculties of reason still lay entirely encased, or, in physiological terms, a small increase in brain mass. From the standpoint of my philosophy, however, it was the splitting of a further part of the motion of the will to life into controller and controlled, as an expression of the will's deep yearning for a new kind of motion.

The new dispositions were consolidated and inherited. One cannot speak of their rapid growth; rather, it must be assumed that in this direction, after many generations, the growth came to a halt. Development lay entirely in the development of individuals, or in other words: the *law of the development of individuality* alone reigned in the first age of humanity. Only once the individuals had multiplied to such an extent that they had to attack and supplant animals did necessity press on the intellect and train it further. It is beyond all doubt that the imagination was the faculty which unfolded itself earliest. With its aid, reason succeeded at thinking in images, joining what had passed with what was present, preserving causal connections in visual connections, and in this way it succeeded first of all at constructing crude weapons and killing with intent. As the development progressed, the tender seed of the faculty of judgment also grew stronger, probably in a *few* select individuals, and the first concepts were formed, from the composition of which crude, uninflected, natural languages arose. In the process, reason practised a sort of coastal navigation; it could not yet set out on the wide sea of abstraction, but had always to keep the indvidual beings of the intuitive world in view.

4.

The multiplication of men—fostered on one hand by a very strong sex-drive, on the other hand by the conditions of the land which the first men occupied, conditions which were advantageous to their maintenance—effected an ever-increasing expansion. Initially, men were still distributed in groups over those abutting regions which offered them livelihood, in constant struggle with the animal world and their fellow men.

The historical gap which lies between these hordes of animal-men and the primitive peoples cannot be filled in with any pretension to certainty. This lengthy period was dominated by the laws of *friction* and of the development of individuality. The first of these laws decisively weakened the will's intensity, albeit very gradually, such that no great difference between successive generations was able to arise. In most of the records of the human species one encounters reports of giant individuals, and there is as little reason to doubt them as to doubt that all extant species were preceded by more enormous kinds, and even the course of humanity familiar to us teaches of a decrease of the life force, which man's increasing longevity does nothing to disprove.

The law of friction, in contrast, strengthened the intelligence, admittedly only very little in this period, since the need of it cannot have been great.

5.

We thus enter the vestibule of civilisation, where we come upon the primitive peoples properly so called: hunting, farming, and agricultural *tribes*. Since it can in no way be ascertained whether the developmental course of prehistoric man proceeded always in groups or, through disintegration, in families which only later reunited, I leave it to each man's discretion to imagine the process as he will. At best, let us assume that it proceeded in families into which the groups dissolved and which nourished themselves on the fruits of trees and on slain animals; for man is essentially unsociable, and only the most extreme need or its opposite—boredom—can make him sociable. It is therefore much more probable that the strong primitive man, when he could rely on weapons and his small but, relative to animals, far superior intelligence, followed his drive for independence and isolated himself, than that he was formed further and without interruption in the group.

If we now consider such a hunter according to his idea only, then he was simple will to life, i.e., his natural egoism comprised no will which had separated in various directions, no qualities of the will. He only wanted to exist in accordance with his particular, simple character and maintain himself in existence. The cause of this is to be sought in the savage's simple mode of life and in his limited mind. The intellect was obligated to make discoverable only those few Objects which satisfied hunger, thirst, and the sex-drive. If his needs were met, then man sank into idleness and torpor.

Corresponding to the simple will, which is not to be thought of other than as wild and independent, was the small number of its states. Aside from the usual state of dull indifference and that of instinctive fear, it was capable only of passionate hatred and of passionate love. The simple will hated everything which obstructed it and sought to annihilate those obstructions; in contrast, it held everything which was able to extend its individuality in a loving embrace and sought to preserve it.

The savage hunter lived together with a woman who perhaps had to accompany him on his expeditions, who perhaps was active only in the hut and guarded the fire as well as the children. The character of the family was crude and still very animalistic. The woman was the man's beast of burden, and once the children were grown, they moved on and established families of their own.

Confronted with the forces of nature, man as hunter behaved with scarce any difference from animals. He pondered the violent elemental forces no further. Now and then perhaps his dependence on nature and his impotence in the face of it entered his consciousness and, like lightning, illuminated the night of his serenity.

Out of this uniform mode of life men were torn by the dearth of nourishment. They had in the meantime multiplied to such a degree that the individual's hunting grounds had suffered a considerable diminution and no longer offered quarry sufficient to sustain him and his kin. Through mere migration this evil could not be eliminated, for the places of the earth favourable to hunters were all inhabited, and apart from each hunter's being hemmed in on all sides, his love for his hunting grounds held him fast to them.

At this juncture, those who lived nearer each other probably came together in a *temporary* union in order not only to repel invaders but also to annihilate them. If the danger was averted, then they parted ways once more. Meanwhile, the character of the family also underwent a change. Firstly, the sons could no longer easily procure shelter for themselves; secondly, it was in the fathers' interest to make use of their sons' power, to strengthen themselves with it. The ties of family were drawn tighter and only now did true hunting tribes emerge, the members of which were imbued with the consciousness that they belonged together, something which was formerly impossible. Since everywhere the same conditions came into being, all families had gradually to unite in hunting tribes, and these were henceforth ever at war with each other. Thenceforth war was among their concerns, and in the constant friction which it created, war raised man's mental powers onto a yet higher level.

War as well as the now communal peacetime concerns demanded strong leadership superior to the coercive power of the heads of the families. The strongest or cleverest man was chosen to be a leader in times of war and a judge in times of peace. Now, too, the immense and consequential difference between justice and injustice entered men's consciousness, a difference which more firmly binds and laces up the individual's will than the animosity of the whole of nature. Within the cooperative, certain actions (theft and murder) were now forbidden which had been allowed outside of it, and the will was subjected to an iron compulsion while in each man's mind the appeal was lodged that he act no longer primarily under his dæmon's sway, but also with reflection and sobre-mindedness.

In this way, to be sure, it was need which cast man into the *legal* cooperative, the first crude form of State, but its organisation was a work of *reason* and rested, all circumstances considereed, on a *contract*. The family elders recognised on one hand that the cooperative could not be dissolved, on the other hand, however, they also recognised that it could exist only on particular foundations, and so they came to the agreement that these foundations ought henceforth to be resolute. One may also say that the laws against murder and theft are the product of an original contract which *had* to be concluded. Constitutions of the State, social conditions, other laws can be established entirely one-sidedly; not, however, these two laws, on which the most complete as well as the most incomplete State has to be founded. These two laws first appeared only by convention and with logical force, and were they abolished today, then after a brief period everyone would once again conclude the same original contract. No far-sightedness, no profound wisdom was needed in order to set up these two necessary legal limits. Once communal living in a vulnerable cooperative became an unavoidable reality, these laws had of necessity to ensue.

6.

Humanity made very important progress when, with the aid of chance, the utility of domesticating certain animals was recognised, and animal husbandry appeared. From hunting tribes, shepherding tribes branched off and these were able to move into all those regions which hitherto had gone unused, and in this way the development of individuals and, connected therewith, the dispersal of humanity became wider again.

The new mode of living brought with it great changes. At first, a general reformation of character took place. It was not that the will had now separated itself out into individual qualities; for that, conditions were still too simple, the intelligence too weak; but the entire will became milder, since the exciting hunt and the wars of annihilation conducted with the utmost brutality had been replaced with a peaceful, monotonous occupation.

At the same time, man became conscious of his relation to the visible world, and the first natural religion arose. On one hand the causal connection of the sun with the seasons, with the fertile pasture was recognised; on the other hand, the precious herds, whose upkeep sustained life, were often seen to be at the mercy of wild animals or devastating and violent elemental forces. In ruminating on these relationships man arrived at notions of good and evil, of powers amicably or adversely disposed towards him, and at the conviction that through worship and sacrifice the latter could be conciliated, the former kept benevolently disposed.

Now, according as the nomads, who were spreading out ever farther, arrived in climes more mild or harsh, this simple natural religion took on a cast more kind or sombre. Where the sun bestowed its blessings on the earth in abundance, the principle of evil receded far into the background, while the principle of good was approached faithfully and in awe. In contrast, where men found themselves in a constant struggle with nature, where predators in great numbers decimated their herds, and where forest fires and scorching desert winds drove men and animals into oblivion, the worried man lost sight of the principle of good completely: all his plans and endeavours were directed at placating through the sacrifice of his most beloved possessions the cruel, wrathful godhead which he had vividly conceived in fancy, and at disposing that godhead to mercy.

The form in which the nomads moved was the patriarchal cooperative. The head of the tribe was prince, judge, and priest, and the reflected glow of this threefold power fell on the father of each family, whereby the character of the family became much firmer and more earnest than it had been amongst the hunting peoples.

7.

Within these simple forms and ways of life all humanity may have moved for millennia. The law of *custom* ruled everyone, and its product, *social convention*, laid itself ever more tightly around the will. The germs of qualities of the will may already have formed in individuals, but they were unable to develop, since all the conditions for their development were yet lacking. Life went by too uniformly. Everyone was free; each man was able to become the father of a family, i.e., to attain authority, and the highest authority was essentially constrained; in short, great contrasts which cut into the mind and stir up the will were lacking.

On the other hand, at the higher level which it had attained, the mind worked on calmly; it became, particularly in mild, temperate climes, more contemplative, more objective, and was thereby able to immerse itself more easily in the contemplation of the essence of things. On this path it had to arrive at many small but important inventions and discoveries, until at long last it recognised the utility of cereal crops and gradually progressed to the cultivation of the relevant kinds of grass.

Firm ground had now been won on which civilisation was able to establish itself and begin its victory march; only now could its supreme law, the law of suffering, reveal itself in ever-growing friction, ennoble the will, and illuminate the mind.

8.

The most immediate consequence of agriculture was a large increase in the number of individuals. The population had to increase significantly because, on one hand, the same piece of land was now able to sustain ten times as many people and, on the other, fewer men were being annihilated in war.

Over the course of time, however, overpopulation occurred, a great evil which was able to be remedied only through mass emigration. It may be assumed that in the Asiatic regions, north of the Hindu Kush and Himalayas, the first transition from nomadic into agricultural life took place and entanglement first entered the scene. From the strong, tough, and valiant Aryan people, large parts loosed themselves early on and, equipped with domesticated animals, plough, and cereals, struck out westward and established for themselves a new home at various loci around Europe. Finally, the whole Aryan people, likely recognising that the land it occupied was not suited to cultivation and that only through a diligent working of the soil a durable and safe existence could be won—and perhaps even beset by nomadic Mongol hordes—resolved to leave its ancient abodes. It moved southward, and while one part turned towards present-day Persia, another took possession of the valleys of the Indus. Here the Indians remained until overpopulation occurred once again; they then began a great military campaign against the half-savage hunting and nomadic peoples occupying the northern half of the peninsula, and carried this campaign to a favourable conclusion. Yet they did not mix with the conquered peoples but established a *caste society*, one of the most important and most necessary forms for the beginning of civilisation, regarding which we shall have occasion to note various new laws.

It is clear that already in the Indus valleys the ancient Indians, when they had for the most part given themselves over to cultivating the land and had become a sedentary people, had to abandon the patriarchal mode of organisation and give themselves a different one. Their work above all had changed. It was more difficult and effortful, and restricted the individual more than the care and defence of livestock. Moreover, the nomadic life has a very special appeal. It is well known that the Tatar, tamed by the Russian, yearns unrelentingly for the occupation of his fathers, and that even the German colonist of the steppe becomes a nomad with head and heart and gladly abandons his plough and horticulture. No wonder! Whoever has savoured a view of the steppe just once understands its irresistible powers of enchantment. How it lies there in the splendours of spring: gently swaying, undulating, solitary, still, endless! How well the man feels who races across it on a fiery steed! How free, how free! – It is therefore no misapprehension to assume there is dissatisfaction and reluctance amongst a large part of the people, which must be vigorously and decisively counteracted.

Furthermore, agriculture demanded a division of labour. Forests had to be cleared away, wild animals fought, equipment made, houses built, roads and canals laid down and, in the process, the field regularly tilled and livestock raised. The neighbouring half-savages had also to be kept out of the captured regions. Meanwhile, the population steadily increased. The existing villages became larger and settlements arose which soon became villages in their own right and remained closely allied with the village of origin. Finally, property relations had also changed fundamentally, since once-roving hordes had acquired lands and these became the source of frequent disputes. These disputes had to be settled according to fixed norms, which had first to be established and then required men with precise knowledge of the law.

All of this mandated the introduction of an authority harsher than that of the family elders, tribal heads and leaders, and led to the despotic monarchy with army, officers, tradespeople, and so on. As development proceeded, the priesthood separated from the monarchy, since the princes now had obligations which laid claim to all their time and the simple natural religion had shaped itself into a religion with a regular cult.

It must therefore be assumed that the Indians, before they pressed on to the mouth of the Ganges, were already a people articulated according to estates but had no castes, for there were not yet slaves. The strict caste society arose only once a half savage, unruly and numerous people had been conquered and incorporated into the framework of society and slavery had been established, and even then it arose only gradually.

The fact that no melding took place is easily explained. In contrast to the half-savage of brutish ways, hateful shape and dark colour, the proud, beautiful Aryan must have felt himself to be a being of a higher kind and must have felt true revulsion at the thought of mixing sexually with the half-savage. He must also have considered it downright dishonourable to maintain social intercourse with those burdened with the harshest and lowest labours and who, in consequence of their recalcitrance and stubbornness, had to be pressed into the dirt with an iron fist. Thus natural revulsion joined with contempt, and both of these made a melding impossible.

If we look now at the basis of caste society, then the *law of development of the part* reveals itself to us first of all, one of the most important laws of civilisation. We could already have recognised it in the fact that parts of tribes emigrated and changed and scaled to a higher level by means of a better constitution of the soil, a more favourable climate, and more noble occupations. In the civilised State, however, it comes more clearly to the fore and shows its full power.

Only by one *part* of the people, at the start of civilisation, being relieved of all the troubles to secure its daily bread was it possible for the mind to grow wings and take free, ingenious flight; for only "idle hands make active heads". In the struggle for existence, necessity may be the mother of invention, but art and science thrive and yield ripe, succulent fruits only in untroubled airs.

We then encounter the *law of the unfolding of the simple will*. This law too I have not discussed until now, because only in the caste system did the contrasts reach their zenith; for it is clear that, already in the first period of a sedentary people which is organised into estates, motives were fully present which must have drawn the will out of its simplicity.

In the individuals arose haughtiness, ambition, thirst for glory, vanity, greed, hedonism, envy, truculence, deceitfulness, malice, fickleness, cruelty, and the like. But the seeds of noble qualities of the will, such as mercifulness, valour, modesty, justice, benevolence, bonhomie, fidelity, allegiance, and the like, also sprouted.

At the same time, the states of the will had to shape themselves more diversely. Fear, sadness, joy, hope, doubt, compassion, schadenfreude, regret, pangs of conscience, aesthetic joy, and the like by turns took possession of the heart and made it more ductile and more malleable.

Of course, the reformation of character was completed (and is still being completed) only gradually under the influence of motives grasped by the mind. Just as everything which is grasped by the will passes, as it were, into the blood, so slight changes were absorbed into the power of procreation, passed according to the *law of the heritability of characteristics* as a germ into the new individual, and there continued to take shape according to the law of custom.

We have furthermore to take notice of the *law of binding* of the new individuality. The simple natural religion was no longer able to satisfy the priests' searching minds, which had become objective. They immersed themselves in the study of nature's fabric, and the short, toilsome life between birth and death became their chief problem. NASCI, LABORARE, MORI. Were they able to commend it? They had to condemn it and brand it an error, a misstep. The recognition that life is worthless is the blossom of all wisdom. The worthlessness of life is the simplest truth, but at the same time the truth most difficult to recognise, because it presents itself to us shrouded in countless veils. It is, as it were, right under our noses; how exactly are we supposed to find it?

The Brahmins, however, had to find this truth because they were relieved entirely of the struggle for existence, they led a life purely contemplative and were able to use all their mental powers for solving the riddle of the world. Furthermore, they assumed the primary position in the State; happier than them (happy in the popular sense of the word) no-one was able to be, and so between them and the truth that shadow which clouds the judgment of those lower in the social order was not cast, namely, the thought that happiness gilds the heights but cannot penetrate into the vales, and that it is therefore really to be met with in the world, just not everywhere. Plunging into their innermost being the Brahmins fathomed the world, and the *empty* hands with which they came up condemned it.

However, the will's recognition that life is worthless, indeed essentially unhappy, must have engendered a yearning for liberation from existence, and the direction in which this was to be attained was indicated by the absolutely necessary constraining of natural egoism by means of the fundamental laws of the State. "Constrain also the drives liberated by the State, constrain natural egoism entirely and you will be set free"—thus had reason to conclude, and it concluded aright.

The pantheism of the Brahmins into which the natural religion of the Indians had reformed itself served merely to support pessimism; it was but the setting for the precious stone. The disintegration of the unity into multiplicity was conceived as a misstep, and, as is made clear in a Vedic hymn, it was taught that three parts of the fallen primordial being had already raised itself out of the world again and only one part remained embodied in the world. The wisdom of the Brahmins assigned to these redeemed parts what every human heart so deeply yearned for and yet was not to be found in the world: rest, peace, and eternal bliss, and this same wisdom taught that only through mortification of the individual will could man be united with the primordial being, otherwise the immortal streak of the primordial being which lived unpurified in every man would by means of reincarnation have to remain in the torment of existence until it was purified and ripe for eternal bliss.

In this way the caste system was also consecrated. It was no work of man, but a divine institution with the imprimatur of the greatest justice conceivable, which had to reconcile everyone with their fate; for through the higher castes flowed constantly a stream of essences which had earned their higher position, and it was put within the power of everyone of low birth to be received into this stream after death.

In accordance with this whole doctrine, the Brahmins now forced themselves to observe the strictest ceremony, which smothered every stirring of their will. They surrendered themselves *completely* unto the *law*, leaving nothing to their own discretion, so that they would be wholly secured against excess. For every hour of the day particular actions such as washing, prayer, meditation, sacrifice were prescribed, and not even a minute remained for each to dispose of as he saw fit. They then went further, adding to very serious fasting the greatest self-torments possible, which aimed at cutting man loose from the world entirely and making will and mind completely indifferent to everything.

In a similar manner they regulated life in the other castes and wrapped unyielding bonds around every individual. To the fear of the harshest punishments in this life was joined the fear of horrible torments after death, and under the influence of these powerful motives even the most tenacious and savage will to life had finally to succumb.

What thus took place in the despotic caste system of the ancient Indians was the raising of man out of his animality and the binding of the simple character, which through political and religious compulsion had separated out into qualities of the will. Similar processes and events occurred of necessity in all other despotic States of the Orient. What was happening was that men in whom the dæmon alone reigned, who were still entirely immersed in a dream-like natural life, who still brimmed with savagery and sloth, were being galvanised, tamed, and with whip and sword driven onto the path of civilisation, on which alone redemption is to be found.

9.

The histories of Babylon, Assyria, and Persia reveal two new laws of civilisation: the *law of decay* and the *law of melding through conquest*.

It is essential to civilisation that, in accordance with the law of development of the part, it begins in small circles and then extends these. Civilisation is not the *opposite* of the motion of primitive peoples; for both kinds of motion have *one* direction. The former is only an *accelerated* motion. The motion of a primitive people is to be compared with that of a ball on an almost horizontal surface, the motion of a civilised people, in contrast, with the plunging of this ball into the abyss. Figuratively speaking, civilisation endeavours to draw *all* peoples into its circle; it has in view humanity *entire* and overlooks not even the smallest cooperative in the most hidden corner of the earth.

To the laws according to which civilisation proceeds in this regard belong the two just mentioned. Every civilised State seeks to maintain itself in its individuality and to strengthen this individuality as much as possible. Thus the

States we are here considering had initially also to turn against the nomadic hordes and hunting peoples—who separated them from other States, unsettled their borders, invaded their territory, robbed, and murdered—and had to seek to render them harmless. They waged war on these nomads and hunters and absorbed them, as slaves, into their community. Once, in this manner, the States were brought to neighbour immediately on each other, each sought to weaken the other, or, as soon as its power allowed and its interest required it, to incorporate the other entirely.

In the former instance, a melding through conquest took place in the lower classes of the State, between savage groups and such as were already subject to laws; in the process, even peoples of diverse races (Aryans, Semites, etc.) were from time to time mixed together; where this happened, members of the higher classes were pushed down into the lower. Through these mixings and meldings the character of many was reshaped.

The motion which executes itself according to the law of conquest is a powerful one originating within the State and directed outwards; that motion, however, which the law of decadence underlies, is a powerful one originating outside the State and directed inwards. The result of both, however, is the same, namely: mixing of peoples, reshaping of individuals; or to express it in quite general terms: expansion of the circle of civilisation.

In the empires we are here considering, lack of discipline eventually took hold of the individuals of the higher classes. Bit by bit, the highly educated individual brushed off all the constraints which social convention, law, and religious commandment had laid upon him, and his drive for bliss, directed at sensual pleasure, thrust him into a state of utter feebleness and effeminacy. Now powerful mountain peoples, or nomads who either stood outside the State or were fettered to it only by a fine thread, encountered no more resistance. Attracted by the accumulated treasures of civilisation, they broke in upon the weakly governed community and either thrust its degenerate members down into the lower ranks or melded with them through sexual intermixing.

10.

The circle of civilisation expanded further and continues to expand according to the *laws of colonisation* and *mental fertilisation*. Amongst the ancient peoples of the Orient it was the Phoenicians in particular who spread civilisation through trade. Overpopulation, strife in the aristocratic families, and other causes effected the establishment of colonies in distant regions, which developed further into independent States and remained closely connected to the motherland.

Between one people and another the Phoenecians also established connections, thereby not only mediating the exchange of surplus products, which caused the wealth of States to grow significantly, but also bringing fresh motion into the mental life of peoples who lacked the power to swing up onto a higher level of cognition themselves—namely, by conveying to them truths discovered by more favoured peoples, i.e., by using the sparks from one fire to kindle another. In this regard the merchants of antiquity are to be compared to those insects which in the economy of nature are designed to fertilise female blossoms with the pollen of male blossoms which has stuck to their wings.

11.

I said above that the principal law of civilisation is suffering, according to which the will is weakened and the mind strengthened. Civilisation continually reshapes man and makes him ever more receptive to suffering. At the same time, it lets unrelentingly powerful motives flow into him through the mind, which give him no rest and magnify his suffering. At these motives—which are commanded by the mind and created from the mind—as they took shape in the Orient, we must now cast a brief glance.

Every people which entered the form of civilised State could not stand still at natural religion: they had to deepen it speculatively; for in the State intelligence grows of necessity and its fruits must therefore be different from those which appear in the loose cooperative.

Whoever can remain clear-eyed and not be blinded by the variety of phenomena will find in every natural religion and every refined religion nothing other than the more or less clear expression of the *feeling of dependency* which every man experiences in confrontation with the universe. Religion is not concerned with the philosophical cognition of the world's dynamic coherence, but with reconciling the individual with the almighty will of a godhead inferred from the phenomena of nature.

In the natural religions of Asia, which fragmented the omnipotence of the world and personified the fragments, the quivering individual conciliated the wrathful gods through *external* sacrifice. In the refined religions, in contrast, he sacrificed to the godhead through the constraining of his *inner* essence. The external sacrifice, which was preserved, was only an allusion to the constraint being imposed internally.

It is extraordinarily significant that such a constraining of the inner man, which with the Indians, as mentioned, went so far as to release the individual completely from the world, was able to be demanded at all and has been demanded almost everywhere. As has been said, what was one able to know of the godhead? Only its will as it revealed itself in nature. Its will showed itself clearly enough, namely, to be omnipotent and in one moment merciful, annihilating in the next. But how was its intention to be apprehended? Why did one not stop at the external sacrifice, but go so far beyond it? I have already given the answer above. The mind of individuals had so developed that human life as such could be judged and, specifically, because the standpoint of those judging had, through favourable circumstances, the requisite height for making a correct judgment. The *intention* of the godhead was now construed to be that the individual should sacrifice his *whole* being to the godhead.

Nevertheless, it remains an admirable fact of history that on the basis of the correct judgment about human life *alone* a religion as magnificent and profound as Indian pantheism was able to be built. This fact cannot be explained any other way than that, for once, the *dæmon* of powerful men played the main role in cognition and, upon the mind's provision of the correct motive (despising of life), let rise from the depths of its feeling intimations which the mind grasped in concepts:

O, I saw it hover above the world like a dove which seeks a nest to brood upon, and the first soul which burst the bonds of its torpor had to receive the idea of redemption.

Hebbel, *Judith*

For the principal truth of Indian pantheism is the unitary course of development, not only of *humanity* but of the *universe*, lying between a start- and end-point. Was the mind alone able to discover that course? Impossible! What was it possible to know of this motion at the time of the Indians? They had an overview only of their own history, which showed neither a beginning nor an end. If they looked at nature then they saw the sun and the stars regularly rise and fall, night regularly follow day and day night, finally they saw organic life tend towards the grave and from the grave arise again. All of this implied a *circle*, not a *spiral*, and the core of Indian pantheism is that the world sprang from a simple primordial essence which lives in it, atones and purifies itself in it, and finally, annihilating it, will return to pure primordial being.

The Indian sages had only *one* firm point of support: *man*. They felt the contrast of their purity with the vulgarity of the savages and the contrast of their peace of heart with the unrest and torment of those who were hungry for life. This gave them a development with a start and an end, but the development of the *entire* world they were able to arrive at only through divination, through an ingenious flight of fancy on the dæmon's wings.

However, this truth of the world's unitary motion, which was not to be proved and therefore had to be *believed*, was bought at the heavy price of having to posit a simple unity *in* the world. Herein lies the weakness of Indian pantheism. With a simple unity in the world the fact of inner and outer experience, which obtrudes time and again into consciousness, that is, the *real individuality*, is incompatible. Religious pantheism and, after it, philosophical pantheism (Vedanta philosophy) solved the contradiction forcibly, at the expense of truth. They denied the reality of the individual and therewith the reality of the whole world, or more precisely: Indian pantheism is pure empirical idealism.

This had to be so. One was not permitted to do without the unitary course of development. On it rested *redemption*. This course, however, called for a simple unity in the world, because otherwise a unitary motion of the universe would not have been explicable, and the simple unity in the world demanded for its part the demotion of the entire real world to a world of illusion, to a deceptive image (veil of Maya); for if a unity is at work in the world, no individual can be real; it is but a dead tool, not a thinking master.

Against this arose the Sankhya doctrine, which denied the unity and stood for the reality of the individual. From it developed the most important religion of Asia: *Buddhism*.

The core of Buddhism lies in the *doctrine of karma*, everything else is fanciful ornament, which must be put on the account of the great man's followers. I will approach this doctrine, which is sublime beyond all praise albeit one-sided, more closely in the Metaphysics, to which I refer the reader. Here I must summarise briefly.

Buddha too, like the pantheists, proceeded from the worthlessness of existence, but he stopped at the *individual*, whose course of development was for him the main concern. He laid all reality in the *individual essence, karma*, and made this *all-powerful*. Merely under the control of its particular character (more precisely: under the control of the sum of evil and the sum of good acts that have flowed from its character in earlier life-courses), the individual creates its own fate, i.e., its course of development. No power lying *outside* the individual has the least influence on its fate.

The individual being's course of development itself is defined by Buddha as the motion out of an incomprehensible primordial being into *non-being*.

From this it is clearly evident that even Buddha's atheism, like the unitary motion of the universe and the simple unity hidden within it of which pantheism taught, had to be *believed*. Moreover, the full *autonomy* of the individual was bought at a heavy price with the denial of chance's dominion, which is actually present in the world and totally independent of the individual. According to Buddhism, everything that we call *chance* is a *deed* of the *individual*, scenery effected from within his karma. Buddha therefore denied, at the expense of truth, the reality of the efficacy of all other things of the world, i.e., nothing less than the reality of all other things, and only a single reality remained: the ego, feeling within its own skin and apprehending itself in self-consciousness.

Like Indian pantheism, Buddhism is therefore crass absolute idealism.

This had to be so. Buddha justly aligned himself with the reality of the individual, the fact of inner and outer experience. However, he had to make the individual completely autonomous, i.e., to deny a unitary course of the world's development, because he would otherwise have been led of necessity to a unity in the world as taught by pantheism—an assumption at which he, like every clear-headed empiricist, bristled. The arrogance of the ego, however, demanded unconditionally the demotion of the remaining world, of the non-ego, to a world of illusion and deception; for if in the world only the ego is real, then the non-ego can only be an illusory appearance, it is decoration, window dressing, scenery, phantasmagoria in the hand of the arrogant individual, who alone is real.

Like pantheism, Buddhism carries within it the poison of contradicting experience. It denies the reality of all things, except that of the individual, and denies in addition the dynamic coherence of the world and a unitary motion of the collective unity; pantheism denies the reality of all things and knows only a simple unity *in* the world with a single motion.

Buddhism, nevertheless, is much closer to the human heart, because the uncognisable unity can *never* take root in our soul, whereas nothing is more real to us than our cognising and our feeling (in short: our ego), which Buddha raised onto the throne of the world.

What is more, the individual motion taught by Buddha, from the primordial being through being (constant becoming, rebirths) into *non-being*, is undeniably correct, whereas with the motion taught by Indian pantheism one must abide the inconceivable *misstep* of positing a primordial essence—a heavy burden indeed.

Both doctrines make *love of one's enemy* possible for their professors; for if the world is only the phenomenal appearance of a simple unity and if every individual deed flows directly from this unity, then the one who offends me, torments and distresses me—in short: my enemy—is entirely innocent of all the evil done me. It is not *he* who causes me pain, but *God* who does it *directly*. If I wanted to hate my enemy, then I would be hating the whip and not my tormentor, which would be preposterous.

And if everything that affects me is *my* doing, then likewise it is not my enemy who offends me, but *I* who have offended *myself* through him. If I wanted to be angry with him, then I would be acting just as irrationally as if I punched my foot because it slipped and caused me to fall.

By teaching exoterically the equality and fraternity of *all* men and thereby breaking through the caste-order, Buddha was also a socio-political reformer; however, this movement did not pervade India. Buddhism was gradually suppressed across that great peninsula and had to flee to the islands and to other lands (Indochina, China, etc.). In India proper, both the caste system and pantheism endured.

12.

In the Persian Zend religion, the evil powers of natural religion are fused into a single evil spirit and the good into a single good spirit. Everything that constrained the individual from *without*: darkness, drought, earthquakes, dangerous animals, storms, and so on, came from Ahriman; in contrast, everything else which promoted the individual's efficacy outwards came from Ormuzd. *Inwards*, however, it was precisely the other way around. The more man constrained his natural egoism, the more powerfully did the pure God of light reveal itself within him; the more, however, he followed his natural drives, the deeper he sank into the web of the evil one. This was only able to be taught based on the recognition that earthly life is futile. The Zend religion also knows a motion of the entire universe, namely the unification of Ahriman with Ormuzd and the establishment of the realm of light through gradual obliteration of everything evil on earth.

These three outstanding religions must have had immense influence on the development of their professors in antiquity. They directed the gaze of man into his innermost being and, based on the certainty which forces itself upon each man that an ungraspable omnipotence determines earthly fates, caused him to be ignited on the well-being depicted by his fancy.

Brahmanism threatened resisters with reincarnation, Buddhism with rebirth, the Zend religion with the unhappiness that shudders through the breast of man when he lies in the embrace of Ahriman; on the other hand, the first one tempted the hesitant with reunification with God, the second with total liberation from existence, and the Zend religion with peace in the lap of the God of light.

Buddhism in particular took firm hold of their souls and made their savage, defiant, stubborn characters soft and mild. Spence Hardy, speaking of all the inhabitans of Ceylon, says:

The carelessness and indifference of the people among whom the system is professed are the most powerful means of its conservation. It is almost impossible to move them, even to wrath. (*Eastern Monachism*, 430)

13.

The Semitic peoples of Asia (with the exception of the Jews), therefore the Babylonians, Assyrians, Phoenecians, did not have the power to deepen their natural religion into an ethical one. They stopped at the external sacrifice, which of course must have touched the individual with extraordinary pain but did not have an enduring effect on his character. The mothers who laid their children in the glowing arms of Moloch, and the maidens who let themselves be dishonoured at the feasts of Mylitta, sacrificed the dearest thing they had to the godhead; for the profound pains of the mother who let her child be incinerated must not be doubted, and Herodotus says expressly that the defiled maiden never again offered herself for intercourse, no matter how much she was offered in return. But what the individual bought with these terrible sacrifices was well-being in this life. The religions did not distract the will from this life and did not give it a firm objective at the end of this path. Furthermore, the gruesome sacrifices were poor motives, and so it came to pass that the people gradually lost all footing and vacillated between immodest sensory indulgence and immodest remorse and wore themselves out.

The ancient Jews, in contrast, attained a purer religion, which is all the more remarkable since Christianity sprouted from it. It was rigid monotheism. God, the uncognisable *extra*mundane essence, the creator of heaven and earth, held creation in His almighty hand. His will, proclaimed by inspired prophets, demanded unconditional obedience, complete surrender to the law, strict justice, constant *fear of God*. The God-fearing man was rewarded in *this* world, the contract-breaker terribly punished in *this* world. But this half-autonomy of the individual in the face of Jehovah was only apparent. The correct relation of God to the individual was the same as in the pantheism of the Indians. The fall of man, derived from the Zend doctrine, gained respect and significance first in Christianity, as original sin. Man was nothing but a plaything in the hand of Jehovah; for even if God did not have an effect directly in him, He did create the ESSENTIA from which man's deeds flow: the ESSENTIA was His work alone.

The Jews too, precisely because of their monotheism, did not arrive at the idea of the motion of the universe:

> One generation passes, another comes; the earth, however, remains eternal.
>
> **Salomo**

The universe has no goal.

14.

Ingenious, objective cognising was then active amongst the ancient oriental peoples (to whom the Egyptians also belong) in the domains of science and art.

Mathematics, mechanics and astronomy found diligent cultivation amongst the Indians, Chaldees, and Egyptians, and although the results gained were wanting in themselves, they yet spurred other peoples, namely the Greeks, onwards.

The faculty of judgment, that important and masterful faculty of the human mind which, on the basis of the drive to research, created the religions of the Orient which are, in practice, so extraordinarily effective and, in theory, so profoundly ethical, also revealed itself very distinctly as a sense of beauty and, in concert with the drive to reproduction, created very significant works of art. But just as in science the powerful fancy essentially constrained the faculty of judgment, so too it trammeled the sense of beauty, and only seldom was the beautiful able to unfold purely and nobly.

In architecture, the formally beautiful of space found earnest and worthy expression, namely in Egypt. The temples, palaces, graves, and suchlike were collossal but symmetrically arranged masses which train the eye and put one's soul in a sublime state. In contrast, the works of plastic art, which stood entirely in the service of religion, were fantastical, immodest, and calculated rather to fill man with fear and cast him *into* the dust than to elevate him. They could not convey him into the blissful state of simple aesthetic contemplation.

Poetry attained a very high degree of completion. The religious hymns, especially the majestic Vedic hymns, had to put the devout in a solemn mood, take firm hold of them and awaken within them a purer striving, whereas the warsongs and heroic poems inspired the devout to bold deeds, bearing courage into their souls.

In general, oriental art depicts the the constraining of the individual by nature's omnipotence; the individual was not yet able to get a word in because he had not yet recognised his own power. This pressing in from without had on the speculative mind an inspiring effect, on the creative mind a depressive one, and we can therefore say that in oriental antiquity the genius of philosophy already flew high above the clouds, whereas the genius of art still grazed the earth with the tips of its wings.

15.

We turn now to the ancient Greeks who, fertilised by oriental art and science, developed a wholly unique culture. The same culture effected great reshapings in contemporary and later States and continues as a mighty ferment to have an effect in the life of civilised nations.

I have above already emphasised the great influence which climate and the constitution of the soil exert on the religious intuitions of a people and thereby on its character. As long as man ventures to approach the godhead—i.e., fate embodied—only contrite and trembling, he will remain unconscious of his power to act and his consciousness of other things will be impaired and deficient. In contrast, if he has recognised Nature's supreme power as disposed towards him overwhelmingly with mercy, then he will look her directly in the eye, gain confidence in her and therefore in himself, and conduct himself calmly and courageously.

Thus the entire political and mental life of the Hellenes was based on the influence of the majestic country they inhabited. Such a rich soil, such a mild, sunny climate was unable to make slaves of men, but had to favour the maintenance of a cheerful natural religion and placed the individual in a dignified relation to the godhead. However, the Greek character thereby gradually became harmonious; the natural, indestructible individuality—so that it did not run wild and degenerate—did not have to be completely bound by laws, but was afforded some latitude in which to be trained into a noble personality.

The first consequence of this free personality was that the Greek nation never achieved political unity. It disintegrated into a heap of independent urban and country communities, which were at first only loosely federated and, later, subordinated themselves to the supremacy of the most powerful State among them. Only their common religion and national festivals joined the communities into an ideal whole.

Crucially, this fragmentation of States over a small region under the protection of a kind of international law favoured the development of all the aptitudes of this richly gifted people; for according to the *law of the rivalry of peoples*, which we here encounter distinctly for the first time, each State was striving to outdo the other through power and had therefore to cause all the strengths of its citizens to unfold and bring those strengths to bear.

A further consequence of the free personality of the Greeks was that the constitution of the State was subjected to modifications until the entire people achieved de facto dominance. Initially in all Greek States there reigned kings, who as the highest judges administered the laws, sacrificed to the gods in the name of the people, and were leaders in war. Their power was constrained by a council whose members were drawn from the nobility. Over against them stood the common people, who enjoyed no influence on the conduct of political affairs. However, these relations changed gradually through internal upheavals which took place according to the *law of melding through revolution*, which we likewise encounter for the first time here.

First the noble families opposed the monarchy, overthrew it, and established in its place an aristocratic republic. But then it was the lower people who struggled for political freedom. However, their efforts were fruitless until conflicts broke out amongst the aristocrats themselves and the defeated ones, in order to exact their revenge, made the people's cause their own. In this way the bond between rulers and ruled was continually weakened until it finally snapped and the people came to hold the power of self-rule.

This internal process of melding was extraordinarily important for the ennoblement of the people. Each man now let his highest well-being coincide with the well-being of the State, and alongside an ardent patriotism, which made even a small people capable of the highest deeds, there arose a system of general education, beneficial for the individual as well as for the totality.

But just as the Greeks' distinct personality was the cause of the common people's elevation to rule and of the tearing down of the boundaries between the social classes, so too, after the Persian wars, it caused the individual to become more and more detached from the whole. Every man overvalued himself, believed himself to know and to understand everything best, and sought to shine. Personality became overripe individuality, in which man waltzes to and fro as in a fever dream. In one moment the life-force flares up, in the next it gutters to the point of going out—a sure sign that the will to life has crossed the summit of its existence and that the beginning of the end is nigh. The individual is doomed to annihilation! The sunny path of the fine, agile Greek of tender feeling seems immeasurably remote from the muddy way of the Asiatic glutton, and they are indeed quite diverse, for on the one path the life-force dissipates in lust and sensual ecstasy, on the other man loses his calm certainty and starts to waver ever more intensely. But both paths have one destination: *absolute death.*

The consequence of this falling away of the individual from the totality was the latter's disintegration. The friction between the parties became ever greater until the decay became so widespread that the law of melding through conquest was able to manifest itself once more. The Greek people, which had reached its twilight years, was defeated by the powerful, hardy Macedonians. In the life of humanity, the same laws are ever at work, but the sphere of civilisation grows ever wider in the process.

16.

We now want to consider briefly the motives which the Greek genius created for all of humanity.

The natural religion of the Hellenes, a cheerful polytheism, was not speculatively deepened, but artistically transfigured. To be sure, the ancient Pelasgians, prior to their mixing with the Greeks, had under Egyptian influence taken a run at developing the religion further (Eleusinian mysteries), for which there was a favourable soil in the cloistered caste of priests; but the movement faltered when the old caste-order collapsed and the priestly office was transferred to the kings. The sole speculative thought which stood out and became dogmatic was the *concept of fate*. The gods were not melded into one godhead which determined mortal lots, rather iron fate was set as a fact *above gods and men*. A splendid unity had been gained, which of course remained intrinsically uncognisable, but to which all the happenings of human life could be effortlessly attributed. In this regard, one must hold the Greeks in the greatest admiration for their abstemiousness. They had very correctly recognised that they stood before something *purely abstract* and their artistic mind, which gave everything a shape, humbly retreated, affectionately embracing on that account the Olympians, who had now come so close to them. (The Erinyes are only personified pangs of conscience, the Fates only a visualisation of the course of human life.) But precisely this shyness before that mysterious power clouded the Greeks' judgment of that power. Fate was not imagined to be a somehow resultant *motion* of the world, but a *rigid* doom presiding over it, a doom which was simply unfathomable.

Now since on one hand natural religion, firstly, was incapable of development in this manner and, secondly, was sacrosanct because it constituted one of the foundations of the State, while on the other hand the advancing intelligence of man engendered a need to fathom his relation to the whole of nature, there arose alongside religion *philosophy*.

It cannot be our task to contemplate the many systems of Greek philosophy. We must be satisfied to focus on a few of them.

Heraclitus, who I am convinced is the most significant philosopher of antiquity, cast a very clear eye upon nature's coherence. He certainly took care not to strike truth in the face and obliterate the real individuals for the benefit of some dreamt-up unity, and he taught that everything is caught in a flux of becoming, has an unceasing motion. However, because he saw life arising wherever death had appeared, he was misled into apprehending the motion of the whole as *aimless*. Using the links being–non-being and non-being–being, he constructed an endless chain or, more precisely, an unceasing *cycle*. The disappearance of one determinate state, process, or thing always entails and is balanced out by the appearance of another, and the way upward (dissolution of the individuality) straight away becomes the way downward (formation of a new individuality).

That said, Heraclitus did not delude himself about the value of life, and so he taught, in addition, that there can be no greater happiness for man than to surrender himself fervently to this endless becoming, to the generality of things, and that there can be no greater pain than to withdraw into one's particularity, into one's own being-for-oneself, to struggle against the sublation of a determinate existence, "to fatten oneself like livestock and to set our true well-being by our stomachs and pudenda, by that which is most despicable in us."

What he therefore demanded was that the individual position himself within the motion of the whole through complete surrender to the general but nevertheless endless process, i.e., that he translate his natural egoism into refined egoism and act morally.

His doctrine is high and pure, but it suffers under its supposition of an *endless* becoming.

Like Heraclitus, Plato taught of an endless cycle. He conceived of the world as composed of the likenesses of ideas living painlessly and blissfully behind the world, in eternal rest. The human soul originates in this pure world of ideas, but cannot over time return to it. If the soul leaves the body, compounded with which it can only lead a polluted life, then—assuming it did not surrender to sensuality but exercised the virtues of wisdom, bravery, modesty, and justice—it enters a state of restful bliss; otherwise it must wander into other bodies until it has regained its original purity and can therefore partake of the aforementioned state. However, the psyche cannot *remain* in this state; after a particular duration, after a thousand years (*Republic*, 614a–621d) it must again elect an earthly lot. The cycle then begins once more.

In the mere assumption of a divine, pure soul which is chained to a reprehensible, sensory faculty of desire lay the condemnation of human life.

If one disregards the cyclical character of their philosophies, then Heraclitus and Plato by means of their teachings cast motives into the world which in some hearts had to awaken yearnings for a purer state and a repugnance at a life of injustice and unrestraint. They thus ennobled the soul and at the same time stimulated the thirst for knowledge, a thirst which is a noble and good thing, since it draws man away from his vulgar doings in this contemptible world.

I mention Aristotle only because he was the first to address himself to the individual in nature and thereby laid the foundation for the natural sciences, without which philosophy would never have moved beyond mere opining and been able to develop into pure knowledge.

I have also to mention Herodotus, the father of history; for history is as necessary for philosophy as the natural sciences. The latter enlarge man's cognition of the world's dynamic coherence, they can however only point uncertainly to an end of becoming at which everything does arrive. In contrast, that overview of the elapsed life of humanity which history provides leads to the most important conclusions; for history confirms what always remains a subjective experience and may for that reason always be doubted—namely, that truth which is evident from the individual's clearly recognised fate: that everything has one particular goal—and it does this by means of *humanity's* fate in such a way that none may doubt it. This is a great gain.

17.

If in the domain of science it therefore fell to the Greek genius merely to give birth to philosophy (as distinct from religion), to the natural sciences and to history, which in their infancy had to be passed on to the coming generations to be nurtured; then in the domain of art, in contrast, the Greek genius attained the greatest heights.

Just as the nature of the country made it possible for the Greek's individuality to be cultivated into a free personality, so too was it the nature of the country which developed the sense of beauty which is indispensible for art and allowed it to ripen quickly to completion. It trained the eye: the splendour of the sea, the brightness of the heavens, the phenomena of the clear air, the form of the coasts and islands, the lines of the mountains, the rich plant world, the luminous beauty of the human forms, the grace of their movements; it trained the ear: the euphony of language. The basis of what is beautiful in things was dispersed extravagantly over the land. No matter the direction in which the eye might look, it had everywhere to objectify harmonic motions. What charm lay in the movement of the individuals during wrestling and fighting, and in the movement of the masses during festive processions! What a great difference was exhibited by the life of this people in contrast to that of the Orientals. In the latter: strict solemnity and anxious deliberateness, indeed, if you will, stiffness created by lacing up, rigid ceremony, profound earnestness; in the former: moderate unrestraint, welling lust for life at the hands of the Charites, simple dignity, alternating with charming gaiety.

When, then, in the souls of the immortal visual artists and poets the creative drive was awakened; when the Homeric ballads inspired bold deeds and the dramas of Sophocles revealed to a mind become objective the power of fate and man's innermost being; when soft Ionian music accompanied the spirited hymns of Pindar; when the marble temples gleamed from afar and the gods themselves descended in transfigured human bodies to dwell amongst the rapturous people—on these occasions, that which lived in each person was merely being put on display, that which suffused all men had merely been condensed into a few indviduals. As if *overnight*, the buds had burst open and the blossoms of the formally beautiful had unfolded in immortal splendour and majesty.

Henceforth the Greeks, and through them all of humanity, had alongside the conceptual law also a figurative one. Whereas the former law, with chains and sword, bears down on the individual and throws to the ground and suppresses the individuality which defies such compulsion, the latter law approaches with friendly countenance, strokes the wild animal within us and, making use of our inexpressible comfort, binds us with unbreakable floral garlands. It casts *aesthetic moderation* over us and thus allows us to feel disgust at excesses and acts of brutality to which, formerly, we were at least indifferent if we were not outright delighted by them.

In this way, art weakens the will directly; indirectly, however, as I showed in the Aesthetics, by awakening in man, after the brief intoxication of pure joy, the yearning for blissful rest, and by referring him to science for the *enduring* satisfaction of that yearning. Art nudges man into the moral domain. Once there, he binds himself through cognition, without the compulsion of the law.

Furthermore, through dramatic poetry, art allows man to gaze into himself and into inexorable fate, enlightening him about the unblissful essence which is at work and struggling in all that exists.

18.

When Alexander the Great had subjugated Greece, he appeared in the Orient as a victorious conquerer and bore Hellenic culture into the empires with despotic constitutions: into Egypt, Persia, and India. A great fusion of Orientalism and Hellenism took place; the rigid formulary, the oppressive ceremony was breached, and a pure, fresh draft of air streamed into the isolated, gloomy lands. On the other hand, oriental wisdom poured into the Occident more profusely than before and fertilised minds.

Alongside this process of mental fertilisation went the process of physical mixing. Both were in keeping with the particular intentions of the youthful hero. He himself married a daughter of the Persian king and in Susa had ten thousand Macedonian men join in matrimony with Persian women.

Even though the great world empire he had established disintegrated again after his death, in individual parts Hellenic education, as the most powerful and most noble of all, yet remained dominant and gradually changed people. The great mass of the people had gained decisively. The Greek was a mild master, and human sympathy became a strict social convention to which even the oriental master had to genuflect. The pressure of the iron hand relented, and the brutish, savage individuality which had been worn down by the law was able to become a striving personality; it had at least gained the greater mobility necessary thereto, the possibility of raising itself out of the mass.

19.

In a manner similar to what occurred in Greece, in Italy, too, beneficent nature prevented the religion of the immigrated peoples of Aryan descent from becoming a power which took hold of and paralysed everything. As in Greece, so in Italy those who were free were able to acquire personality and thereby found States of great vital power and with a civilising vocation.

The struggle of the lower people for rights consistent with their obligations, a struggle which takes place according to the law of melding through inner upheaval, was more tenacious with the Romans than with the Greeks, because the former had a harder and more rugged character than the latter. Piece by piece, the plebeians had to wrest for themselves a share in the government of the State and nearly five centuries passed before all political offices were opened to them. When the constitutional disputes had ended—disputes which had on both sides the most beneficial consequences, since the intelligence was thereby sharpened—the golden age of the Roman State began, the age of genuine civic virtue.

The individual weal now coincided with the common weal, and this harmony must have given the citizen great inner peace and extraordinary fortitude. Obedience to the laws was elevated into the most heartfelt patriotism; every man had only the one ambition: to strengthen the power of the community and to maintain the State at its height. In this way, according to the law of the rivalry of peoples, Rome had to start down the path of conquest, which it was likewise of necessity unable to abandon before it had dominated the world; for every new addition to the empire brought the State into contact with new elements, the power of which, owing to the drive for self-preservation, it was unable to tolerate alongside its own. And thus arose gradually the great Roman Empire, which united within itself almost all of the civilised States of antiquity. In this immense State the most varied peoples with the most varied mores and religious views and in the most varied states of civilisation moved amongst each other. Now the laws of mental fertilisation and of melding came once more to the fore and in part engendered new characters, in part caused the old ones to be polished and reshaped, all under the influence of the general culture which was gradually taking shape.

This and the ever accruing wealth then effected the greatest process of decay recorded in history. The conventions of the ancient republicans—cultivation, simplicity, modesty, and resilience—increasingly disappeared, and idleness, hedonism, and lack of restraint took their place. Henceforth the individual was no longer subordinated to the whole:

> The elements once fused in mighty life
> No longer will reciprocally join
> With force of love in unity renew'd
> Continually. Scattering, forth they fly,
> And each returns unto itself in coldness.
>
> **Goethe** (*The Natural Daughter*, Act V, Scene VIII)

Each man thought only of himself and his merest advantage and was not satisfied with his share in the sum of goods which, as in a beehive, is produced by the individual's surrender to the totality. In consequence of its growth, the intelligence had further disrupted the sure motion of man, for the more the entire motion divides itself, that is, the greater sensibility and irritability become, the more vacillating becomes the will. The dimwit has the surest motion.

There was nothing holy anymore: neither the will of the godhead, which was ridiculed, nor the fatherland, whose protection was left to mercenaries, remained holy. Every man believed he was allowed, in respect of his own person, to abrogate the venerable covenants. There was but one goal yet able to bring a few Romans to inner composure and set their hearts aglow: *domination*. The majority took hold of one thing, then the other, wanted now this, now that, and snatched at everything. It had lost all earnestnesss and had arrived at the precipice leading to annihilation. Friction reached its zenith and with its iron hands wore down the men who ran riot in the most crazed passion. The bloodiest civil wars broke out; these were succeeded by the total fatigue of the people, which led to the establishment of the despotic empire.

20.

Whoever immerses himself in the study of the process of decay and extinction of the Asiatic military despotisms, of Greece, and of Rome, and holds merely the basic motion in view, will recognise and never again lose sight of the fact that the progress of humanity is not the phenomenal appearance of a so-called *moral* world-order, but is the pure motion out of life into absolute death, which, everywhere and everywhen, by a route entirely natural, has arisen from effective causes alone. In the Physics we were unable to arrive at any other result than that ever more organised beings arise from the struggle for existence, that organised life ever renews itself, and an end to the motion was not to be discovered. We might say that in the Physics we found ourselves in the vale. In the Politics, however, we find ourselves on an unobstructed summit and do descry an end to that motion. To be sure, in the period of the Roman Republic's downfall we do not yet see this end clearly. The mists of humanity have not yet cleared entirely and only here and there does the golden sign of *everyone's* redemption gleam through the veil which obscures it; for not all of humanity was contained in the form of the Babylonian, Assyrian and Persian State, nor in that of the Greek and Roman State. Indeed, not even all the peoples of these empires have died off. It was, so to speak, only the tips of the great tree's branches which withered. But in the course of events we discern clearly the important truth: *that civilisation kills*. Every people which enters civilisation, i.e., transitions into a *faster* motion, falls and is dashed to pieces far below. Not one can preserve its virile strength, each must grow decrepit with age, degenerate, and live out its life.

It is quite irrelevant *how* the individuals who constitute a people and are doomed to absolute death sink into annihilation; be it according to the law of decay: gone to rack and ruin, wallowing in the mud and excrement of refined lust; or according to the law of individualism: discarding in disgust all delectable fruits because they no longer give any satisfaction, dissipating themselves in excess and boredom, wavering to and fro because they have lost their firm will and clear goals:

> Though not choked, in Life not sharing,
> Not resigned, and not despairing;
>
> **Goethe** (*Faust II*, Act V, Scene VI)

or through morality: sighing their lives out in the aether of bliss. Civilisation takes hold of them and *kills* them. As bleached bones mark the ways through the desert, so the monuments of disintegrated cultures, proclaiming the deaths of millions, mark the path of civilisation.

But all those who have been dashed to pieces have found *redemption* and they have all of them earned it. For what reasonable man would dare say: Only they shall partake of redemption who have acquired it through charity or chastity? All whom fate thrusts into the night of utter annihilation have dearly purchased liberation from themselves through *suffering* alone. To the last heller they have paid the stipulated ransom by the mere fact of having lived—for life is torment. Through thousands of centuries they, as hungry will to life, had to persevere without rest, now in this, now in that shape, always feeling the whip at their backs, shoved, kicked, flayed; for they lacked the liberating principle: thinking reason. Not until this precious good had at long last come into their possession did friction and want grow in earnest with their growing intelligence. And the will's blazing flame became ever smaller until it had shrunk into a flickering will-o'-the-wisp that went out in the lightest breath of wind. Their hearts became peaceful, they had been redeemed. On their long path most of them had found pure, genuine happiness only for a brief time, namely, when they surrendered themselves entirely to the State and their patriotism had bound everything cruel within them and cast it down to the bottom of their souls. The rest of their lives was all blind urge and, in the mind's consciousness, compulsion, tribulation, and heartache.

21.

Into this process of dissolution and extinction, which took place in the historical form of empire, there fell, like oil into the fire, *joyful tidings from the kingdom of God*.

What did Christ teach?

The ancient Greeks and Romans knew no higher virtue than justice. Furthermore, their ambitions were incorporated into the State. They clung to life in *this* world. When they thought of the immortality of their souls and the kingdom of shadows, their eyes glazed over. What was the most beautiful life in the underworld against the bustle of life under the sun?

Christ, in contrast, taught love of one's neighbour and of one's enemy and demanded the unconditional turning away of man from life: *hatred* of one's own life. He thus demanded the dissolution of man's innermost essence, which is insatiable will to life, he set nothing more in man free; he bound and tied off natural egoism entirely, or in other words: He demanded *slow suicide*.

However, since man, precisely because he is hungry will to life, esteems life the highest good, Christ had to give the drive for earthly life a countermotive which had the power to draw man away from the world, and this powerful countermotive was the *kingdom of God*, eternal life full of rest and bliss. The effectiveness of this countermotive was increased through the threat of hell; yet hell faded far into the background, its only purpose was to terrify the most brutish men, to harrow the heart so that the hope of a pure life of light from eternity to eternity could take root.

Nothing more absurd could be conceived than the claim that Christ did not demand the individual's *complete detachment* from the world. The gospels leave no room whatsoever to doubt his demand. With reference to the *virtues* he preached, I want now to give the indirect proof of this demand:

Ye have heard that it hath been said, Thou shalt love thy neighbour, and hate thine enemy. But I say unto you, Love your enemies, bless them that curse you, do good to them that hate you, and pray for them which despitefully use you, and persecute you. (Matt 5:43-44)

Can that man in whom the will to life is still powerful love his enemy? Then:

All *men* cannot receive this saying, save *they* to whom it is given. For there are some eunuchs, which were so born from *their* mother's womb: and there are some eunuchs, which were made eunuchs of men: and there be eunuchs, which have made themselves eunuchs for the kingdom of heaven's sake. He that is able to receive *it*, let him receive *it*. (Matt 19:11-12)

Can that man who remains chained to the world by even just a single, fine thread exercise the virtue of virginity?

The direct proof is evident in the following passages:

So likewise, whosoever he be of you that forsaketh not all that he hath, he cannot be my disciple. (Luke 14:33)

If thou wilt be perfect, go *and* sell that thou hast, and give to the poor, and thou shalt have treasure in heaven: and come *and* follow me. (Matt 19:21)

It is easier for a camel to go through the eye of a needle, than for a rich man to enter into the kingdom of God. (Matt 19:24)

In these passages is demanded above all the detachment of man from all *external* possessions which chain him so firmly to the world. The difficulty of the demand was expressed most naïvely and eloquently by the disciples of Christ, when they asked their master, in respect of the latter pronouncement:

Who then can be saved?

But Christ demands *much, much more*:

And another also said, Lord, I will follow thee; but let me first go bid them farewell, which are at home at my house. And Jesus said unto him, No man, having put his hand to the plough, and looking back, is fit for the kingdom of God. (Luke 9:61-62)

If any *man* come to me, and hate not his father, and mother, and wife, and children, and brethren, and sisters, yea, and his own life also, he cannot be my disciple. (Luke 14:26)

He that loveth his life shall lose it; and he that hateth his life in this world shall keep it unto life eternal. (John 12:25)

Here, therefore, Christ demands in addition: firstly, the cutting of all sweet ties of the heart; then, from the man who now stands there entirely alone and completely free, *hatred* of himself, of his own life.

Whoever wants to be a *genuine* Christian must not and cannot make any compromise with life. Either – Or: TERTIUM NON DATUR.

The reward for complete resignation was the kingdom of heaven, i.e., *peace of heart*:

Take my yoke upon you, and learn of me; for I am meek and lowly in heart: and ye shall find rest unto your souls. (Matt 11:29)

The kingdom of heaven is peace of soul and not at all anything lying beyond the world, such as a city of peace, a new Jerusalem:

> For, behold, the kingdom of God is within you. (Luke 17:21)

The genuine follower of Christ enters paradise through death, i.e., enters absolute nothingness—he is freed from himself, is completely redeemed.

Here it is also evident that hell is nothing other than *torment of heart, pain of existence*. In death, the child of this world only appears to depart hell, for it had already delivered itself into hell's power entirely:

These things I have spoken unto you, that in me ye might have peace. In the world ye shall have tribulation. (John 16:33)

The relationship of the individual to nature, of man to God, cannot be more *profoundly* or more *truly* conceived than it is in Christianity. It is merely veiled, and to remove this veil is the task of philosophy.

As we have seen, the gods came about merely through the personification of discrete activities of nature's undeniable power. The unity, God, arose from the melding of these gods. Always, however, fate, the unitary motion resulting from the motion of all individuals of the world, was either partly or entirely apprehended and correspondingly *personified*. Giving shape in this way to an *abstract* relation was in line with a mind in which imagination outweighed judgment.

And *complete* power was given always to the godhead; the individual understood himself to be utterly dependent and therefore held himself to be *nothing*.

In the pantheism of the Indians, this relation of the individual to the unity manifests itself quite nakedly. But even in the monotheism of the Jews it is unmistakable. Fate is an essentially merciless, terrible power, and the Jews were completely right to imagine God as a wrathful, fervent spirit which they *feared*.

Now, Christ *altered* this relation with a *firm* hand.

Taking his lead from the fall of man, he taught *original sin*. Man is born a sinner:

For from within, out of the heart of men, proceed evil thoughts, adulteries, fornications, murders, thefts, covetousness, wickedness, deceit, lasciviousness, an evil eye, blasphemy, pride, foolishness. (Mark 7:21-22)

Accordingly, his individual fate takes shape first and foremost from within himself, and all unhappiness that affects him, all want and pain, is due to the sin of Adam, in which *all* men have sinned.

In this way, Christ took from God all cruelty and mercilessness and made him into a *God of love* and mercy, into a faithful *father* of men who could be approached confidently, *without fear.*

And this pure God now guides men so that they will *all* be redeemed:

For God sent not his Son into the world to condemn the world; but that the world through him might be saved. (John 3:17)

And I, if I be lifted up from the earth, will draw all *men* unto me. (John 12:32)

This redemption of *all* men will take place over the entire course of the world, to which we shall shortly turn our attention, and it will do so gradually as God, bit by bit, mercifully awakens the hearts of *all* individuals. This direct intervention of God in man's soul, which has become obdurate through original sin, is called providence:

Are not two sparrows sold for a farthing? and one of them shall not fall on the ground without your Father. But the very hairs of your head are all numbered. (Matt 10:29-30)

The *effect of grace* is a snippet of providence, it is, as it were, the blossom:

No man can come to me, except the Father which hath sent me draw him . . . (John 6:44)

Let us pause here for a moment. What had happened? Had fate as such, the world's motion, become suddenly mild and peaceful? Did no more evil henceforth appear in the world: no plagues, no sicknesses, no earthquakes, no floods, no wars? Had all men become peaceable? Had struggle in society ceased? No! All that had remained. The course of the world retained its terrible character. *But the individual's attitude to God had been totally changed.* The course of the world was no longer the emanation of a unitary power; it now arose from *factors*, and these factors from which it was created had been strictly separated. On one side stood the sinful creature which alone bears the guilt for its unhappiness, which acts from its own will; and on the other side stood the merciful Father-God, who governed everything for the best.

Henceforth, individual fate was the product of original sin and of providence (effect of grace): the individual acted *half* autonomously, and was *half* controlled by God. A great and beautiful truth.

Christianity therefore occupies the *correct* middle-ground between Brahmanism and Buddhism, and all three are based on the *correct* judgment about life's value.

But not only did Christ teach the individual's motion out of earthly life into paradise, but also a unitary motion of the universe out of being into non-being:

And this gospel of the kingdom shall be preached in all the world for a witness unto all nations; and then shall the end come. (Matt 24:14)

Heaven and earth shall pass away: but my words shall not pass away. But of that day and *that* hour knoweth no man, no, not the angels which are in heaven, neither the Son, but the Father. (Mark 13:31-32)

Here, too, Christianity unites the two one-sided truths of pantheism and Buddhism; it joins the real motion of the individual (individual fate), which Buddha alone recognised, with the real motion of the entire world (universal fate), which pantheism alone admitted.

Thus, Christ had looked most profoundly into the dynamic coherence of the universe, and this places him high above the wise pantheists of India and above Buddha.

There can be no doubt that Christ was thoroughly acquainted, on one hand, with Brahmanism and Buddhism and, on the other hand, with humanity's history in ages past. Yet, this significant knowledge is insufficient to explain the emergence of that most splendid and best of all religions. Assistance must be sought through reference to the saviour's prodigious dæmon which, in the form of intuitions, supported his mind. For the determination of men's individual fates, all necessary points of reference were present in the pure and magnificent personality of Christ, not however for the determination of the universe's fate, whose course he nevertheless ascertains without faltering, even if he also confesses openly his ignorance in regard to the end times:

But of that day and *that* hour knoweth no man, . . . neither the Son, but the Father. (Mark 13:32)

With what apodictic certainty, in contrast, he speaks of that factor of fate which, independently of man, helps to shape individual fate!

I speak that which I have seen with my Father. (John 8:38)

And then the sublime passage:

But I know him: and if I should say, I know him not, I shall be a liar like unto you: but I know him, and keep his saying. (John 8:55)

Compare this with the judgment of the pantheistic poet about the uncognisable, hidden unity *in* the world:

> Who dare express Him?
> And who profess Him,
> Saying: I believe in Him!
> Who, feeling, seeing,
> Deny His being,
> Saying: I believe Him not!
> The All-enfolding,
> The All-upholding,
> Folds and upholds he not
> Thee, me, Himself?
>
> **Goethe** (*Faust I*, Scene XVI)

Whoever judges the teachings of Christ without prejudice will find only *immanent* material: peace of heart and torment of heart; individual will and dynamic coherence of the world; individual motion and universal motion.

Kingdom of heaven and hell; soul, Satan, and God; original sin, providence, and working of grace; Father, Son, and Holy Ghost. All this is but the dogmatic shroud for truths which can be known. But in Christ's day these truths were *not* able to be known, and for that reason they had to be objects of *faith* and appear in such shrouds as were *effective*. John's question:

> Who is he that overcometh the world, but he that believeth that Jesus is the Son of God? (1 John 5:5)

was therefore fully justified.

22.

The new doctrine had a powerful effect. The wondrous, moving words of the saviour:

> I am come to send fire on the earth; and what will I, if it be already kindled? But I have a baptism to be baptized with; and how am I straitened till it be accomplished! Suppose ye that I am come to give peace on earth? I tell you, Nay; but rather division. (Luke 12:49-50)

were fulfilled. "Every great idea, as soon as it appears, has a tyrannical effect." Their truth has therefore extraordinary power because it passes straight away into *conscience*. Man henceforth *knows* a greater good; it clings to his heart and, no matter how he shakes himself, it no longer lets him go. And so too the teachings of Christ, once they had been cast into the world as a new motive, were no longer to be annihilated. They took hold first of the lowdown, the despised, the rejected. "*All* men are brothers, are children of a loving father in the heavens and *every* man is called to partake of God's majesty." For the first time in the Occident, the equality of all men was being taught; for the first time it was being solemly declared that a person's public esteem had no currency before God; and for the first time religion was leaning down to *each* individual, taking him affectionately into its arms, and consoling him. It redirected his gaze from his fast-expiring life in this world to an eternal life, and it clearly and firmly set the price at which that eternal life was to be attained: "Love thy neighbour as thyself; if, however, you wish to be quite sure of obtaining the immortal crown of life, *then never touch a woman*." The yearning for the kingdom of heaven in the hearts of those languishing in chains must have become all the greater when there was no prospect whatsoever that through inner upheavals the personal, civic, and political freeedom of *all* would ever become a truth. But then why should it become a truth at all? How soon this brief life is over and then freedom is secured for eternity!

The new doctrine then took hold of women in particular. The character of woman, due to millennia of constant oppression, also in part due to being made tender in civilisation, is much milder than the character of man. Woman is especially merciful. The religion of life must then have exerted the greatest authority over the, as it were, predisposed souls of the women who came within its province. They became Christianity's principal propagators. Their example, their life-change was infectious. And how the new generation must have shown the nobility of their souls. I remind the reader merely of Macrina and Emmelia, the grandmother and mother of Basilius; of Nonna, the mother of Gregory of Nazianzus; of Anthusa, the mother of Chrysostomos; of Monica, the mother of Augustine; and of the Hellenist Libanius's exclamation: What women the Christians have!

Finally the doctrine took hold of the educated, who felt a dreadful emptiness within themselves and must have been unspeakably unhappy. In order not to sink completely into the mud and because the mind, like the body, demands nourishment, they threw themselves into the arms of the crassest supersition, gave their fancy free rein, and snatched at phantoms in great fear and trepidation. Christianity gave them a *firm goal* and therewith a *definite direction*. In place of Heraclitus' *infinite* development and Plato's *infinite* wanderings—in whose views man felt like a wanderer in the desert afflicted with a burning thirst—it put a *conclusion*: delightful rest in the kingdom of God. The ignorant, the brutish man lets himself be driven ever onwards, like a wilted leaf by the autumn wind, and is seldom conscious of his pain. But in the man who has escaped want and has recognised and felt painfully the restlessness which is essentially connected with life, the yearning for rest, for removal from the shallow, disgusting goings-on of the world is awakened and grows ever more intense. But Greek philosophy was unable to slake that thirst. It always flung the languishing man who sought consolation in it back into the process of the whole, which it lacked the means to set an end to. Christianity, in contrast, gave the weary wanderer a point of rest full of bliss. Who under those circumstances would not have put up with the inconceivable dogmas?

For *all* those of whom it took hold, however, Christianity proved itself a great force that can really make man happy. In the best ages of Greece and Rome there was only *one* moral ignition of the will which was possible on the basis of cognition, namely, patriotism. Whoever had recognised and learned to treasure the goods which the State offered him had to catch fire, and surrendering himself to the State gave him great satisfaction. Than the welfare of the State there was no other higher motive which the will could have taken hold of. Now, however, faith in blissful, eternal life was internalised by men, set them aglow and purified them, let them accomplish works of pure charity, and made them blissful already in this life.

23.

The extinction process of the Romans was then accelerated by *Neoplatonism*, which is to be traced back to Brahmanic wisdom. It taught, in an entirely Indian vein, of a primordial unity whose emanation is the world, yet polluted by matter. For the soul of man to be able to free itself of its sensory additives, however, the exercise of the four Platonic virtues is insufficient; rather, sensuality must be killed by asceticism. A soul thus purified must now no longer, as with Plato, return into the world, but sinks into the pure part of the godhead and is lost in unconscious potentiality. Neoplatonism, which bears a certain resemblance to the Christian doctrine, is the consummation of the philosophy of the ancients and, as against the systems of Plato and Heraclitus, an immense step forward. The law of intellectual fertilisation has never come more significantly and consequentially to the fore than in those first centuries after Christ.

Neoplatonism took control of those educated persons who placed philosophy above religion and accelerated their extinction. Later it had an effect on the Church Fathers and thereby on the dogmatic development of Christ's doctrine. The truth is extraordinarily simple. It can be summarised in a few words: "Remain chaste and you will have the greatest happiness on earth and find redemption after death." But how difficult it is for this truth to be victorious! How often it has had to change form! In what guises it had to appear in order to gain a foothold in the world at all!

24.

Neoplatonism and Christianity turned the gaze of their professors from the world, which is why I said above that they not only did not impede the decline of the Roman Empire, but brought it about. "My kingdom is not of this world," Christ said. The Christians of the first centuries took this pronouncement to heart. They let themselves be slaughtered by the thousands rather than surrender to the State. Each man was concerned only for the salvation of his soul and that of his brothers in faith. Let earthly things take whatever form they wished—what could the Christian lose? At most his life, and death was precisely his gain; for the end of the brief earthly life was the beginning of the eternal blissful life. This view had so permeated everyone's thinking that a martyr's deathday was generally celebrated as his birthday.

Even when Christianity had been elevated to the religion of the State, the Christians did not change their attitude. The bishops merely used their influence in order to abolish the bloody combat of the gladiators, to have almshouses and hospitals established everywhere, and in order to convert the barbarians living at the borders of the Empire more easily.

Thus the destiny of the Roman Empire was at last realised, and upon the most splendid decay followed the most splendid melding of which history tells.

Already in the second century before Christ, parts of the powerful peoples of Germanic descent living in the north of the Roman Empire, the Cimbri and the Teutons, had sought to smash the Empire to pieces. But the time had not yet come when fresh wild blood, in which the healthy fragrant air of the steppe lived, was to regenerate the infirm Romans. The aforementioned hordes were defeated by Marius and in large part destroyed. But five hundred years later the tide was no longer able to be stemmed. Vandals, Visigoths, Ostrogoths, Lombards, Burgundians, Suebi, Alans, Franks, Saxons and the rest broke in from all sides upon the State, which had previously been separated into an Eastern and Western Roman Empire. The atrocities of the Migration Period defy all description. Wherever the savage peoples arrived, they destroyed the works of art for which they had no understanding, let the cities go up in flames, murdered the greater part of the native peoples, and desolated the land. Fate revealed its objective and confirmed the Christian teaching, which ever louder and more forcefully demanded a turning away from the horrific struggle for existence and the individual's detachment from the world.

Gradually, however, the barbarian hordes established themselves and mixed with the remaining civilised peoples of the Western Roman Empire. Everywhere there emerged new idiosyncratic characters and powerful mixed peoples, which formed larger autonomous States. Only those Germans who had in part remained in Germany and in part been repelled thither maintained themselves unmixed in their full original power. Bit by bit, Christianity became the reigning religion in every new State and under its influence brutal ways died out, and hearts softened and were bridled.

Into the abandoned abodes of the Germans came the Slavs, who were drawn into the sphere of civilisation sometimes through peaceful contact with the neighbouring Germans and mixed peoples, sometimes through subjugation by those same peoples.

25.

Shortly after that mixing of peoples which came about through a violent impetus from the north had somewhat subsided and produced new empires, from the south, too, half savage peoples pressed their way into the sphere of civilisation. The Arab Mohammed had on trade journeys become acquainted with Christianity and the Jewish religion, and out of these he formed for himself a worldview that ignited him. *Fate* has a prominent place in that worldview and is correctly identified—but only when seen from the *periphery*, where it reveals itself as an inexorable, unstoppable motion of the world occuring of necessity. It floats *above* the world, as with the Greeks, and no individual in the world helps, from within its own nature, to shape it, every essence having, upon Allah's impetus, to carry out what is supposed to take place; whereas the correct view of fate is that which sees it as a motion of the world resulting from the motions of *all* individuals, of the motes of solar dust as well as of man; that therefore sees it as arising from the world alone, through the intertwining of *all* the necessary actions of *all* individuals.

The prophet was urged to inform his tribesmen of the salvation he had found and to lead them at the same time into the higher forms of life of civilisation, which he had learned to treasure. He founded a new religion, Mohammedanism, with its alluring paradise, inspired the imaginative nomads of Arabia, and gave them motives which drove them abroad to the peoples of Asia Minor, Egypt, Persia, and Northern India, which were all going extinct. Like the Germanic peoples, they subjugated in fervent fanaticism all the countries into which they penetrated until they came up against the Roman-Germanic kingdoms of Spain and France and found in them an obstacle. They nevertheless established themselves in southern Spain. Here, and everywhere else, they partly mixed with the old inhabitants, and partly let themselves be fertilised by the high culture they had there found. Thus a quite idiosyncratic, so-called Moorish culture gradually arose, which exerted a great influence on the peoples of the Occident. The Moors cultivated the natural sciences, particularly mathematics, astronomy, philosophy, and medicine, produced outstanding works of poetry, and developed a graceful architecture which revealed in the most noble way and in a new direction the formally beautiful of space.

26.

The law of intellectual fertilisation shows itself very distinctly in the simple Christian doctrine. This doctrine has its roots in the Jewish religion, which is a natural religion purified under Egyptian and Persian influences, and in the Indian religions (probably through Egyptian transmission).

With the continued development of the Christian doctrine there came to accompany the abovementioned law the *law of intellectual friction*. For the first time in the Occident, a religion was left to itself, it served not as a firm foundation for the State, but floated above the State quite freely and addressed itself to the individuals without earthly help, taking hold of this individual in one moment, of that individual in the next. Now, if the professors of this doctrine had held with childish sense to the simple truth of salvation, which can in no way be misunderstood, then it would have been impossible for sects to arise at all. But the brooding mind immersed itself with passion in the study of the divine mysteries, the dual nature of Christ, the relation of the Holy Ghost to God and Christ, the essence of sin and mercy, and so on, and obviously opinions on such matters had to diverge significantly from each other, because the holy scriptures are ambiguous in that regard. Compounding this was the ambition of the learned (of the superficial "know-it-alls" as the sombre Heraclitus calls them with contempt) to fuse all the good elements of philosophical knowledge of that age with God's revelation through Christ. One-sided doctrines thus took shape; a unitary Christianity existed no longer and the various doctrinal opinions stood in stark opposition to each other.

The danger for Christianity was great. It awakened men, who mobilised everything in order to avert it. Skilfully they advocated for the unitary faith, and finally—when the doctrine became the religion of the State and it was therefore necessary to make the religion into a firm, unassailable basis for the body politic—their efforts succeeded, during religious councils, in trapping the fine ethical fragrance of Christianity in the sturdy vessels of dogma. The heretics were persecuted, and even if the sects were not able to be wiped out entirely, they still lost all their influence on the destiny of humanity.

However, later peripheral conflicts between the bishop of Rome and the patriarch of Constantinople, aggravated mainly by the varying interpretations of the trinity, led to a splitting of the Church into a Roman Catholic and a Greek Catholic branch.

So that the struggle with the Greek Church, which was powerfully supported by the Byzantine Emperor, could be successfully executed, the Roman

Church had the Roman Empire resurrected, and invested Charles the Great first of all with imperial majesty. The Emperor was supposed to be God's representative on earth, a highest referee in earthly affairs, and to make this world into the reflected splendour of God's kingdom. "Glory to God in the highest, and on earth peace." (Luke 2:14) However, the Church revered this view of the matter only as long as it felt weak. When, by the victories of devoted princes and the self-sacrificing activity of divinely inspired missionaries, it saw the greater part of European countries subjected to the Christian faith, it made the Pope God's sole representative on earth. The Pope merely transferred his power to the Emperor and only for as long as the Empreror acted in accordance with his instructions. At this juncture arose the long discord between papal and imperial prerogative, between spiritual and temporal power, which even to this day has not been settled.

27.

We have now to consider briefly the conditions of the Middle Ages in political, economic, and intellectual domains.

Occidental Christendom disintegrated into a great number of autonomous States which in principle acknowledged the emperor as the highest authority. In him apparently, but in the pope actually, the unwritten law of nations was embodied, such that wars of extermination against Christians were impossible and according to the law of rivalry of peoples, an animated political life could gain ground.

The form of these States was the feudal State. The king was viewed as the possessor of the entire conquered land. Of it he gave parts to the high nobility, to the high clergy, and to the cities, i.e., he thus enfeoffed them, and received in exchange military service and particular dues. For their part, the enfeoffed in turn gave parts of their fief to their men and to the peasants, who in exchange were obligated to them in service.

From this general feudal union, in time, the highest nobility, the princes of the Church, and the free cities separated off. They used their power to turn their fiefs into freeholds, while intensifying the conditions of dependency below them. Most peasants were reduced to serfs, and they sank into want and misery.

In this way, the king's power was crippled. He was then able to continue promoting the weal of the State only insofar as it agreed with the private interest of the lords.

The feudal State was therefore the breeding ground of the most unrestrained fragmentation. The law of the development of the part, which is here best called the *law of particularism*, manifested itself powerfully within the feudal form. Every man separated himself off with his dependants and developed his personality one-sidedly. There arose a profusion of genuine, defiant characters who were preserved from decay because there was no wealth and the high degree of friction in such circumstances kept their forces constantly in tension and protected them from slackening. Sharp-edged, defiant, iron men who would sooner break into pieces than surrender their self-will! But they were not forgotten by civilisation! Civilisation let those men step to one side and separate themselves off in order to prepare great suffering for themselves and others. Then came the flood which tore them into the stream of becoming, dissolved them, and let them shoot up as new crystals of a softer nature.

28.

If we now enter the economic domain of the Middle Ages, then we have first of all to take a look at *work* in antiquity.

The economic character of the ancient world is that of *slavery*. The ruling classes of priests and nobles, the former in possession of the mysterious science, the latter with sword in hand, had the lower classes work for them and so grew rich. While the common people lived in want because they were only allocated the meagre minimum necessary for the continuation of an arduous life, the ruling classes indulged in excess. The economic focus lay on agriculture, which occupied the majority of slaves. The rest were used for producing necessary objects such as clothing, weapons, equipment, and the like. The surplus of such products was exchanged by the ancient lord, by means of merchants, for the luxury goods of other countries.

The economic relations of the Middle Ages took on a similar shape. Slavery had indeed been abolished by Christianity, but in its place there came serfdom and bondage. The freer peasants had to provide their lord natural services and surrender to him parts of their harvest, of their livestock, etc.

The trade associations, when they were not in the service of the feudal lords, could not escape the reigning spirit of the times and organised themselves according to strictly separated guilds. For every location the number of trade associations and for every trade association the number of masters was fixed; furthermore, it was precisely determined in what way one could become a master, what number of apprentices he was allowed to retain, and how much he was permitted to produce.

29.

In the intellectual domain, the Church reigned. Its position in relation to the vital mixed peoples and pure Germans was a different one from that of the Christian doctrine to the Roman people. This doctrine had to lead downhill fragments of a nation which was going extinct; that Church had to usher all individuals uphill and to dampen and make milder their vitality.

The effect had by the Church was at first extraordinarily beneficial. In the main, it never grew unfaithful to the doctrine of its sublime founder, but, like him, it addressed itself immediately to the individual, whose significance it did not lose sight of. To all men it preached the truth of salvation, to all men the way to it was always open, to all men it gave whatever it had, and all men it accompanied from cradle to grave. Into brutish men it introduced the dichotomy between natural egoism and God's clear commandments, gave them a stricter conscience and, along with that stricter conscience, anxiety of conscience, fear, and terrors—the best means of taming wild blood. Over the worn-out soil, however, it scattered by the handful the truth that life is worthless, and the seeds of hope, of love, and of faith in eternal bliss.

It turned man's gaze towards an imperishable good and pointed to the correct path on which the creature can make peace with its creator. *Borne by the genuine Christian spirit*, it forbade its priests marriage and, in a Christian spirit equally genuine, it facilitated the founding of cloisters, which were a necessity and kept themselves long in purity. The essence which expressed itself in the cloisters was, is, and will ever exist. The great congregation, the invisible order of ascetics extends itself day by day.

Since the Church had nothing yet to fear from science, it acquired for itself in those times the credit of having rescued as much of ancient literature as it could. It hid those treasures in the cloisters, where they were copied and thereby conserved for the people. To the cloisters it joined schools where science, if only as a small flame, was protected and could wait for better days. The priests had been convinced of the high truth of religion and of its invincible strength. That made them patient. The ambition of the Church Fathers to cultivate Hellenic science was carried on. Later, the Church ossified, and the view that whatever is not written in the Bible is false and dangerous gained the upper hand.

In contrast, the Church fostered art by all its means. There arose the extraordinarily significant, entirely idiosyncratic genre of Christian art which, as an essential element of education, took its place next to religion. The artists inspired by genuine faith depicted the effects of divine mercy on man, and on their works men's souls were ignited. Art led them deeper into religion, brought them closer to the liberating principle embodied in Christ and gave them inner peace through faith.

The cathedrals which were everywhere erected had a similar effect. The high, heaven-aspiring vaults put the soul in a sublime mood, and the soul, freed of all pressure, let itself be carried before the throne of God on the wings of Church music, which was constantly developing. The heart humbled itself and the recognition that, in comparison with the pure life in Christ's kingdom, all earthly joy, all happiness comes to nought struck that heart like a bolt of lightning and ignited it.

The Church also had an effect through the dramatic passion plays which imposed themselves with devastating power upon the mind of the spectator, earnestly and successfully reminding him that he is a stranger on this earth.

The power of the Church revealed itself most magnificently and most distinctly in the Crusades, from which we derive that important law of civilisation, the *law of intellectual contagion*. High-born and low, hundreds upon hundreds of thousands took up the cross and, with certain death in view, ventured abroad to liberate the Redeemer's grave. An electric current passed through all of Christendom and enabled man to defy all difficulties, to bear all tribulations. The Crusades are a very curious phenomenon. Whoever immerses himself in the study of them has the impression of receiving a pledge that some day, in a similar atmosphere, all of humanity shall be redeemed. Men were taken hold of not by a sensory, but rather by an ideal motive and elevated above themselves. The spirit that reigned in the first three centuries of the Church was revived and caused life to be cast off with relish as one casts off a heavy burden.

In no period of history has the boundedness in all domains been greater than in the Middle Ages. All life moved in stiff, oppressive forms. Man went about laced up from head to toe. The mind was bound, the will and labour were bound. The apparently free men, the clergy and the knights, were slaves like all others, for they were bound by mutual constraint and the universal intellectual bondage.

This being-bound in all directions bears a great resemblance to that being-bound which prevailed in the old States of the Orient, States in which natural brutality and savagery also had first to be broken by means of despotism, in which "the animal-man [had first to be made] from nothing into something". In the new realms, the will was being prepared to follow a great intellectual impulse so that humanity would be able to take a new, great step forward.

30.

The invention of gunpowder first breached this fixed organisation of peoples in the Middle Ages—in political, economic, and intellectual domains—and instigated the reformation of the feudal State into the territorial principality, later into the absolute State.

The power of the lords great and small was broken and the nobility forced to enter the standing armies (which since that time had been increasing) and the administration of the princes. However, nothing about the legal standing of the privileged classes was changed. Legally, the nobility and priesthood were the two ruling estates, but the individual had lost his autonomy and gravitated towards the heads of the State, like planets towards the sun. The motion peaked in the absolute State, in which the prince was identified with the State (*l'etat c'est moi*). In the prince, the whole State was condensed, on him alone the weal and woe of his subjects depended, and the nobility, like the priesthood, was but a tool in his hand for the carrying out of his thoughts, plans, epiphanies, and moods (*tel est mon plaisir*). The form of the absolute State was the same as that of the despotic State of antiquity; although a great difference between them lies in the fact that the latter was necessary for the beginnings of culture, the former in contrast was called to draw those parts which had reached the farthest possible limit of particular development back into the stream of becoming. Here the *law of levelling* was manifested.

31.

The fixed forms in the economic domain were exploded by great discoveries and inventions: the invention of the compass, the discovery of maritime routes to East India and America. The means of production of goods were totally reshaped. As the undulations of the sea will erode a cliff-face until the overhang succumbs to its own gravity and falls into the ocean, so the newly arisen global trade powerfully and relentlessly ran up against the guild constitution. Now the needs newly awakened in new lands—such as clothing, equipment, and the like—and the needs of the constantly growing European population had to be satisfied. The demands placed on the guilds became ever greater; but how were these supposed to be met when the number of masters remained fixed and none of them was permitted to produce a greater quantity of objects than was legally stipulated? The constraints had to be loosened. Alongside the persisting workshops of the guild masters, who still worked to fulfill local demand, factories, which were ever more loosely associated with the guilds, took their place, and the historical form called *industry* arose.

Its immediate consequence was that the law of the development of individuality could again and with renewed force govern phenomena. Marriage in the Middle Ages was extraordinarily restricted. A journeyman almost never entered into marriage, and those who were married, inhibited by the difficulty of procuring nourishment, concieved only a few children. But civilisation wants all men as much as possible to spread themselves out in new individuals, so that immediately and mediately the will is weakened—immediately through fragmentation, mediately through greater friction. The beneficial consequences of the struggle for existence inundate those caught in the struggle only when they are pressed together in the narrowest space and well and truly step on each other's toes.

Let us here also draw attention to the effect produced by the potato's introduction into Europe. The population rose rapidly, quadrupling itself in Ireland, for example, thanks to this new source of nourishment. What a multiplication of friction!

Another consequence of industry which made itself felt in the political domain—the most important consequence—was the strenghtening of the third estate of the bourgeoisie. Already in the earliest Middle Ages, trade and commerce had brought about the flourishing of cities and enabled their citizens to make themselves independent of the nobility of the surrounding regions and then also of the nobility in their midst. Now, however, the power of the citizens was growing day by day because they were becoming wealthier day by day, such that the nobility even deigned to enter the armies of the established trading companies and to serve the bourgeoisie in order to have a share in the mobile goods which the diligent and skilful merchant produced as if by magic.

32.

In the intellectual domain, the Church still reigned without constraint. The space which the sciences had to move within was defined by the Church, and they bore distinct traces of that iron compulsion. What a withered blossom Scholasticism was!

But already long before the Reformation, sects had begun to unsettle the dominion of the Church and produced the first cracks in the great, steely historical form. The occasion was provided by the process of decay which had appeared at the highest levels of the priesthood. While the lower clerics were in a situation of dire need, the princes of the Church debauched themselves, and in particular the profligacy, opulence, and immorality of most popes no longer had any limits. They used the Church for personal and nepotistic ends and shamelessly desecrated the teachings of Christ. Peter Waldo, who founded the congregation of Waldensians, was the first to rise up against this degeneracy. Waldensians renounced the pope and elected their chaplains. In the bloody Albigensian Crusade they were indeed almost all annihilated, but the first impetus had been given and had to create new motions. A new, good motive had again been given and it had an igniting effect on individuals. Wycliffe, Hus, and Savonarola entered the scene. The latter two were also rendered harmless by the Church and the traces of their efficacy obliterated. But the fire was no longer to be smothered; ostensibly stamped out, it glimmered on, and finally flared up as a bright blaze when Luther published his theses against Rome in Wittenberg (31 October 1517).

Favoured by the political attitude of the princes of Germany to each other, he hacked the form of the papacy to pieces, liberated a large part of those for whom the stiff walls had made welling life long ago into an agony, and placed next to the shattered form another which afforded their minds greater room to play.

The Reformation effected two great reshapings. First it gave intellectual life a healthy soil in which to grow and detached science from religion; then it turned the soul inward by stoking faith to a new blaze and directing man's gaze once again to a higher, better life than the earthly one.

A spring breeze passed through the civilised world. Shortly beforehand, the Turks had destroyed the Byzantine Empire and many learned Greeks had fled to the Occident, where they awakened the enthusiasm for ancient education. A new fertilisation of minds took place; people immersed themselves in the study of ancient works and grafted the noble Greek rice onto the strong German stem—classical antiquity and the contemplative Middle Ages were wed. Thus was joined to the new religion a new art and a new autonomous science, which at the many newly established universities found a protected, favourable soil in which to grow.

The intellectual movement grew day by day, accelerated by the newly discovered art of printing. Philosophy took an entirely different direction. If, up to that point, one had uselessly tortured oneself in metaphysical ruminations, one now began to investigate how the mind had arrived at all of these wonderful concepts. It was the only correct path. One doubted everything, left the "shoreless ocean" and placed onself on the sure ground of experience and nature. The British in particular were active in this direction and in this connection Bacon, Locke, Berkeley, Hume, and Hobbes must be mentioned.

In the field of pure natural science, the great men: Copernicus, Kepler, Galileo, and Newton produced the well-known great revolutions.

Furthermore, a new style of art arose. The Renaissance style introduced fresh, undulating life into architecture, and everywhere, especially in Italy, the most splendid churches and palaces appeared. Sculpture experienced a magnificent second flourishing under the influence of the antique masterworks which once again saw the light of day, and painting for the first time attained the clear heights of perfection (Leonardo da Vinci, Michelangelo, Raphael, Titian, Correggio).

Like painting, realistic poetry also swung to the highest level (Shakespeare), and music more powerful than any before appeared and was henceforth a truly great power for the soul (Bach, Händel, Haydn, Gluck, Mozart, Beethoven).

Under the influence of the great sum of these new motives, the intellectual life of the bourgeoisie took on an ever freer and more profound shape and the life of the dæmon an ever nobler one. The development of the mind weakens the will directly because the mind can strengthen itself only at the expense of the will (modification of the factors of motion). Indirectly, however, this development weakens the will even more by means of multiplied suffering (elevation of sensibility and irritability: passionateness) and by means of the yearning for rest which is born in the more frequently recurring state of pure contemplation.

Now, too, the developmental course of humanity revealed itself with increasing clarity. Outstanding minds, tracing all motions, saw one ideal end: the State under the rule of law and a more complete international law, and, ablaze with moral enthusiasm, they adjusted themselves to the motion, accelerating it.

33.

In the face of Protestantism, the Catholic Church collected itself and took immense pains to overcome the schism (emergence of the Jesuit order; wars of religion). But it did not succeed, even though the opponents had disintegrated (Reformers, Lutherans, etc.). The only consequence of the bloodiest, most devastating conflicts was that in a few countries, like France, Austria, and Hungary, the new doctrine was stamped out.

The friction in the intellectual domain was great and the motion in the States became ever fresher and livelier. All the fruits of the new period fell into the laps of the bourgeoisie, to which everyone belonged who was prominent through wealth and the attainments of heart and head. And this third estate had as good as no political rights in the State, since the nobility and the clergy closed ranks to secure their privileges. This situation of things was untenable. Firstly, in the Netherlands and England the bourgeoisie wrested for itself greater freedom and a determining influence on the governing of the State. Then the motion took hold of the French citizenry. The most able and brilliant men, like Voltaire, Montesquieu, Rousseau, and Helvetius, attacked the status quo in all domains. The third estate made its cause the cause of all humanity; the seed of Christianity ("All men are brothers") had been powerfully developed, and all life in the State pressed with coercive force towards the one point: complete legal recognition of the third estate.

34.

The time had now come where the law of inner melding was again able to come into effect through the pulling down of all differences between the estates, and the storm, strengthened by the free air which wafted across the sea from the gloriously established American federation, all of a sudden broke. It swept away all the burdens of the feudal State: serfdom, natural servitude, payment in kind, ecclesiastical tithe, guild coercion, constraint of settlement, and so on. On the *unforgettable day* of 4 August 1789 all of these chains were stripped from the people and human rights declared. Later, the estates of the Church and of all those nobles who did not want to comply with the new order of things were taken over and a peasant estate was established. At its side stood the estate of free workers.

35.

The attainments of the French Revolution could not remain confined to France; for civilisation has all of mankind in view, and this fact had revealed itself more purely than ever precisely during that great revolution. The occasional cause of these attainments' propagation was the military campaign of many princes, who feared the consequences of the revolution and sought to smother it. The real propagator of the new institutions was Napoleon. He bore the holy fire at the tip of his sword through a sea of blood into most of the lands of Europe. And once again the peoples of Europe heaved through each other, but this time the genius of humanity floated in a clearer shape above the immense turmoil.

The general agitation, however, aimed above all only at the loosening of the soil and the sowing of the seed. The seed prospered in peacetime, and gradually the chains of the feudal State were removed from the peoples of all civilised States.

36.

While these reconfigurations in political and economic domains spread, a German man, Kant, brought about the greatest revolution in the intellectual domain. His immortal deed, the composition of the *Critique of Pure Reason* (completed on 29 March 1781), was greater and more consequential than Luther's. He referred the inquisitive mind once and for all to the soil of experience; he in fact ended for all insightful men the human struggle with spectral forms in, above, or behind the world, and dashed to pieces the remnants of all natural religions which fear engendered.

It was through Kant that the revolution first became a complete one. In the economic domain had arisen freedom of labour; in the political domain had arisen personal, bourgeois, and political freedom; and in the intellectual domain had arisen independence of all faith and superstition. For insightful men, the last form of a church had also been destroyed and the foundation of the temple of genuine, pure science, into which all of humanity will some day enter, had been laid.

37.

The French Revolution and the Napoleonic Wars, with their sorrow on one hand, their attainments on the other, belong to the historical events wherein the fundamental motion of the human species out of life into absolute death reveals itself, wherein the genius of humanity unveils its visage, so to speak, with the earnest, mysterious eyes, and in consolation utters the promise:

Through a red sea of blood and war we wade towards the Promised Land, and our wilderness is long.
 Jean Paul

After the violent action a reaction necessarily occurred, which made use of the state of fatigue in which everyone found themselves in order to curtail the freedoms gained. But they could not be entirely annihilated; for the bourgeoisie was too powerful and, moreover, lent its own hand to reversing the concessions to a degree commensurate with its interest. Only temporarily had it made its cause the cause of humanity; now, in peacetime, it effected a divorce and excluded the lowborn completely from government.

In most lands, following England's example, *constitutional monarchy* was introduced, according to which the power in the State was distributed amongst the bourgeoisie, nobility, clergy, and the princes. The second chamber, which was supposed to represent the people, represented only a small portion of it, namely the rich bourgeoisie, for a strict census was introduced, which once again deprived the poor man of political rights.

In the economic field, however, the worker and his power were free, but the *yield* of his labour was a limited one, and thus the worker again became effectively unfree. In place of a master in one form or other, for whom one worked in exchange for the meeting of vital needs, appeared *capital*, the coldest and most dreadful of all tyrants. The serfs, bondsmen, and journeymen, who had been declared legally free, were in fact without means and, despite their freedom, had to enter once again into the relation of slave to master in order not to starve. More they did not receive. Every surplus which the worker's labour yields beyond his wages flows as a rule into the pockets of a few individuals who, like the slaveholders of antiquity, accumulate immense riches. Except that in this new relation there exists the disgraceful state of affairs that the modern slave, during trade crises, is mercilessly abandoned to his fate and pushed into the torments of hunger and squalor by his employer, whereas the slaveholder of antiquity had to maintain his slaves in times of inflation and hardship due to a bad harvest just as he did in times of plenty. The chastisement which is meted out to the employers precisely during such crises for their heartlessness and, all things considered, also their narrow-mindedness, and the fact that the workers in good times temporarily gain a better wage for themselves, do not modify this dreadful basic relation.

In this circumstance, that great law of civilisation, the *law of social misery*, manifests itself. "The heart is bettered through tribulation." Social suffering wears the *will* down more and more, anneals it, melts it, makes it softer and more plastic, and prepares it to be receptive to those motives which an enlightened science will proffer it.

Furthermore, social suffering has a rousing and honing influence on the mental powers: it heightens the *power of the mind*. One need only look at country folk and at the inhabitants of large cities. The difference in physical build, since the body is nothing other than the thing-in-itself which has passed through the subjective forms, is based in the idea. The proletarian appears as a weak individual with a relatively large brain, an appearance which is the *embodied* effect of the *principal law of politics*. The proletarian is a product of the ever-growing friction in the State, which first prepares the way for redemption and then redeems. Whereas hedonism weakens the higher classes, suffering weakens the lower, and *all* individuals are thereby enabled to seek their happiness somewhere entirely other than in this life amongst its empty, inflated, paltry charms.

That greater intelligence turns many proletarians into criminals—because in their more vivid minds the will, through neglectful rearing and deficient education, flares up for motives which it would otherwise not see or would abhor—merely provides evidence of the law of friction. On the other hand, this necessary aberration awakens charity and the endeavour to raise those lower down onto a higher level of cognition. Only a fantasist can complain about the increasing corruption; *the noble man will provide help*. For one need spend no time seeking out the basis of evil; it is there in the plain light of day and merely demands *strong* hands in order to render it harmless.

The law of social misery and the *law of luxury* (under which one can place a principal motion of the *higher* classes) are the expression of the harms of the whole society, of its irrational mode of production and life. From a particular standpoint, both laws can also be called the *law of nervousness*. Sensibility, which constantly grows according to other great laws of civilisation, is, according to this law, artificially *stimulated*, or in other words: One of the factors of motion is made to act with greater intensity, and the whole motion of the individual thereby becomes a different one, an essentially more intense and more rapid one. Here belong those stimulants, such as alcohol, tobacco, opium, spices, tea, coffee and the like, which according to the laws of contagion and custom have become a necessity for everyone. They weaken the life-force in general by heightening sensibility immediately and irritability mediately. For example, the alcoholic drinks consumed in the United States of North America in 1870 represent a value of 1,487,000,000 dollars. It has been calculated that the fluid mass would fill a canal 80 English miles in length, 4 feet deep and 14 feet wide!

In the intellectual domain, after the Revolution, the natural sciences above all unfolded. Nature was at last approached without bias and preconceptions, and interrogated honestly, and the binding of physics to a metaphysics was anxiously avoided. Kant's moral theology, in which an extramundane power underwent the highest conceivable refinement, was soon set aside and *materialism*, which is a thoroughly untenable philosophical system, took its place. I have already illuminated the chief defect of materialism in the Physics; here I have to cite another, namely, that materialism, although it recognises changes in the world, recognises no *course* of the world. It can therefore not arrive at an *ethics*.

On the other hand, materialism is a very important and beneficial historical form in the intellectual field. It is to be compared with an acid which destroys all the debris of centuries, all the residues of destroyed forms, all superstition, an acid which certainly makes the heart of man unhappy but in exchange purifies the mind. It is what John the Baptist was for Christ, the forerunner of genuine philosophy, for which Kant's ingenious successor, Schopenhauer, laid the foundation. For no other task at all can be set up for philosophy than that of establishing the core of Christianity on a *rational* foundation, or, as Fichte expresses it:

For what is the highest and final task of philosophy if not that of establishing the Christian doctrine on a proper foundation, or even of amending it?

However, it was Schopenhauer who first attempted this successfully.

Natural science then reached deeper into practical life and reshaped it. What changes those two important inventions: the steam engine and the electrical telegraph, wrought in the world! By means of these inventions, the motion of humanity has acquired a ten-fold faster tempo, the struggle for existence has become ten times more intense, the life of the individual ten times more restless than before.

38.

The conditions in the economic domain enlarged the chasm between the three upper estates and the new fourth estate more each day, until in the fourth estate class consciousness awoke. In France, the workers demanded electoral reform because the parliament was not the adequate expression of the people's will. The king's refusal caused a storm, and on 24 February 1848 revolution broke out. A worker was appointed to the provisional government, the State was obligated to improve the situation of the lower working class, and direct and universal sufferage was proclaimed, whereby every citizen without a criminal record and above the age of twenty-one gained an influence on the will of the State.

Yet the Republic went under owing to the splitting of the socialist parties as well as the intrigues of the bourgeoisie, which had recognised that the reforms threatened its power. But the people had seen a bright dawn, and since then the certainty has lived in them that the sun will break forth and shine over a *levelled society*, which is humanity entire.

Goethe says quite rightly:

The world is not supposed to approach its goal as quickly as we think and wish it would. There are always retarding dæmons, which are everywhere intervening and everywhere opposing, such that things do indeed move forwards, but very slowly.

As stars seem to stand still, even to move backwards, so too humanity seems to the mind immersed in the study of individual phenomena to stand still in one moment, to move backwards in the next. But the philosopher sees everywhere only resultant motion, and specifically a steady forward motion of humanity.

39.

We have now, with foresight and circumspection, to cast a glance into humanity's future, tracing the direction of those trends presently dominating in the purely political, economic (socio-political), and purely intellectual domains.

In Europe, the purely political phenomena of the present time are subject to three great laws: the *law of nationality*, the *law of humanism*, and the *law of the liberation of the State from the Church*, i.e., the *law of the annihilation of the Church*.

According to the first law, all small States which either originate in the Middle Ages and have maintained themselves in artificial segregation, or were created on a whim after the Napoleonic Wars, are being wrenched into the universal stream of becoming, half drawn, half driven into it from within themselves. People with a common language, common mores, and a common culture seek, with irresistible force, national unity, so that they do not perish and are not oppressed in the terrible struggle of nations for political existence. This striving also presses against the walls of large States which comprise peoples of various nationalities.

The second law reveals itself in very diverse phenomena. First and foremost *within* civilised States; every man, whatever his station be, is viewed as the most valuable, most important, and most sacrosanct being in the world:

But what then is the community of man if one of its members can vanish like a leaf carried away on the wind?

Souvestre

If, somewhere or other, a man is beset in a manner that contravenes the un|written codex of humanity, which is very incomplete and extraordinarily unclearly composed, then the whole of educated humanity trembles and cries aloud. So must it be if redemption is to take place. The more the individual's life loses value in his own eyes, the higher must its significance climb in the eyes of the totality. In antiquity it was the direct opposite; there the individual knew nothing more valuable than his life, which the totality valued no higher than that of a leaf or a rat. To this law the emancipation of the Jews must also be attributed, which was an event of the utmost importance in world history. The Jews appear everywhere with their minds which have been extraordinarily developed through long pressure, and they make the motion *more intense* wherever they set foot.

The law then reveals itself in the efficacy of the States *abroad*. Wherever the representatives of great nations set foot, the personal freedom of the individual is demanded. There shall be no more personally unfree men in the world; slavery shall cease on the whole surface of the earth.

Furthermore, all civilised States seek gradually to leave the state of nature in which they stand to each other. Already multiple small conflicts between States have been mediated by referees (the Alabama Claims, etc.), and multiple powerful associations ensure that things proceed ever onwards in the direction indicated. On this path lies a code of international law; and if the motion is not diverted through socio-political currents, then it will finally bring about the "United States of Europe"—about this there can be no doubt.

The most effective means of humanity is the good press. It mercilessly uncovers all harms and demands, steadfastly, the elimination of evil.

The struggle of the State with the Church has currently broken out in a manner which makes a healthy peace agreement impossible; it is comparable to a duel, in which one man must remain standing. That the State will be victorious lies in the course of humanity's development. In the victorious State, absolute philosophy, flourishing in the meantime in the intellectual domain, will finally take the place of religion.

In *Asia*, the old laws of melding through conquest and of intellectual fertilisation will govern events. It is a matter of gradually winning over all the people of the great part of the world to European civilisation.

Russia and England are called to lay the groundwork. The former encroaches relentlessly on the wide steppe and restrains the last residues of that unsettled force which, in the Middle Ages, had so often broken in upon the civilised realms with devastating consequences.

England for the time being confines itself to India. Over its great empire, governed by a petty but nevertheless beneficial politics, it casts a network of railroads, highways, canals and telegraph lines, and everywhere spreads European culture.

How relations will be shaped once the Asiatic possessions of England and Russia border on each other can in no way be determined and is irrelevant in any case. China will by then have emerged from its isolation and powerfully encroach upon the development of things, which development will also be subject to the influence of all the great nations of the world.

It is very probable that, as at the time of the Migration Period but without its horrors, a melding will occur and new empires of powerful mixed peoples will arise; for it may be deemed impossible that a complete extinction of the remainders of the old oriental civilisations will occur.

In *America*, the youthful mixed people which inhabits the United States is spreading farther and farther. In the Union, the law of melding found and still finds constantly the greatest application. Who can follow the crossings that arise from the sexual mixing of Frenchmen, Germans, Englishmen, Irishmen, Italians, and so on, or that of whites with blacks, Chinese, American Indians, etc.? How the qualities of the will are there bound, awakened, strengthened, and weakened, and every generation is essentially a different one.

In time, the Americans of the Union will inundate all of North America and perhaps spread over South America too.

Meanwhile, in America and Australia the half savage aborigines are progressively dying out. They lack the strength to bear contact with higher culture, and civilisation is callously toppling them into death.

That land which is hardest of all to draw into the sphere of culture and will enter it last of all is *Africa*. For the time being it is enclosed by a belt of colonies which will gradually expand more and more, until the whole land is exploited. Perhaps the Republic of Liberia is destined to become in later times the main outpost of civilisation in Africa. It would be odd if amongst the educated blacks of the Union apostles did not emerge for the raising of their poor brothers into a more humane form of life.

Egypt too seems destined to reshape the interior of that part of the world.

Those noble explorers of Africa must also be mentioned who endeavour to investigate the mysterious lands of the interior. Perhaps in time their efforts will succeed in casting such motives into the Old World that streams of emigrants will flow into Africa's interior and colonise it. Finally, we must mention the Christian missionaries, who in Africa are exactly where they ought to be. As much as one must condemn their workings in India, where they want the Christian religion to replace ethical systems of equal standing, so much must their efforts with the brutish negro tribes be acknowledged.

Now, if the sphere of civilisation has not yet been closed, then it must at least be clearly recognised from the causes now active that some day it will be closed. Its continued expansion is effected by the railways and shipping lines which daily multiply. Emigration is underway and is becoming ever greater. Today it is the gold and diamond fields that entice Europeans abroad, tomorrow the freer forms of life. The laws of melding and of the development of individuality preside over the motion and quicken its pace.

40.

In the economic (socio-political) domain, we are confronted with the so-called social question. At its foundation lies the law of melding through inner upheaval, which, as soon as the question is solved, will govern not one phenomenon more in the life of humanity—for then the beginning of the end will have arrived.

The social question is nothing other than a *question of education*, even if it has an entirely different appearance on the surface; for it is merely a question of *bringing all men to those cognitive heights upon which alone life can be correctly judged*. Since, however, the way to those heights is barred by purely political and economic hindrances, so the social question presents itself at present not as a pure question of education, but foremost as a question of *politics*, then as one of *economics*.

Accordingly, in the immediate future, the hindrances in the way of humanity must first of all be done away with.

The hindrance in the purely political field is the exclusion of the unpropertied classes from the government of the State. It will be eliminated through the granting of universal and direct suffrage.

The demand for this suffrage has in many States already been granted, and all others must in time follow this example—they cannot lag behind.

The demand was able to be met by the conservative elements in the State, firstly, because in consequence of the persistent division of political authority, the will of the people is not an absolute one, resolutions have therefore not always to be carried out; secondly, because the very ignorance of the masses made the law provisionally into a blunt weapon. There was no danger whatsoever that the people would now straight away topple all the institutions of the State by means of the law. On the other hand, the people had been completely satisfied because in fact no higher, purely political right can be demanded, and the rest was able to be left to the development of things. Every legislative assembly which is based on the universal and direct franchise is the adequate expression of the will of the people, for it is such an expression even when the majority is adversely disposed towards the people, for the electors betray fear, lack of insight, and so on, and evince their troubled spirit.

No better electoral law can therefore be given to the people. But its application can become more extended. If we keep our attention focused on Germany, then only the elections to the national parliament will be effected according to that law. However, all elections ought to take place according to that law: the elections to the state parliaments, to the provincial and district parliaments, to the parish councils, to the courts of assizes, and so on. Such an extension, however, depends on the *education* of the individuals.

Here we stand before the economic hindrance through which the true essence of the social question can already be clearly discerned. The common man is supposed to be able to *administer* his political offices.

For this purpose he must gain *time*. He must have time in order to be able to educate himself. Here lies the fountainhead of the whole question. The worker in fact currently lacks the time to educate himself. He must—because the whole profit of his labour does not accrue to him, for ruling capital takes the lion's share of it—work long hours in order that he might live at all, such long hours that, returning home of an evening, he has no more energy to cultivate his mind. The task of the worker is therefore: To wrest for himself a *shorter* working day while maintaining an adequate existence. In this way, however, not only does the price of the products he has created increase, but also the price of all the necessities of life, since in the economic chain one link depends on the other, and for that reason he must of necessity demand a *wage increase with a simultaneous shortening of his working hours*; for the wage increase will be absorbed by the generally increased prices, and his *sole* gain remains only the shortened working hours.

The recognition of these facts is the basis of all the strikes of the present day. One must not allow oneself to be misled into believing that the time gained, like the suffrage granted, will not be correctly used by most people.

The recognised advantage will *gradually* urge *each* man to collect his thoughts, just as at present many—whose names (as is written in the catacombs of Naples) *God alone knows*—are already using the time gained appropriately. (The inscription, at once beautiful and sublime, runs: Votum solviums nos quorum nomina Deus scit.)

Let us now assume that the workers would have to solve their task alone, without any help at all; then the consequence of everything would be that old and young would gain clear insight into their interests and thus gradually come to delegate a *strong minority* to the legislative bodies, which time and again would have to make two demands:

1) *free* schooling;
2) *legal* reconciliation between capital and labour.

By means of the time gained the individual can at present not achieve a comprehensive education. Only here and there can he reap a grain. The main thing is and remains that he be ignited by his interest, gain clarity about social conditions, enlighten others about them, hold firm to the totality, and in this way obtain through worthy representatives a determining influence on the will of the State. Now, these representatives have firstly the obligation to take hold of evil at its root and loudly demand free schooling, i.e., free *scientific* instruction for *every* man. There is no greater prejudice than the assumption that someone cannot be a good farmer, tradesman, soldier, etc. who speaks English and French, or who can read Homer in the original Greek.

However, so that this demand, when it is granted, be executable, the parents must be in such a position with regard to their earnings that they can not only do without their children's labour, but can also provide for their maintenance until they are completely educated, i.e., the wage conditions must be radically changed.

Lassalle, that great talent in theoretical and practical regard but without a trace of genius, has suggested making trade-based labour associations possible by means of granting public credit, which associations could then compete with the capital-owning classes. The existing capital would remain untouched, and competition using said capital would only be granted insofar as the workers could come to own the absolutely necessary instruments of their labour by means of the credit.

As incontestible as it is that such means would help, so certain is it also that the State would not lend a hand to that end (for, as above: "the world is not supposed to approach its aim as quickly as we think and wish it would").

Now, what else can be demanded of the State, which in any case is obligated to sanction the just demands of its taxpayers?

The incorporation of small workshops into large factories is a consequence of major capital. It lies in the tendency of our times, a tendency which is strengthened by minor capital (the crisis of 1873 and its consequences have only *temporarily* weakened this tendency), that the factories will be transformed into stock companies. Now, it is firstly to be demanded of the State that it facilitate this transformation of the factories, *but subject to the condition that the worker share in the profits of the business*. Furthermore, one can demand of the State that it compel autonomous manufacturers likewise to give the workers a share in the profits. (Several manufacturers, correctly recognising their advantage, have already done this.) Interest would then be paid on the equity at a customary rate and, on the other side of things, the wage of the workers would be paid out according to merit. The pure profit would then be divided into equal halves between capital and labour; the distribution amongst the workers would have to occur in accordance with their wage.

One could then, at stipulated junctures, gradually reduce the rate of interest paid to the capitalists more and more; and also gradually set the modulus of distribution of the pure profit more and more in the workers' favour; indeed, one could through gradual amortisation of the shares using a certain portion of the pure profit bring the factory entirely into the hands of all those who participate in the business.

Banks and trading companies and agriculture could be organised in a similar way, always proceeding according to the law of the development of the part, for social conditions cannot be reformed at a single stroke.

That the current mode of economic exploitation of the land is untenable the insightful men of all parties concede. I need only recall the admirable Riehl, who would like to have conserved, albeit remodeled, the *forms of the Middle Ages*. He says:

The question has been posed, how long the agricultural preconditions will remain of that kind which make possible an estate of small landowners, the peasantry depicted by us? For with the enormous strides in agricultural chemistry, in rational cultivation of the land, and with population growth which shall soon stand in no correct relation to the still superficial exploitation of the soil, the incompleteness, cumbersomeness and limited abundance of the economic exploitation method ... must in the short or long term give way to an, as it were, factory-like, large-scale cultivation of the land, which would then drain the peasantry in the same way as the industrial factory system has already in large part drained the small trades. That this eventuality must at some point come to pass we doubt not in the least.

If this were achieved, then the stock companies of a branch of labour could for specific purposes join together; groups could have their mutual bank, their insurance society for various incidents (illness, invalidity, death, loss of all kinds, etc.), and so on.

Furthermore, all the commercial shops of a city, of a suburb, could be organised along similar principles, in short, commerce as it now is would on the whole remain the same and only be extraordinarily *simplified*. However, the main thing would be that an actual *reconciliation between capital and labour* would eventuate and education would essentially ennoble the life of all.

Another good consequence of this simplification would be a change in the legislating of taxes; for the State would now have clear insight into the income of all, and by taxing the *companies* it would have taxed the *individual*.

41.

In this way, the social question could be solved in a slow, peaceful developmental course of things, if the workers pursued their objectives tenaciously and without excesses. But can this be assumed? Just as the half-savage Germanic peoples rattled on the frontiers of the Roman Empire, so the workers now rattle, wrathful and eager, on the social conditions, which bear the mark of capital. Impatience lays itself like a veil over the mind's clear eye, and desire surges unrestrained after a pleasure-filled life.

Accordingly, if the workers stood alone, then it could be foretold with certainty that a *peaceful solution* of the social question is not possible. *Such a solution*, however, is all that we presently have in mind, and we have therefore to discover those elements which are, so to speak, a counterweight to the impatience of the lower classes and can influence the social motion in such a way that its course remains a *steady* one.

These elements are supplied by the *higher classes*.

We have compared the motion of humanity, as civilisation, to the falling of a ball into the abyss, and whoever has followed attentively what we have been saying will have recognised that the conflict and strife in the progressing of humanity grows ever more intense. The original disintegration of the unity into multiplicity gave all subsequent motions this tendency, and so the oppositions in all domains multiplied continually. Consider even superficially the intellectual field of the present day. Whereas in the first century of the Middle Ages man simply believed and attempts to attack the established order were made very rarely by some brave, free individual, now in every direction opinion is opposed by opinion. In not one field of the intellectual domain does peace reign. In the religious field one finds a thousand sects; in the philosophical a thousand different banners; in the natural-scientific a thousand hypotheses; in the aesthetic a thousand systems; in the political a thousand parties; in the mercantile a thousand opinions; in the economic a thousand theories.

Now, each party in the purely political domain seeks to exploit the social question to its advantage and joins together with the workers in the pursuit now of one, now of the other of its aims. In this way, the social motion is first made to flow *more swiftly*.

And, since time immemorial, ambition, imperiousness, and the craving for fame have given men from the higher strata of society occasion to abandon their idle lives and make the people's cause their own. The material is extraordinarily brittle: the fingers bleed, and the arms often droop with exhaustion; but is that not happiness we see there rolling by, holding high the laurel wreath or the insignia of power?

But immanent philosophy grounds its hope principally on the insight of the reasonable employer and on the *good* and *just* men from the higher estates. The untenability of the social conditions forces itself upon every thinking and unprejudiced mind. This fact is even recognised in the "sovereign" strata of society, and I cite in evidence the words of the unfortunate Maximilian von Habsburg:

> What I still cannot accustom myself to is the sight of the rich, exploitative factory-owner producing in great quantities what satisfies the immoderate luxury of the rich and tickles their love of grandeur while the workers are serfs subjugated by his money, pale shadows of real men who in utter stultification and mechanical rhythm sacrifice their bodies to his moneybag in order to sate the needs of their stomachs.
>
> (*From My Life*)

Humanity's *redemption* depends on the *solution* of the social question—this is a truth on which a noble heart *must* be ignited. The social motion lies within humanity's motion, is a part of humanity's fate, which coerces the willing and the counter-striving alike into its immutable course. Herein lies the call for every man not under the spell of the narrow, barren sphere of natural egoism to offer himself with blood and treasure, with all his force to fate as its instrument, to adjust himself *to* that motion and to attain in exchange the highest happiness on this earth: peace of heart, which arises from the conscious harmonisation of the individual will with the course of the totality, with the developmental course of humanity, which has taken the place of God's divine will. Truly, whoever feels this happiness even transiently within himself must flare up in moral enthusiasm, his clear head must set his powerful heart aflame such that from within him the blaze of charity breaks forth irresistibly, for:

> the fruit of the Spirit is love. (Galatians 5:22)

Sursum Corda! Arise and descend from the luminous heights whence you have seen with intoxicated eyes the Promised Land of eternal peace; whence you *had* to recognise that life is essentially unhappy; where the blindfold *had* to fall from your eyes; descend now into the dark vale through which the troubled stream of the disinherited wends its way, and take in your tender but *true, pure, valiant* hands the calloused hands of your *brothers*. "They are brutish." Then give them motives that ennoble them. "Their manners are repellent." Then change them. "They believe that life has worth. They hold the rich to be happy because they eat better, drink better, because they hold feasts and are boisterous. They think the heart beats more peacefully under silk than under a coarse tunic." Then *disillusion* them, not with *figures of speech*, but through *deeds*. Let them experience, let them taste for themselves the fact that neither wealth, honour, fame, nor a comfortable life make happiness. Tear down the barriers that keep these besotted men from their alleged happiness; then clasp them, disillusioned, to your breast and open to them the trove of your wisdom; for now there is nothing more on this wide, wide earth that they could desire and want than *redemption from themselves*.

Once this happens, once the good and just regulate the social motion, then and only then will civilisation be *able* to take its course, its necessary, determinate, unstoppable course, avoiding mountains of corpses and rivers of blood.

42.

If we look back from our current vantage point, then we see that the principle of nationality, the struggle of the State with the Church, and the social motion will bring forth great upheavals which *can* altogether take a bloodless course.

However, is it probable that the conditions for this will eventuate? Is it probable that through congresses and courts of arbitration, States will be destroyed and peoples united who *want* to be united? Is it probable that the struggle of the State with the Church will be mediated through laws alone? Does the highest authority in *every* State stand on the side of the pure concept of State? Finally, is it probable that the capitalists will some day have such a day as the feudalists had on 4 August 1789?

No! All this is not probable. On the contrary, it is probable that the upheavals will all be violent. Humanity can bring the *form* and the *law* of a *new* period into existence only amidst intense birth pangs, amidst lightning and thunder, in an air thick with the stench of decay and miasmas of blood. Such is the lesson of history, "the self-consciousness of humanity". But the upheavals will be effected more swiftly and be accompanied by fewer atrocities—the good and just or, in other words, humaneness, *which will have become a great power*, will ensure it.

It is the task of philosophical politics to sketch in broad strokes and from wide points of view the course of humanity, for only philosophical politics can do so. But it would be presumptuous to want to specify the individual events.

In this direction, philosophical politics, if it wishes to do its dignity no harm, may give only general intimations and, looking at the fullness of effective causes at their root, characterise certain groupings as probable.

Firstly, it is clear that in the near future none of the upheavals presently discussed will take place completely unadulterated. Endeavours rooted in the principle of nationality will encroach on the State's struggle with the Church, and at the same time the banner of social democracy will be unfurled.

In the foreground, however, stands the struggle of the State with the Church, of reason with ignorance, of science with faith, of philosophy with religion, of light with darkness, and this struggle will leave its mark on the next period of history.

We have therefore to contemplate this struggle first of all.

Which European nations will oppose each other in this struggle no-one can predict. That said, it is certain that Germany will represent the idea of State, France will stand on the side of the Church.

Who the victor will be is debatable; but however the war may turn out, humanity will take a very great step forward.

We must substantiate this claim.

If France conducts a pure war of vengeance under Rome's banner, supported by all who under the splinters of exploded historical categories lead a light-shunning, obstinate, vengeful, pathetic, and narrow-minded life, then it can be predicted with certainty that France, whether it stand alone or with powerful allies, must succumb. For how could France be the victor over a power which, because under the given conditions it stands in the motion of humanity, increases its force a thousandfold through the moral enthusiasm with which its armies will glow? Will it not roar in Germany when the igniting watchword is spoken: *final* and *definitive* reckoning with Rome, with priestly lies and priestly deception? Would there be a single *judicious* social democrat who would not then take up the sword and say: First Rome, then my own cause!? O, what a day that would be!

If, in contrast, France writes the solution of the social question on its banner, likewise supported by Rome and by all scheming romantics who are caught in the illusion that, after the victory, they could banish the spirits they invoked; then it is not certain but very probable that Germany will not be successful; for then France stands *in* the motion of humanity, whereas Germany will not be a power held firmly together.

However, in the latter as in the former case, Rome is doomed to extinction; for a France that has been victorious under a social-democratic banner *must* cast aside that fragile form so that it shatters into pieces that can never be glued back together.

The great, powerful historical form of the Roman Catholic Church is ripe for absolute death. That it drives itself to this end and is not driven to it, that it pressed the sign of annihilation onto its own brow, is what makes its fall so deeply tragic and poignant. It has, one may admit, had an exceedingly beneficial effect for humanity. It has, as a political power, *increased strife*—a *great achievement*—and, specifically, it has acted successfully on the side of the will. It did not cast a cloud over the mind, it merely left a cloud cast over it; but the hearts, the defiant, wild and rebellious hearts, it broke with its iron hands and keen weapons.

If we consider both cases attentively, then we will find that the first is the more probable; for how ought France to be able to enter the struggle against Germany under the social-democratic banner? The conditions in that disjointed country give no sign of it at the present time.

43.

Now, however the new war with France, which is inevitable and lies in the development of things, may turn out, it is certain that not only the power of the Church will be annihilated but the social question will also be brought very close to its solution.

If France is victorious, then it must solve the question. If, in contrast, Germany is victorious, then two outcomes are possible.

Either the social motion will develop powerfully out of France, which will have been completely destroyed in itself—a blaze will arise within it which will take hold of all civilised peoples; or Germany will magnanimously thank all those whose sons have made up the greatest part of its victorious armies by stripping them of the heaviest fetters of capital. Is Germany supposed to be called to solve only intellectual problems? Is it impotent in the economic domain and can it there only ever *follow in the wake* of others? Why should the people that gave birth to Luther, Kant, and Schopenhauer, to Copernicus, Kepler, and Humboldt, to Lessing, Schiller, and Goethe not add to the laurel it earned for defeating Rome a second time (and this time destroying it) another laurel for having solved the social question?

Here too is the place to elucidate cosmopolitanism and modern patriotism and to establish the healthy connection between them. In our age, the first is to be retained *only* in principle, i.e., we must not lose sight of the fact that all men are brothers and called to be redeemed. But presently the laws of development of the part and of the rivalry of peoples still reign. The fundamental motion has not come to the surface as a unitary motion, but still separates itself there into various motions. These must first be consolidated in order to yield the form of that other motion, i.e., that other motion must be *created* out of the many and varied strivings of the individual nations. The will of the individual must therefore be ignited on the mission of his fatherland, keeping the whole of humanity in view. In every people there reigns the belief in such a mission, only it is in one moment a higher mission, in the next a lower one; for immediate need decides, and the present is proved right. Thus the mission of a people which still lacks unity is, firstly, to achieve unity, and its citizens may champion this proximate aim, confident that a fraternal people more favourably situated is in the meantime achieving the higher one, whereupon the fertilisation of the one by the other cannot fail to materialise.

For the period of history in which we are living, these words hold true: *For the sake of cosmopolitanism*, every man is a self-sacrificing *patriot*.

44.

I cannot repeat often enough, and every insightful man who pursues the threads which reach out of the darkness of antiquity into the present, showing clearly the direction they shall take in the future, will agree: that the social motion lies in the motion of humanity, and that—even if it now executes itself half peacefully or, like the French Revolution, amidst horrific atrocities and the whimpering of all whom the tree of life has shed violently into the night of death—it *cannot be held back*.

Just as Marius succeeded in annihilating the Cimbrian and Teutonic peoples, so the bourgeoisie succeeded in repelling the workers in 1848 and suppressing other socialist revolts which took place in several countries in the intervening periods. But can at least four fifths of the people remain excluded in the long term from the treasures of science by means of the current mode of production? Certainly not, as little as the plebeians of Rome were able to be denied political offices in the long term, as little as the bourgeoisie itself was able to remain excluded from the government of the State in the long term.

I said above that civilisation *kills*. In accordance with nature it weakens the higher strata of society more than the lower, because the individuals of the higher strata can live out their lives more swiftly. They are subject to the influence of many motives which awaken many desires, and these consume their life-force.

Barren scarcity is the best soil for the human plant, says the conservative statesman.

The *warmth of the greenhouse* is what the human plant requires, says the immanent philosopher:

> The oldest original lineages of the high nobility almost all died out towards the end of the Middle Ages. As the individual man passes away once he has fulfilled his mission, so too yield the lineages and families once they have had their effect in full measure. The proudest house, to which countless scions seem to promise a duration of many centuries yet, often dies out all of a sudden.
>
> **Riehl**

The corruption and depravity in the upper classes of present-day society is great. The attentive man finds in them once again all those phenomena of decay which I have already pointed out with regard to the Romans in the period of their extinction.

Now, wherever decay appears in society, the law of melding reveals itself; for civilisation—as I earlier said, expressing myself figuratively—endeavours to extend its sphere and it creates decay, so to speak, in order that savage peoples of nature, so enticed, give up their slow motion in exchange for the swift motion of civilisation.

But where are the savage peoples of nature who could now invade the States?

It is true: The life-force of the Romanic nations is smaller than that of the Germanic ones, and the force of the latter has been weakened more than that of the Slavic peoples. But a mass migration of peoples can no longer take place; for all these nations are already in a closed sphere of civilisation and in *each* of these nations, in Russia as well as in France, decay is already present.

Regeneration can therefore occur only *from the bottom up*, according to the law of internal melding, the consequences of which, however, will be different this time from what they were in Greece and in Rome. Firstly, no more personally unfree men exist; secondly, the barriers between the estates already lie half in rubble. The law will therefore bring about the *levelling* of all of society:

> Once the noonday sun of civilisation has scorched the plains, then from the uncivilised mountains and highlands the life-breath of an unbroken spirit of the people, fresh as nature, will blow like a forest air over civilisation, revitalising it.
>
> **Riehl**

Not only the peasants, but also the workers, the frenzied but at the same time unbroken workers, driven irresistibly by the genius of humanity, will tear down the artificial levees, and in every State a single, levelled society will exist.

45.

It is clear the social question would not exist, a solution of it would therefore not be able to be striven for, if all men were wise (or even just *good Christians*); but precisely because all men shall become wise, since only *as such* can they find redemption, the social question exists and must be solved.

Let us now assume the highest standpoint.

It is utterly foolish to say that social circumstances are not capable of any radical improvement. But it is just as foolish to say that a radical change of those circumstances would establish a paradisaical life.

Man must always work, but the organisation of work must be such that *all* the enjoyments that the world has to offer are accessible to *each* man.

There lies in luxury neither happiness nor satisfaction; consequently, it is also no unhappiness to have to abjure luxury. But it is a *great unhappiness* to place happiness in luxury and not be able to *learn through experience* that *no* happiness lies therein.

And this unhappiness, the gnawing unhappiness that spasms through the heart, is the driving force in the life of the lower social groups, which whips them onto the path of redemption. The poor are consumed with yearning for houses, gardens, estates, riding horses, state coaches, champagne, and the rhinestones and daughters of the rich.

Now, give to the poor all this frippery and they will fall as if out of the clouds. They will then complain: We believed ourselves so happy, but *in* us nothing has essentially changed.

All men must be *sated* with all the pleasures the world can offer before humanity can become ripe for redemption, and since their redemption is their *destiny*, men *must* be sated, and only the solution of the social question will bring this about.

The success of the social motion can thus be deduced from the principle of justice (humaneness), from the pure political rivalry of nations, from the decay in the State itself, and from the universal fate of humanity. The modern social motion is a necessary motion, and as it has arisen of necessity, so of necessity it shall also arrive at its goal: the *ideal State*.

46.

Hitherto we have sought in general to define the changes which will eventuate in the political and economic domain; we now want to trace the development of purely intellectual life in the future.

Let us first consider art.

To art only a limited further development can be attributed. In architecture, the formally beautiful of space has almost, if not completely, been exhausted by oriental, Greek, Roman, Moorish and Gothic art. Only the combination of forms and the shifting of the dimensional proportions offer some room to move.

The beauty of the human form has been depicted by the Greek sculptors and great Italian painters unsurpassably and with consummate skill. The human species daily declines in beauty, and so another, better ideal can never be set up. However, inasmuch as what is innermost in man's essence shines forth in phenomena, Christian sculpture and painting cannot be surpassed. Only realistic plastic arts have yet some leeway for emphasising great historical moments and the depiction of great men.

In music one may—after Bach, Händel, Gluck, Haydn, Mozart and Beethoven—justly concede a further development only within narrow limits.

Only for poetry is there yet a high goal. Alongside the optimistic Faust, who, active and creative, found apparent satisfaction in life as such:

> The empty moment that amused him last,
> Infatuated, he would fain hold fast!

poetry has yet to place the pessimistic Faust, who won for himself genuine peace of soul. An ingenious master will find his way to this.

The natural sciences still have a wide field of work before them; but they must and will draw to a close. Nature can be fathomed, for it is *purely immanent*, and nothing transcendent, whatever its name may be, coexists with and encroaches upon it.

Religion, to the same extent that science grows, will find ever fewer professors. The connection of *rationalism* with religion (German Catholicism, Ancient Catholicism, New Protestantism, Reform Judaism, etc.) hastens its downfall and, like materialism, leads to unbelief.

Pure knowledge, in contrast, does not destroy faith, but is its *metamorphosis*; for pure philosophy is only the religion of love, refined through reason but confirmed in its foundation. Pure knowledge is therefore not the opposite of faith. Formerly one had, because of impure cognition, to *believe* or *have faith in* the redemption of humanity; now one *knows* that humanity will be redeemed.

The motion of humanity, with a view to the principal infuence of thought on will, can also be defined as the motion through superstition (fear) to belief (blissful internalisation), through this to unbelief (desolate bleakness) and through unbelief finally to pure knowledge (moral love).

Likewise, philosophy itself will at long last come to an end. Its final link will be absolute philosophy:

When at last the absolute philosophy has been found, then the right time for judgment day has come.

So declared Riehl facetiously. We'll hold on to this cheeky expression, but *in earnest*.

Thus everything in the intellectual domain also tends towards completion, closure, towards pure labour.

However, the coming periods of history will distinguish themselves from past ones in that art and science will diffuse ever more widely amongst the people until they pervade the whole of humanity. The people's understanding for the works of the ingenious artist will become ever more developed. Aesthetic joy will thus enter more frequently into the life of each man and his character will become ever more moderate. Science, furthermore, will become a common good and the enlightenment of the masses will become a fact.

47.

In this way the *ideal* State will at last appear.

What is the ideal State?

It will be the historical form that embraces the *whole* of humanity. However, we will not define this form more closely, for that is a quite minor concern. The main concern is the *citizen* of the ideal State.

He will be what individuals have been since the beginning of history: a thoroughly free man.

He will have outgrown completely the taskmasters that are the historical laws and forms and will stand, free of all political, economic and spiritual fetters, *above* the law. All external forms will be shattered—man will be completely emancipated.

All *driving forces* will gradually have disappeared from the life of humanity: power, property, fame, honour; all *bonds of feeling* will gradually have been torn asunder: *man will be weary*.

His mind will now judge life correctly and his will shall be ignited on this judgment. Now his heart will be filled with only the one yearning: to be obliterated forever from the great book of life. And the will shall attain its goal: absolute death.

48.

In the ideal State, humanity will make the "great sacrifice", as the Indians say, i.e., it will *die*. No-one can specify in what way the sacrifice will be made. It could be based on a general moral resolution which is immediately carried out, or whose carrying out one leaves to nature. It could, however, also be contrived to occur in some other way. In any case the *law of intellectual contagion*, which revealed itself so powerfully when Christianity came on the scene, during the Crusades, and more recently in the pilgrimages in France and in the "praying plague" in America, will govern the final processes in humanity. It will be as it was in Dante's time, when the people marched through the streets of Florence crying:

Morte alla nostra vita! Eviva la nostra morte!

(Death to our life! And long live our death!)

Here the question can also be posed, *when* the great sacrifice will be made.

If one merely considers the dæmonic power of the sex-drive and the great love of life that almost all men show, then one is tempted to place the moment of redemption in the farthest, farthest future.

If, in contrast, one considers the strength of the currents in every domain of the State; the haste and impatience which set every breast dæmonically aquiver; the yearning for rest in the depths of the soul; if, furthermore, one considers the fact that around all people untearable threads have already been spun which daily multiply, such that no people can have a slow, *isolated* course of civilisation any longer; that savage peoples, driven into the maelstrom of civilisation, end up in a state of agitation which eats at the marrow of their force, that they become ill with fever, so to speak; finally, if one considers the immense power of intellectual contagion—then one will grant the course of civilisation a duration no longer than one Platonic year, which can be reckoned from 5000 years before Christ. However, if we consider that according to this calculation humanity would still have to drag itself along for another 3000 years, then we ignore this calculation too and it seems a duration of but a few centuries is the longest we may assume.

49.

If we cast a glance back over the ground we have covered, then we find confirmation that civilisation is the motion of humanity entire and is the motion out of life into absolute death. It executes itself in a *single* form, the State, which assumes various configurations, and according to a *single* law, the law of suffering, whose consequence is the weakening of the will and the growth of the mind (reconfiguration of the factors of motion). This law may be disaggregated into various laws which I now want to set out. However, this scheme lays no claim to completeness:

>Law of the development of individuality;
>Law of intellectual friction;
>Law of custom;
>Law of development of the part;
>Law of particularism;
>Law of unfolding of the simple will;
>Law of binding of the qualities of the will;
>Law of inheritance of characteristics;
>Law of decay;
>Law of individualism;
>Law of melding through conquest;
>Law of melding through revolution;
>Law of colonisation (emigration);
>Law of intellectual fertilisation;
>Law of rivalry of peoples;
>Law of social misery;
>Law of luxury;
>Law of nervousness;
>Law of levelling;
>Law of intellectual contagion;
>Law of nationality;
>Law of humanism;
>Law of intellectual emancipation.

The historical forms are the following:

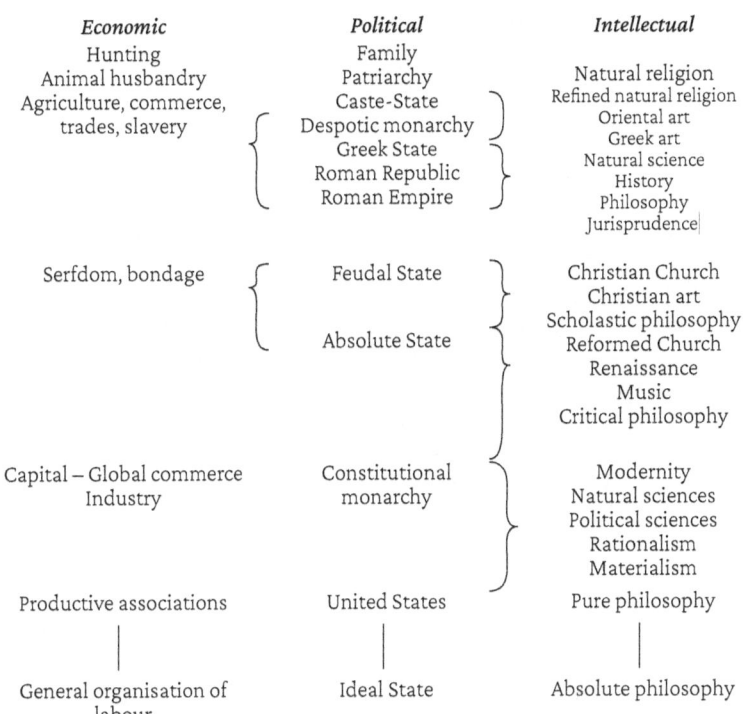

50.

Humanity is above all a concept. Corresponding to it in reality is a totality of individuals who alone are real and keep themselves in existence by means of procreation. The *individual's* motion out of life into death, in conjunction with his motion out of life into life, yields the motion out of life into *relative* death. But this motion, since in the continuous transitions which it entails the will grows weaker and the intelligence stronger, is the helical motion out of life into *absolute* death.

Humanity must have the same motion since it is in fact nothing more than the totality of individuals. Every definition of its motion which does not contain absolute death as its goal falls short because it does not cover all of the processes. Were the true motion unable to be distinctly recognised, then immanent philosophy would have to postulate absolute death as its goal.

All individual life-courses: the short life-time of children and of adults whom death annihilates before they were able to procreate, and the long life-time of such men as look upon the children of their children's children, must, like all the life-courses of human groupings (of Indian tribes, of South Sea Islanders), allow themselves to be worked effortlessly into the postulated motion of humanity. If this is not possible in a single instance, then the definition is *false*.

Now, the motion of humanity out of being into non-being coincides with each and every particular motion. The thinker who has recognised that motion will not read another page of history in astonishment, nor will he complain. He will neither ask: What guilt did the inhabitants of Sodom and Gomorrah incur that they had to perish? What guilt did the 30,000 men incur who were annihilated in a few minutes by the earthquake of Riobamba? What guilt the 40,000 who at the destruction of Sidon were burned to death? Nor will he complain about the millions whom the Migration Period, the Crusades, and all wars have thrust into the night of death. *All of humanity is ordained to die.*

The motion itself of our species (if we disregard the other influences of nature) results from the strivings of *all* men, as I already said at the beginning of the Politics. It arises out of the motions of the good and the bad, the wise and the foolish, the ardent and the cold, the bold and the timid, and can therefore bear no mark of morality. In its course it *creates* men who are good and bad, wise and foolish, morally ardent and despicable, wise heroes and villains, arch-knaves and saints, and is *created* out of these motions in turn. At its end, however, stand only *weary, exhausted, deathly tired* and *debilitated* men.

And then the still night of absolute death descends upon all. How in the moment of transition they shall all shudder in bliss: they have been redeemed, redeemed forever!

Metaphysics

And you, ye Gods, I thank, that ye resolve
Childless to root me hence. Thee let me counsel
To view too fondly neither sun nor stars.
Come follow me to the gloomy realms below!

Childless and guiltless come below with me!

Goethe

1.

Immanent philosophy, which in the foregoing chapters has drawn from only two sources: nature in the broadest sense and self-consciousness, does not enter upon its last chapter, Metaphysics, in order to be able, free of all restraint, to "go wild with reason". In the Metaphysics it simply places itself on the *highest immanent* standpoint. Hitherto it has assumed the highest point of observation for each discipline, whence it was able to look out over the whole staked-off domain; however, if it wanted to let its glance wander beyond the boundary into the distance, then higher peaks obstructed its view. Now, however, it stands on the highest summit—it stands *above* all disciplines, i.e., it looks out *over* the entire world and embraces everything in *one* point of view.

We will therefore uphold the honesty of inquiry in the Metaphysics too.

Now, because immanent philosophy in the individual doctrines of the foregoing chapters always assumed a correct but nevertheless one-sided perspective, some results had also to be one-sided. We have, therefore, in the Metaphysics not only to set the capstone atop the pyramid, but also to supplement half-results and to smooth out others which protrude at irregular angles. Or more precisely: From the highest immanent standpoint, we have once again to consider the entire immanent domain, from the moment in which it arose down to the present day, and to judge its future soberly.

2.

Already in the Analytics, pursuing the developmental chains of things-in-themselves (with the aid of time) A PARTE ANTE, we found a simple, premundane unity, before which our cognitive faculty went lame. According to the individual faculties of cognition, we defined that unity negatively as: inactive, extensionless, undifferentiated, unfragmented, motionless, timeless. We then placed ourselves before this unity once again in the Physics, hoping to catch a glance of it in the mirror of those principles of will and mind which we had found in the meantime, but there too our efforts were completely unsuccessful: *nothing* revealed itself in our mirror. There too we had therefore to define things once again only negatively, as a simple unity at rest and free, which was neither will nor mind, nor an interpenetration of will and mind.

On the other hand, we obtained three extraordinarily important *positive* results. We recognised that this simple unity, God, fragmenting itself into a world, perished and disappeared entirely; further, that the world which arose from God, precisely because it originated in a simple unity, stands without exception in a dynamic coherence and, in connection with this, that the motion creating itself continuously from the efficacy of all individual beings is fate; finally, that the premundane unity *existed*.

Existence was the thin thread which bridged the chasm between the immanent and transcendent domains, and to existence we have first to turn our attention.

The simple unity existed, we can predicate of it no more than this. Of what type this existence, this being was, is veiled from us entirely. If we want nevertheless to define it more closely, then we must again take refuge in negation and state that it bears no resemblance to any kind of being with which we are familiar, for all being with which we are familiar is *moved* being, is a *becoming*, whereas the simple unity was motionless, in absolute rest. Its being was *supra-being*.

Our positive recognition that the simple unity existed remains entirely untouched by this fact; for the negation does not affect existence as such, but only the kind of existence, a kind which we cannot make comprehensible to ourselves.

Now, from this positive recognition that the simple unity existed flows of its own accord that other, very important realisation that the simple unity also had to have a particular *essence*, for every EXISTENTIA posits an ESSENTIA, and it is simply inconceivable that a premundane unity existed but was in itself without an essence, i.e., that it was nothingness.

But of the essence, the ESSENTIA of God, as of His EXISTENTIA, we can also form for ourselves not the slightest notion. Everything which we apprehend and cognise *in* the world as the essence of individual things is inseparably connected with motion, and God was at rest. If, however, we want to define His essence, then this can only be done negatively, and we must state that the essence of God was an incomprehensible but in itself quite *definite supra-essence*.

Even our positive recognition that the simple unity had a definite essence remains entirely untouched by this negation.

Thus far everything is clear. But it also seems as if human wisdom had here reached an end and the disintegration of the unity into multiplicity were quite simply unfathomable.

But we are not yet entirely helpless. We have precisely the disintegration of the unity into multiplicity, the transition of the transcendent into the immanent domain, God's death and the birth of the world. We are confronted with a *deed*, the first and sole deed of the simple unity. The immanent domain *followed* on the transcendent, something has become which previously was not. Should it not be possible here to fathom the deed itself, without becom-

METAPHYSICS

ing fantastical and wandering off into wretched hallucinations? We want to be very careful indeed.

3.

We are nevertheless confronted with a process which we can conceive of in no other way than as a deed; we are also thoroughly justified in calling that same process a deed, for we are still standing entirely in the immanent domain, which is nothing other than this very deed.

If, however, we ask after the *factors* which brought this deed about, then we leave the immanent domain and find ourselves on the "shoreless ocean" of the transcendent, which is forbidden us, forbidden because all our faculties of cognition go lame in that domain.

In the immanent domain, *in* the world, the factors (in themselves) of one deed or another are always known to us. We have constantly on one hand an individual will of a quite distinct character and on the other hand a sufficient motive. Now, if we wanted to use this unshakeable fact in addressing the present question, then we would simply have to describe the world as a deed which sprang from a divine *will* and a divine *intelligence*, i.e., we would be placing ourselves in complete contradiction with the results of immanent philosophy; for we have found that the simple unity was neither will, nor mind, nor an interpenetration of will and mind; or, in Kant's words, we would in the most arbitrary and sophistical manner be making immanent principles into *constitutive* principles in the transcendent domain, which is TOTO GENERE different from the immanent.

But here all of a sudden there is opened to us a way out, which we may take without reservation.

4.

We are confronted, as I have mentioned, with a *deed* of the simple unity. If we wanted to call this deed of deeds, as we call all the deeds known to us in the world, a *motivated act of will*, then we would become unfaithful to our vocation, betray the truth, and be simplistic dreamers; for we may attribute to God neither will nor mind. The immanent principles, will and mind, cannot at all be transferred onto the premundane essence, we are not allowed to make them into *constitutive* principles for the *derivation* of the deed.

In contrast, we may make these same immanent principles into *regulative* principles for "the mere *judgment*" of the deed, i.e., we may attempt to explain the arising of the world by conceiving it *as if* it had been a motivated act of will.

The difference is patent.

In the latter case we merely make a problematic judgment, by analogy with the deeds in this world, without madly presuming to render any kind of apodictic judgment about God's essence. In the former case, in contrast, it is claimed without the slightest hesitation that the essence of God, like that of man, was an inextricable compound of will and mind. Whether one says this or expresses oneself more vaguely and calls the will of God POTENTIA-will, resting, inactive will, and the mind of God POTENTIA-mind, resting, inactive mind—one is always striking the results of honest inquiry in the face: for *will* implies *motion* and mind is a part of the will which has precipitated out and has a particular motion. A resting will is a CONTRADICTIO IN ADJECTO and bears the mark of logical contradiction.

5.

Accordingly, we set foot upon no forbidden path if we conceive God's deed *as if* it had been a motivated act of will and thus, merely for judging the deed, *temporarily* ascribe will and mind to His essence.

That we must ascribe to it will *and* mind and not will alone is clear, for God was in absolute solitude, and nothing existed besides Him. He was unable to be motivated from *without*, but only by means of Himself. In His self-consciousness were mirrored His essence and its existence, nothing more.

It follows from this with logical compulsion that God was able to exercise his freedom (the LIBERUM ARBITRIUM INDIFFERENTIAE) in only a *single* choice, namely: either to *remain* as He was or *not to be*. To be sure, He also had the freedom *to be other* than He was; but in all directions of this being-other, freedom had to remain latent, because we can conceive no more complete and better being than that of a simple unity.

Thus, only one deed was possible for God, and specifically one *free* deed, because He was subject to no compulsion whatever, because He was able to forgo that deed as well as carry it out, namely, to enter *absolute nothingness*, the NIHIL NEGATIVUM, i.e., to annihilate Himself completely, to cease to exist.

Now, if this was His only possible deed and we, in contrast, face an entirely different deed, the *world*, whose being is a constant becoming, then the question is raised: Why did God, if He wanted not to be, not crumble into nothingness *directly*? You all must ascribe omnipotence to God, for nothing constrained His power; consequently, if He wanted not to be, then He had also to be annihilated straight away. But instead there arose a world of multiplicity, a world of struggle. This is an obvious contradiction. How do you all propose to solve it?

METAPHYSICS

The response to this is firstly: It is on one hand certainly established logically that only a single deed was possible for the simple unity: to annihilate itself completely; on the other hand, the world proves that this deed did not occur. But this contradiction can only be an apparent one. Both deeds—the only one logically possible and the actual one—must at root be capable of unification. But how?

It is clear that they can only be unified if it can be proven that God's direct annihilation was impossible due to some *obstacle* or other.

We have therefore to search for this obstacle.

In the question above it was remarked: "You all must ascribe omnipotence to God, for nothing constrained His power." This sentence, however, is false in its generality. God existed alone, in absolute solitude, and it is consequently correct that He was not constrained by anything outside Him; His power was therefore an omnipotence in the sense that nothing lying *outside* Him constrained it. But it was no omnipotence with respect to His *own* power, or in other words, His power was not to be annihilated by itself, the simple unity was unable, by means of itself, to cease to exist.

God had the freedom to *be* as He wanted, but He was not free of His own particular *essence*. God had the omnipotence to carry out His will to *be* some way or other; but He did not have the power *not* to be all at once.

The simple unity had the power to be, in some way or other, other than it was, but it did not have the power suddenly not to be at all. In the former case it remained in *being*, in the latter case it was supposed *not* to be; in this latter case, however, it stood in its own way; for even if we cannot fathom God's essence, we do at least know *that* it was a particular supra-essence, and that this particular supra-essence, reposing in a particular supra-being, was, as a simple unity, not by means of itself able not to be. This was the obstacle.

Theologians of every age have unreservedly predicated omnipotence of God, i.e., they attributed to Him the power to carry out His every will. In doing this, however, none of those theologians thought of the possibility that God can also will Himself to become nothingness. No one has ever considered this possibility. But if one considers it seriously, then one sees that in this *single* case God's omnipotence was constrained by nothing other than itself, that it was no omnipotence in relation to itself.

According to this view, God's one deed, the disintegration into multiplicity, presents itself as the *carrying out* of the logical deed, of the *resolution* not to be, or in other words: The world is the *means* to the *end* of non-being, and specifically the world is the *sole means possible* to that end. God recognised that only by means of the *becoming* of a real world of multiplicity, only by means of the immanent domain, by means of the world, would He be able to pass over from *supra-being* into *non-being*.

Incidentally, were it not clear that God's essence was the obstacle to His dissolution into nothingness, then our ignorance of the obstacle would be no cause for concern. We would then simply have to postulate an uncognisable obstacle in the transcendent domain; for in what follows we shall, in the purely immanent domain and leaving no room to doubt, obtain the result that the *universe* is in fact moving out of being into non-being.

The questions which one could here raise, namely, why God did not want non-being *sooner*, and why He preferred non-being to supra-being at all, are devoid of all meaning; for as to the first question, "sooner" is a temporal concept, which in the context of eternity lacks all sense, and as to the second, it is adequately answered by the *fact of the world*. Non-being must simply have earned preference over supra-being, or else God in his perfect wisdom would not have chosen it. And this all the more when one considers the torments experienced by the higher ideas familiar to us, by the animals nearest to us and by men, torments with which alone non-being can be purchased.

6.

We have only provisionally attributed will and mind to God's essence and conceived God's deed *as if* it had been a motivated act of will in order to gain a regulative principle for the mere judgment of the deed. By this route we also arrived at our objective, and speculative reason may rest content.|

However, we are not allowed to leave our idiosyncratic standpoint between the immanent and transcendent domains (we are hanging from the thin thread of existence over the bottomless abyss separating both domains) in order to set foot once more in the firm world, on the sure ground of experience, until we have *declared loudly* once again that God's essence is neither a compound of will and mind, like man's, nor was it an interpenetration of will and mind. The world's true origin will therefore *never* be fathomed by a human mind. All that we can and may do—a warrant of which we too have made use—is infer the divine act through analogy with deeds in the world, but always keeping in mind and never losing sight of the fact that:

> we see through a glass, darkly (1 Cor 13:12);

and that, according to our limited endowments, we concoct piecemeal an act which, as the unitary act of a simple unity, can *never* be apprehended by a human mind.

Yet the result of this piecemeal composition is satisfactory. Let us also not forget that we could be equally satisfied if the ability to see the divine act through a glass darkly were denied us; for the transcendent domain and its simple unity have vanished without a trace in our world, in which only individual wills exist and beside or behind which nothing more exists, just as *before* the world *only* the simple unity existed. And this world is so rich, it responds so distinctly and clearly to an honest interrogation that the soberminded thinker turns with a light heart away from the "shoreless ocean" and devotes all his mental power to the divine act, to the book of nature, which lies at all times open before him.

7.

Before we proceed, we want to summarise these results:

1) God wanted not to be;
2) His essence was the obtsacle to His instant entry into non-being;
3) this essence had to disintegrate into a world of multiplicity whose individual essences all strive for non-being;
4) in this striving they impede each other mutually, they struggle with each other and in this way *weaken* their force;
5) God's whole essence passed into the world in a modified form, as a particular sum of force;
6) the whole world, the universe, has *one* objective: not to be, and achieves it through continuous weakening of its sum of force;
7) every individual, through weakening of its force, will be brought to a point in its developmental course where its striving for annihilation can be fulfilled.

8.

Of these results, those which relate to the immanent domain must now be subjected to a test.

In the inorganic realm we have gases, liquids, and solid bodies.

Gas has only one striving: to spread out in all directions. If it could exercise this striving unimpeded, then it would not be annihilated, but would become ever weaker; it would approach annihilation ever closer but never attain it, or: gas has the striving for annihilation, but it cannot achieve it.

In this sense we have also to conceive the state of the universe in its earliest periods. In absolute nothingness, the individuals, in the form of a fiery nebula rotating with utmost speed, expanded their spheres of force (which, subjectively, we cannot define in spatial terms) ever further, all the while struggling unceasingly with each other until the exhaustion of a select few became so great that they were no longer able to preserve their gaseous state and, drop by drop, became liquids. The physicists say that in the *cold void of space* they lost a portion of their heat. What a feeble explanation! Through their striving itself and through the struggle with each other they were so weakened that, had a cognising Subject been present, it would only have been able to objectify their striving, their essence, as liquid.

Liquid has but one striving: It wants to flow apart horizontally in all directions towards an ideal point lying outside itself. However, it is clear that to strive towards an ideal point is quite patently to strive towards non-being; for any liquid which succeeded in attaining the goal for which it strives would straight away be annihilated.

In the periods of the universe when gaseous individuals changed into liquid ones, the formation of the celestial bodies began. Each and every liquid only ever strove towards some particular centre-point which, however, it could not attain. If we focus exclusively on our solar system, then a single, immense sphere of gas was on all sides enclosed by a sea of liquid fire (like a soap bubble). Every gas within the sphere strove to break through the sea and to spread out in every direction; the sea, on the other hand, strove towards the centre-point of the sphere of gas. The result of this was an extraordinarily great tension, a violent pressure and counter-pressure, with no other result than a gradual weakening of the individual forces, until a firm crust formed around the whole.

Every *solid body* has but one striving, namely, towards an ideal point lying outside it. On our earth this point is the extensionless centre-point of the earth itself. If a solid body were able to reach the centre-point of the earth unimpeded, then in the moment in which it arrived it would be completely and forever dead.

The periods of the universe which followed immediately on those in which solid crusts had formed around the celestial bodies were filled with transformations. Since the whole universe was rotating from its beginning, the (arguably less dense) solid bodies loosed themselves and orbited in the form of rings around the central sun until, as the transformations proceeded, they shaped themselves into planets; at the same time, according to the Kantian-Laplacian hypothesis, the central body proceeded to solidify as it cooled and contracted (weakening of force).

9.

The primordial state of the universe presents itself to our thinking as an unconscious yearning of individuals for absolute death, which found only

METAPHYSICS

piecemeal fulfilment in the ever-increasing weakening of the definite sum of force.

Reflected in the universe of that time, as also in every gas of our universe today, is the transcendent obstacle God found in His own essence when He wanted not to be, or in other words, the *retarding element*. Out of every gas peers the reflected image of the transcendent doom: that God wanted not to be but was unable to find fulfilment straight away.

In subsequent periods, we encounter *particular* individuals for whom the wholehearted satisfaction of their yearning would arguably have come about had they been able to reach their goal unimpeded.

The universe at present, however, cannot be thought of except as a finite, but to our minds immeasurably large sphere with a liquid or extraordinarily light, solid shell within which every inorganic individual is *inhibited* from reaching the goal of its striving, or, in other words, the universe is kept in pervasive, violent tension which continually weakens its definite sum of force.

10.

In the entire inorganic realm of the universe there is nothing other than individual will with a particular striving (motion). It is *blind*, i.e., its goal lies in its striving, is of itself already contained in the motion. Its essence is pure drive, pure will, always following the *impulse* which it *acquired* when the unity disintegrated into multiplicity.

Accordingly, if we say: Gases want to spread out IN INDEFINITUM, liquids and solid bodies also want to move towards an ideal point lying outside themselves; then in saying so we only express the fact that a *cognising Subject*, following the direction of the striving, comes to a definite goal. Independently of a cognising Subject, every inorganic body has only a particular motion, is pure, genuine drive, is mere blind will.

And I now ask: How, *in light of all this*, must the will of the chemical idea be reflected in man's mind? As will to *life*? Not at all! According to all that has been said up to this point, it is *pure will to death*.

This is a very important result. In the inorganic realm, through and through, not *life* is *willed*, but annihilation; *death* is *willed*. The only reason we have to do with a *will* at all is because something is supposed to be acquired which still *has not been*, because a *retarding element* is present which makes its instant attainment impossible. *Life* is not *willed* but is only the *phenomenon of the will to death*; and specifically, in the primordial state of the universe and in every gas of the present, it is the phenomenon of the retarding element in the individual; and in every liquid and every solid body, it is the phenomenon of a striving *impeded from without*. For this reason, in the inorganic realm too, not the *life* of the individual is the *means* to an end, but the *struggle* as such—or, the multiplicity which occasions that struggle, as the case may be—is the *means*. Life in the inorganic realm is only ever phenomenon, is the gradual motion of the chemical ideas towards death.

As long as there are gaseous ideas in the world, (and even now they outweigh all others), so long is the sum of force in the world not *ripe* for death. All liquids and solid bodies are ripe for death, but the universe is a fixed whole, a collective unity standing without exception in dynamic coherence and with a single goal: non-being; and for this reason the liquids and solid bodies cannot fulfil their striving until each and every gas has been weakened to the point where they too become solid or liquid, or in other words: The universe cannot become nothingness until the entire sum of force contained in it is ripe for death.

Now, from this vantage point, with the *whole* in view, the life of the liquids and solid bodies, therefore their striving impeded from without, appears as a *means*, namely, as a means to achieving the purpose of the *whole*.

In the Physics we therefore assumed a too-low standpoint with respect to the chemical ideas and only acquired a half-result. We recognised the impeded striving of all ideas quite rightly as *life*, but, since we stopped at that point or, more precisely, had to stop at that point for want of a metaphysics, we erred in our explanation of the will. The chemical idea wants *death*, yet it can only attain death through struggle, and for this reason it lives. In its innermost core it is *will to death*.

11.

We now enter the organic realm. In doing so, we have to remember from the Physics that this realm is nothing other than a form for the weakening of the sum of force in the universe. We now call it more precisely: the most perfect form for the *extinction of force*. This is sufficient for us at this point. In what follows, we will find a place where we can once again immerse ourselves in the study of organisation and apprehend its whole significance.

The *plant* grows, reproduces (in some way or other) and *dies* (after a certain lifespan). If we now look past every particular, then what here leaps out at us first of all is the great fact of real *death*, which was unable to appear as a phenomenon anywhere in the inorganic realm. *Could* the plant die if it did not *want* to die in the deepest core of its essence? It merely follows its fundamental drive, which drew its entire striving from God's yearning not to be.

But the plant's death is only a *relative* death, its striving finds fulfilment only piecemeal. It *reproduced*, and through reproduction it lives on.

Now, since reproduction, the maintenance of life, is indeed induced from without and depends on other ideas, but in its most essential aspect springs from the innermost idea of the plant itself, so the life of the plant is a phenomenon entirely distinct from that of the chemical idea. Whereas with the chemical idea life is but an obstacle to the will to death, induced and conditioned from within or without, *life* in the plant is directly *willed*. The plant therefore shows us will to life *alongside* will to death, or more precisely, because it wants absolute death but cannot have it, it wants life directly as a *means* to absolute death, and what results is *relative death*.

This all is phenomenon of its drive, which is governed by no cognition, i.e., in the cognising *Subject* its drive is reflected in the manner specified. The plant is pure will, pure drive, following the impulse which the simple chemical ideas constituting it acquired during the disintegration of the unity into multiplicity.

In the Physics we defined the plant as will to life with a particular motion (growth). This explanation requires amendment. The plant is will to death, like the chemical idea, *and* will to life, and the resultant of these strivings is relative death, which is bestowed on the plant too.

12.

The *animal* is first of all a plant, and everything that we have said of the plant is valid also for the animal. As plant it is will to death *and* will to life, and from these strivings relative death results. The animal wills life as a means to absolute death.

The animal, however, is also a combination of will and mind (at a particular level). The will has partly divided itself, and each part has an idiosyncratic divided motion. The animal's plant-life is hereby modified.

The animal's mind perceives an Object and instinctively feels the danger threatening it. The animal has, with respect to particular Objects, an *instinctive fear of death*.

We are confronted with an extraordinarily peculiar phenomenon. In the innermost depths of its essence, the animal wants annihilation, and yet by virtue of its mind it fears death; for mind is a precondition of this fear, because the dangerous Object must in some way or other be perceived. If it is not perceived, then the animal remains peaceful and does not fear death. How is this odd phenomenon to be explained?

We have seen in the Physics that the individual is constrained—he is not completely independent. His power is only half complete. He has an effect directly and indirectly on all ideas, but he also experiences the influence of all other ideas. He is a member of a collective unity standing in the firmest dynamic coherence and for this reason leads no thoroughly autonomous life, but rather a *cosmic* one.

Thus, already above we found, in the inorganic realm, that discrete individualities are ripe for death and would be extinguished if their drives were given free reign. But, as a means to achieving the purpose of the whole, they must live.

Things are the same way with the animal. The animal is a means to achieving the purpose of the whole, just as the entire organic realm is only a means to achieving the purpose of the inorganic. And specifically, its constitution corresponds to the particular purpose which it is meant to fulfil.

Now we can place this purpose in nothing other than a *more effective* extinction of force, which extinction is only to be attained through fear of death (more intense will to *life*), and this fear, in turn, is a means to achieving the purpose of the *whole*, is a means to absolute death.

Whereas therefore in the plant the will to life still stands *alongside* the will to death, in the animal the will to life stands *in front of* the will to death and obscures it entirely: the means has stepped in front of the end. Thus, on the surface the animal wants only life, is pure will to life and fears death, which in the depths of its essence is all it wants. For here too I ask: *Could* the animal die if it did not *want* to die?

13.

Man is first of all an animal, and what we have said of the animal is valid also for man. Since man is an animal, in man the will to life stands *in front of* the will to death, and the life is dæmonically willed and death is dæmonically feared.

In man, however, a further division of the will and thereby a further division of its motion has taken place. To reason, which synthesises the manifold elements of perception, was added thought, i.e., reflecting reason, reflection. In this way, man's animal-life is essentially modified and, specifically, in *two entirely different* directions.

First of all, the fear of death on one hand and the love of life on the other hand are increased.

Fear of death is increased: The animal does not know death and it fears it instinctively when it perceives a dangerous Object. Man, in contrast, knows death and also knows what it signifies. He then surveys the past and gazes into the future. He thus surveys extraordinarily more—I might say: infinitely more—dangers than the animal.

Love of life is increased: The animal for the most part follows its main drives, which are restricted to hunger, thirst, the need for sleep, and everything pertaining to mating. It lives in a narrow sphere. In contrast, by means of his reason, man encounters life in such forms as wealth, women, honour, power, fame, and so on, which stoke his will to life into lust for life. Reflecting reason multiplies his drives, intensifies them, and speculates on the means to their satisfaction. Artificially, it turns their satisfaction into *refined enjoyments*.

In this way, man comes to hate death with all his soul and at the mere mention of death most people's hearts are seized by agony, and fear of death becomes both anxiety of death and despair when men stare death in the eyes; life, in contrast, is loved with a passion.

With man, the will to death, the drive of his innermost essence is therefore no longer simply concealed by the will to life, as with the animal, but disappears completely into the depths, where it expresses itself from time to time only as a profound yearning for rest. The will loses sight of its *end* completely and *holds fast* merely to the *means*.

In the second direction, however, the animal-life, through reason, is modified in another way. Before the thinker's mind and from the depths of his heart arises, radiant and illuminated, the *pure purpose of existence*, while the means disappears entirely. The invigorating image now fills his eyes entirely and ignites his will. Powerfully, the yearning for death flares up and, without shuddering, the will, in moral enthusiasm, takes hold of the *better* means to achieving the recognised purpose: *virginity*. Such a man is the sole idea in the world which, by willing *absolute death*, can also achieve it.

14.

If we summarise, then *everything* in the world is *will* to *death*, which in the organic realm appears more or less veiled as will to life. Life is willed by pure vegetative drive, by instinct, and finally dæmonically and consciously, because in this way the objective of the whole, and thus the objective of every individuality, is *more quickly* achieved.

At the world's beginning, life was the phenomenon of the will to death, of the individuals' striving for non-being, which was slowed down by a retarding element *within* them.

In the structured universe, which through all its regions is kept in the utmost tension, one can, with the chemical ideas as such in view, call life the inhibited striving for non-being and say that it presents itself as the means to achieving the purpose of *the whole*.

The organisms, in contrast, will life from within themselves, they veil their will to death in the will to life, i.e., they will from within themselves the means which shall lead first *them*, and then through them the whole, to absolute death.

We have then, after all, found a superficial difference between the inorganic and the organic realms which is very important.

But at root the immanent philosopher sees in the entire universe only the deepest yearning for absolute annihilation, and for him it is as if he heard distinctly, piercing all the heavenly spheres, the cry: "Redemption! Redemption! Death to our life!", and the consoling response: "You *all* shall find annihilation and be redeemed."

15.

In the Physics, we traced the purposiveness of nature, which no rational person can deny, back to the first motion, the disintegration of the unity into multiplicity, from which first motion all subsequent motions were and are but continuations. This was completely satisfactory. Now, however, we connect the purposiveness immediately to the *resolution* of the premundane unity to pass over from supra-being into non-being.

The simple unity was denied the *instant* attainment of its objective, but not the attainment of its objective altogether. A process (a developmental course, a gradual weakening) was necessary, and the whole progression of this process lay VIRTUALITER in the disintegration.

Everything in the world has therefore *one* objective, or better: To the human *mind*, nature presents itself *as if* it were moving towards one objective. At root, however, everything is only following the first blind impulse wherein what we must hold apart as means and end lay inseparably united. Everything in the world is not drawn by something *in front of* it or governed by something *from above*, but is driven from within itself.

Everything is thus interlinked, each thing is dependent on every other; all individualities compel and are compelled, and the resultant motion of all individual motions is the very same as if a simple unity had a unitary motion.

Teleology is a merely *regulative* principle for judging the course of the world (the world is thought of as springing from a will governed by the highest wisdom); however, even as a merely regulative principle, everything that clear, empirical minds considered obnoxious about teleology disappears only when the world is traced back to a simple, premundane unity *which no longer exists*. Hitherto one has had a choice between only two paths, and on neither was satisfaction to be found. Either one had to deny purposiveness, i.e., to strike experience in the face in order to preserve an unhaunted, purely immanent domain; or one had to honour truth, i.e., acknowledge purposiveness but then also accept a unity in, above, or behind the world.

Immanent philosophy, with its radical cut between the immanent and transcendent domains, has solved the problem in a thoroughly satisfying way. The world is the unitary act of a simple unity which is no longer, and for this reason it stands in an insoluble dynamic coherence from which a unitary motion arises.

16.

We have now, on the sure basis of the results gained, to immerse ourselves once more in the contemplation of *organic* life.

Natural scientists trace organic life back to a spontaneous generation, and the view now prevalent is that a GENERATIO ÆQUIVOCA no longer takes place in nature.

As we will recall from the Physics, there is for immanent philosophy no gulf between inorganic bodies and organisms. What distinguishes them from each other is their motion. If one wished to assume a gulf existed, then it would neither be wider nor offer grounds for greater astonishment than that between a gas and a liquid.

The motion of the organism is growth, i.e., maintenance and development of a particular *type*, through ongoing assimilation and excretion of chemical forces which constitute the type.

Every organism is a self-contained idea, like copper oxide is an idea. Like copper oxide, so also the organism holds simple chemical forces bound together, or more precisely, it preserves them in a simple, undifferentiated unity.

However, whereas the chemical compound has no other striving than what flows from the nature of the combined forces composing it, than that particular coherence; the organism behaves towards those chemical ideas, parts of which form its type, with overwhelming assimilation, and forces those ideas first to enter its type, preserving and developing it, and then to leave it. This is the essence of growth and, in a broader sense, of reproduction.

The foundation of every organism is therefore a *type*, a particular chemical combination, which has a particular motion that cannot be found in the inorganic realm.

But every organic type is a link in a developmental chain and, as such, is essentially different from the *first* link in the chain.

How, then, did the first organism arise?

That it arose through the compounding of simple chemical ideas or from compounds already present is clear. But these ideas or compounds had to find themselves in a very particular *state*, and this state was able to be present on our earth only *once* in the developmental course of the general cosmic life. It appeared of necessity, and of necessity soon afterwards the first organism, i.e., a chemical compound moving in a new way came into existence, precisely as the liquid and then the solid were able to be formed for the first time only in the necessary developmental course of the *universe*.

For this reason, the GENERATIO ÆQUIVOCA was able to occur on our planet only *once*, for in the continued progression of cosmic life there came *not one day* more when the chemical ideas would have had a *state* necessary to allow them to coalesce into an organism.

This origin, and the fact that organic life can only be ignited upon itself, place every organism on that level of constrained autonomy which the simple chemical ideas occupy, and lend the organism the *dignity*, so to speak, which these ideas have, even if the organism can only maintain itself in existence by means of them.

In what quantity the first organisms arose is a matter of complete irrelevance. Organisation, the new form, was present. Of necessity it had arisen, of necessity it maintained itself in existence, of necessity it developed in the course of the universe's further evolution, and of necessity it will some day break into pieces and vanish again once its work is done.

Our investigations hitherto illuminate the fact that the whole realm of organisms is only a superior form for the killing off of the sum of force active in the universe. Every organism follows its drive, but in doing so it is a part in service of the whole. It is a form which leads its individual life and follows its drives, which yet, in dynamic coherence with all other individualities, admits chemical ideas, draws them into the maelstrom of its individual motion, and then expels them *no longer as the same chemical ideas*, but weakened, even if the weakening eludes observation and does not unveil itself to synthetic perception until the end of long developmental phases.

Here it might seem as if the man who, in moral enthusiasm, takes passionate hold of virginity in order to attain absolute death, wholehearted redemption from existence, were in the grip of a deplorable madness; furthermore, as if, completely or partially denying the will to life (*affirming the will to death*), he acted *against* nature, against the universe and its motion out of being into non-being. But we may be consoled, for it only seems so, as I shall now show.

17.

He who effectively denies the will to life reaps in death the utter annihilation of the *type*. He shatters his form, and *no power* in the universe can build it anew. In its idiosyncrasy and the torment and pain of existence connected therewith, it is forever struck from the book of life. And more he cannot demand, more he also does not demand. Through abstinence from sexual pleasures he has freed himself from rebirth, before which his will shrinks back like the savage before death. His *type has been redeemed*—that is his sweet reward.

In contrast, he who has effectively affirmed his will finds no redemption in death. Certainly, his type has also been destroyed and dissolves into its elements; but in reality he has already set out on his new, arduous journey, on a path whose length cannot be determined.

Now, the elements of which the type is composed persist in its death. They lose the typic impression, the typic particularity, join once more in the general cosmic life, form chemical compounds or enter into other organisms whose life they support. That they persist, however, cannot upset the wise man; for firstly they can *never* again coalesce into *his* individual type; secondly, he knows himself to be on the sure path to redemption.

18.

Let us now turn to the second objection. He who denies the will to life is supposed to be acting *contrary* to nature by suppressing the sex-drive.

Now, to this one may answer in general that in a universe which stands in a resolute dynamic coherence and is ruled through and through by *necessity*, absolutely *nothing* which would be contrary to nature can happen. The saint entered life with a quite particular character and a quite particular mind, and both were developed in the current of the world. Thus, the moment when his will *had* to be ignited on cognition and enter denial came of necessity. Where in this entire individual developmental course is there even the smallest hook on which this foolish second objection could be hung? Far from acting contrary to nature, the saint in fact stands in the midst of the universe's motion, and when in his death his type falls away from the universe, then this, in view of the purpose of the whole, is precisely what *had* to happen.

We have next to point to the fact that he who suppresses his sex-drive is contesting a struggle whereby the sum of force in the universe is *more effectively* weakened than it would be through his utter devotion to life. As Montaigne very correctly remarks, it is easier to wear a cuirass one's life long than to be chaste:

I hold it more easy to carry a suit of armour all the days of one's life than a maidenhead; and the vow of virginity of all others is the most noble, as being the hardest to keep. (*Upon Some Verses of Virgil*)

And the Indians say: It is easier to tear a tiger's prey from its jaws than to leave the sex-drive unsatisfied. However, if this is the case, then in this regard too the saint stands in the service of nature, he sacrifices to it faithfully and thereby accelerates nature's course in the most effective manner.

Whereas he who is drunk on life makes force into:

> the fodder of his passion,

and is:

> the rider whose horses consume him (**Hebbel**, *Judith*),

the chaste man uses force in order to master himself.

That struggle with the world which the child of the world conducts and then carries on in his progeny, reacting unceasingly to actions originating outside him, is relocated by the child of light, at once humbly and proudly, with unmatched courage, *into his own breast*, where he fights it out, bleeding from a thousand wounds. Whereas the child of the world cries out in wild exultation:

It is so matchless sweet to die of life itself, to let the stream so swell that the vein which should contain it bursts, to mingle the extremity of bliss with the shudder of annihilation (**Hebbel**, *Judith*);

the wise man, contemplating absolute nothingness, chooses the shudder of annihilation alone and forgoes the bliss; for after the night comes the day, after the storm comes sweet peace of heart, after the leaden skies comes the clear aetherial vault on whose splendour a little cloud (the disturbance of the sex-drive) is an ever shrinking blemish, and then at last comes absolute death: *redemption from life, liberation from oneself!*

The wise hero, the purest and most magnificent phenomenon in the world, creates for himself in this world true and genuine happiness, and in so doing he, like no other, promotes the universe's motion out of being into non-being. For he knows that in death his form will be broken into pieces, and "bearing in his bosom this safe treasure", completely satisfied and seeking for himself nothing else in the world, he devotes his life to the life of humanity. In this way, however, and by means of the victoriously concluded struggle in his own breast, he also, once he leaves the heavenly kingdom of his peace of heart and enters annihilation, has performed gloriously the labour which as an *organism* he had to perform for the *universe*.

19.

We have recognised that the organic realm is the most complete form for the extermination of the chemical ideas coursing through it, and remarked that it will some day break into pieces and vanish of the same necessity of which it arose. On this event and on the universe's demise, the utter annihilation of the sum of force active in the world, we have now to focus.

We concluded the Physics with the implication to which it gave rise:

METAPHYSICS

The world is indestructible. The motion of the inorganic realm is an endless chain of compositions and decompositions; the motion of the organic realm is a progressive and endless development of lower into higher forms of life; but in this motion, the force contained in the world is weakening continually.

At the same time, we reserved to ourselves the right to check this result once again in the Metaphysics. We already did this *indirectly* in the foregoing sections and have therefore to declare that the result of the Physics was an essentially one-sided one. The *whole* universe is moving, all the while weakening its force steadily, out of being into non-being, and the developmental chains to which we had in the Analytics to give a *beginning* will also have an *end*; they are not endless, but issue in pure absolute nothingness, in the NIHIL NEGATIVUM.

If even in the Politics, where we traced the developmental course of humanity, the surest part of our experience, we did not venture to define in detail its progression out of the present towards the ideal objective in the future, but only made known a few prominent forms through which it must pass; then here in the Metaphysics, where we are supposed to construct the entire universe's progression further into the future, of which universe only a vanishingly small part is given to us as experience, we will proceed with the utmost caution, supporting ourselves only on what is logically certain.

Although we know only very few processes in the universe and our knowledge, regarding the whole of nature, is fragmentary and merely a work in progress, we do have the unshakeable certainty that everything in the world has happened, is happening, and will happen *of necessity*. Every event, be it known or unknown to us, came to pass of necessity and had necessary consequences. Everything, however, happened and is happening (to speak figuratively) for the sake of a single objective, for the sake of non-being.

Accordingly, our ignorance of the revolutions which have taken place on all the stars can cause us no pain. Whether organic life has arisen on all or on most or even on none at all, or whether it has already gone extinct again—it is all the same to us. We are familiar with the world's objective, and know that the means by which to reach that objective have been chosen with the utmost wisdom.

We therefore disregard for the time being the universe at large and direct our gaze exclusively at our planet.

It is *humanity* which here gives us the first point of reference. I have shown in the Politics that humanity, subject to the great law of suffering which makes the will of the individuals ever weaker but their minds ever brighter and more encompassing, must of necessity enter the ideal State and then non-being. There is no other way. It is humanity's inexorable, unalterable fate, and happy shall be humanity when it sinks into the arms of Death.

It is a matter of complete indifference, as I already remarked in the Politics, whether humanity makes the "great sacrifice" (as the Indians say) or brings about "the revelation of the children of God, for which all creation *anxiously yearns*" (as Paul says) in moral enthusiasm, or through impotence, or in a wild, fantastic flaring up of the final life-force. Who can foretell how it shall happen? It is enough that the sacrifice will be made, because it *must* be made, because it is a transition point for the necessary development of the *world*.

If, however, the sacrifice is made, then nothing less will eventuate than what at the theatre they call a sensation. Neither the sun, nor the moon, nor a single star will vanish; rather, nature will calmly continue on its course *but under the influence* of the modification which humanity's death has produced and which previously was not present.

Here, too, we are cautious and do not rush on ahead with our faculty of reason. Lichtenberg once said that a pea thrown into the North Sea would raise the level of the sea on the Japanese coast, although the change in level would be imperceptible to the human eye. It is likewise logically certain that the shot of a pistol fired on our earth will make its effect felt on Sirius, indeed at the outermost limits of the immeasurable universe; for this universe finds itself pervaded by the most violent tension and is no limp, foolish, paltry so-called infinite. We will therefore do well to refrain from proposing a hypothesis in which, step by step, we seek out the consequences of the great sacrifice; for what would we thus contrive but a fantastical image alike in value to some fairytale which, in a night of twinkling stars, the Bedouin tells his tribesmen? We content ourselves with simply confirming *that* the departure of humanity from the world stage will have effects which lie in the one and only direction of the universe.

However, we can with near certainty state that nature will not allow any new humanoid beings to arise from the remaining animals; for what nature aimed at with humanity—i.e., with the sum of individual essences, which are the highest essences conceivable in the entire universe because they can dissolve their innermost kernel (on other stars beings of equal worth may exist, but none which are higher)—also finds in humanity its complete fulfilment. No work will remain to be done which a *new* humanity would have to perform.

Furthermore, we can say that the death of humanity will have as a consequence the death of all organic life on our planet. Already before humanity's entry into the ideal State, certainly within it, humanity will probably hold the life of most animals (and plants) in its hand, and it will not forget its "immature brothers", especially its faithful pets, when it redeems itself. Such will be the case for the higher organisms. The lower, however, due to the change brought about on the planet, will lose the prerequisites of their existence and go extinct.

If we now look once more at the whole universe, then we first of all let the effect flow into it which the extinction of all organic life on the earth must exert on it, in all its parts, without presuming to specify the "*why*". We then keep to that fact which we owe to the astronomers, that the orbit of each and every celestial body, through the resistance of the aether, will gradually decay and that, finally, all of them will fall into the true central sun.

The new formations which will arise from these partial universal conflagrations must not concern us here. We place ourselves straight away on that link of the developmental chain which continues to show us only solid or liquid bodies. All *gases* have disappeared from the universe, i.e., the tenacious sum of force has weakened itself to such an extent that only solid and liquid bodies constitute the universe. At best we can assume that everything still existing at that time is only *liquid*.

Now absolutely nothing more stands in the way of these liquids being redeemed. Each has a free path, every conceived part of them passes through the ideal point and its striving is fulfilled, i.e., it is annihilated in its innermost essence.

And then?

Then God has in fact passed over from supra-being, through becoming, into non-being; through the world-process He has found what He was unable to achieve *directly* because His own essence inhibited Him: non-being.

First the transcendent domain perished, now (in our thoughts) the immanent too has passed; and, depending on our worldview, we gaze aghast or in profound satisfaction upon absolute nothingness, absolute emptiness, upon the NIHIL NEGATIVUM.

It is finished! The deed is done!

20.

We have thus supplemented all the half-results of the Physics and can proceed.

The Aesthetics shows itself, from the highest immanent standpoint, exactly as we apprehended it from the lower. This can hardly cause surprise: for the foundation of what is beautiful in the things-in-themselves has indeed its magnificent explanatory basis solely in the simple unity or, as the case may be, in its first harmonic motion. In the realm of what is beautiful nothing more is anticipated: there is nothing more to come! What is beautiful lies entirely in the delightful splendour of God's premundane existence, indeed, it is the delightful splendour itself of God's essence (which is entirely *at rest* in itself), of the simple unity (with regard to the contemplative Subject), it is the objectification of the continuations of that miraculous and harmonic first motion, when God died and the world was born.

21.

In contrast, the Ethics yields multiple results in need of supplementation. Metaphysically supplemented, however, they present themselves as solutions of the most difficult philosophical problems. Truth lets fall its final veil and shows us the true *co-existence of freedom and necessity, the individual's full autonomy* and *the pure essence of fate*, from the cognisance of which a consolation, a confidence, a trust flows such as Christianity and Buddhism cannot offer their professors; for from a truth which man *cognises*, he reaps a satisfaction wholly different from that yielded by a truth in which he must *have faith*.

In the Ethics we assumed the harshest position with respect to the *will to life*. We condemned it and pressed upon its forehead the mark of insanity. We shrank back before the struggle for existence and placed the *denial* of the will to life in complete *opposition* to the will's *affirmation*.

In doing this, our judgments were not rash and unsober but only one-sided, because we lacked the correct overview.

Now, however, the entire immanent domain lies before us in the mild light of cognition, cognition which we, searching in the gulf between the transcendent and immanent domains, have gained for ourselves. And here we must declare that the denial of the will to life does *not* stand in opposition to its affirmation.

The true relation of the one to the other will become evident in what follows.

We have seen that a single great law presided over nature from the beginning, presides over it now, and will continue to preside over it until its annihilation: the law of the weakening of force. Nature grows old. Whoever speaks of an *éternelle* (!) *jeunesse*, of an "eternal" youth of nature (might one at least express oneself with logical correctness and say "endless"!) judges like the blind man judges colour and stands at the lowest level of cognition.

Under the dominion of this great law stands everything in the world, thus also man. He is at his foundation will to death because the chemical ideas which constitute his type and, coming and going, maintain him in existence want death. But since they can only attain it through weakening and there is no more effective means to this than the willing of life, so the means steps dæmonically in front of the end, life in front of death, and man manifests himself as pure will to life.

Now, by devoting himself solely to life, by being ever hungry and full of desire for life, he acts in nature's interest and *at the same time* in his own; for he weakens the sum of force of the universe and at the same time his *type*, his individuality, which, being a particular idea, has half-autocracy. He finds himself on the path of redemption, there can be no doubt about this; but it is a *long* path, the end of which cannot be seen.

On the other hand, he who had to turn away from life of the same necessity whereof the brutish man clings to it with a thousand arms, he for whom the end has stepped *in front of* the means, death *in front of* life by means of clear, cold cognition; he too acts in nature's interest and in his own, but he *more effectively* weakens the universe's sum of force as well as his type, which in life enjoys the blissfulness of peace of heart and in death finds absolute annihilation, for which everything in nature yearns. Far from the great *military road* of redemption, he walks on the short *path* of redemption—the summit lies before him bathed in golden light, he sees it and he will reach it.

The former man, through the affirmation of the will to life, by a dark and sultry way where the thronging is terrible and everything pushes and is pushed, therefore achieves the same objective as the latter does through the denial of the will, by a bright track only at first thorny and steep, then even and magnificent, where there is no thronging, no crying, no whimpering. But the former achieves the objective only after an indefinite period during which he is always unsatisfied, full of cares, concern, and torment, whereas the latter at the end of his individual career lays his hand on the objective and, on his way to it, is free of cares, concerns, and torments and lives in the profoundest peace of soul, in imperturbable serenity.

The former drags himself effortfully on, always inhibited, wanting to go on and not being able to; the latter is carried up, as it were, by hosts of angels, and because he cannot turn his gaze from the lighted summit and loses himself entirely in contemplating the view, he is suddenly at his objective he knows not how. It seemed at first so distant, now it has already been reached!

Both therefore want the *same* thing, and both get what they want; the difference between them lies only in the *type of their motion*. The denial of the will to life is a *quicker* motion than that of its affirmation. It is the same relation as that which we identified in the politics between civilisation and the state of nature. In civilisation, humanity moves more rapidly than in the state of nature; in both forms, however, it has the same objective.

It can also be said: The key switches from *major* to *minor*, and the tempo of the life-course changes from *adagio* and *andante* to *vivace* and *prestissimo*.

He who denies life spurns only the *means* of him who affirms it; and he does so specifically because he has found a *better* means to their common end.

And herewith the wise man's attitude towards his fellow men is also given. He will not insult them, nor haughtily deride them in the conceit of his superior insight. He sees how, in order to cope, they flounder with a tool which will rob them of weeks. Here he offers them a different tool, which demands somewhat more exertion but leads to their objective in a few minutes. If they become obstinate at this offer, then he should try to win them over. If this does not succeed, then he should let them move on. Now, at least, they are *acquainted* with the truth, and it works on quietly within them, for:

Magna est vis veritatis et praevalebit!

The time will therefore come when from their eyes too the scales shall fall.

Likewise, he will not roll his eyes when he sees merry men who carouse in wild jubilation. He will think: *Pauvre humanité!* But then: Carry on! Dance, skip, court, and let yourselves be courted! The fatigue and crapulence will set in soon enough; and then for you too the end will come.

It is as bright as the light of the sun. Optimism is supposed to be the *opposite* of pessimism? What a paltry and confused notion! The whole life of the universe, *prior to* the appearance of a wise, contemplative faculty of reason, is supposed to have been a senseless game, the waltzing to and fro of a fever-sick man? How insane! Is a brain five to six pounds in weight, once it arises, allowed to sit in judgment on the world's developmental course during an inexpressibly long span of time and condemn that course? That would be pure absurdity!

What is an optimist, then? An optimist, of necessity, is that man whose will is not yet *ripe* for death. His thoughts and maxims (his worldview) are the blossoms of his urge and hunger for life. If superior cognition is given him from *without*, but if it takes no root in his mind or if it does indeed take charge of his mind but thence emits only so-called *cold flashes* into his heart because that heart is obstinate and hard—what ought he to do? Therefore carry on! His hour too will come, for all men have, everything in nature has a single goal.

And what is a pessimist? Who *must* be one? Whoever is *ripe* for death. He is as little able to love life as the optimist to turn away from it. If he ignores the fact that he would live on in his children, a fact which obscures the *cruel* character of procreation, he like Humboldt will recoil in horror from the idea of purchasing a few minutes' pleasure with those torments which a *strange* being would have to endure perhaps eighty years long, and he will rightly consider the begetting of children a *crime*.

So let fall your weapons and quarrel no more, for your struggle has provoked a misunderstanding. You both want the same thing.

22.

It then remains for us to specify the attitude of immanent philosophy towards the man who takes his own life and towards the criminal.

How easily the stone falls from one's hand onto the grave of the man who has killed himself, how difficult in contrast was the struggle of the poor man who laid himself so well to rest. First he cast from afar an anxious glance at Death and turned away in horror; then, trembling, he skirted Him in wide arcs; but with each day the distance grew smaller and smaller until finally he threw his tired arms around Death's neck and looked Him in the eye: and in those eyes was peace, sweet peace.

Whoever can bear the burden of life no more, let him cast it off. Whoever can hold out no longer in the carnival hall of life—or, as Jean Paul says, in the great servants' quarters of the world—let him step out through the "ever opened" door into the still night.

To be sure, immanent philosophy with its *ethics* also addresses itself to the men tired of life and seeks to draw them back from the edge with friendly words of persuasion, urging them to be ignited on the world's course and to help accelerate it by working for the sake of others; but when even this motive has no effect, when it is insufficient for the relevant character, then immanent philosophy quietly withdraws and genuflects to the world's course, which *requires* the death of this particular individual and must for that reason and of necessity extinguish him; for take even the *most insignificant* being out of the world and the course of the world will become a *different* one from what it would have been if that being had remained in the world.

Immanent philosophy must not condemn; it cannot do this. It does not demand suicide; but, serving truth alone, it had to destroy terribly coercive-countermotives to suicide. For what does the poet say?

> Who would these fardels bear,
> To grunt and sweat under a weary life,
> But that the dread of something after death,
> The undiscovered country, from whose bourn
> No traveller returns, puzzles the will,
> And makes us rather bear those ills we have
> Than fly to others that we know not of?
>
> **Shakespeare**

This undiscovered country, whose supposed mysteries caused many a man to loosen his hold on the dagger in his gripe—this country with its horrors had to be annihilated *completely* by immanent philosophy. There was once a transcendent domain—it is no more. The world-weary man who poses himself the question: To be or not to be? should draw his reasons for and against merely from *this* world, but from the entire world; he should also bear in mind his hopeless brothers, whom he can help not so much by producing shoes or planting cabbage for them, but by helping them to gain for themselves a better situation. Beyond the world is no place of peace nor one of torment, but only nothingness. Whoever enters it has neither rest nor motion, he is stateless as in sleep, but with the great difference that what in sleep is stateless in death exists no longer: the will has been completely annihilated.

This can be a new countermotive as well as a new motive. This truth can drive the one man back into the affirmation of will, and draw the other powerfully into death. However, the truth itself must *never* be denied. And if hitherto the notion of an individual after-life in some hell or heavenly kingdom held many back from death, whereas immanent philosophy will lead many into death—then this latter *should* henceforth be so, just as the former was meant ere now to be, for every motive which enters the world appears and has its effect of necessity.

23.

In the State, the criminal is ostracised and rightly so; for the State is the form which has entered the life of humanity of necessity, the form in which the great law of the weakening of force reveals itself as the law of suffering, and the form in which alone man can be quickly redeemed. *The motion of the universe sanctifies the State and its fundamental laws*. It compels men to legal actions, and whoever injures the fundamental laws sows division between himself and his fellow citizens which persist until death. "He stole", "he murdered"—these are invisible chains in which the criminal is buried.

But in the State there is one free, beautiful standpoint from which the criminal is embraced by faithful arms, and faithful hands are laid over the mark on his forehead and conceal it. It is the standpoint of pure religion.

When Christ was supposed to condemn the adulteress, he urged the accusers to stone her if they felt themselves pure, and when he hung on the cross between two murderers, he promised one of them the kingdom of heaven, the place where, according to his own promise, only the *good* were supposed to live.

Immanent philosophy upholds this standpoint in its metaphysics.

If we ignore the criminal who acts out of desperation and focus only on those who, compelled by their dæmon and despite every countermotive, injured the law, then we must confess that they have acted of the same necessity whereof a good will does works of justice and philanthropy.

The criminal, like the saint, helps only to shape a necessary course of the world which is not in itself moral. Both serve the whole. This is what first calls for *leniency*.

Secondly, the criminal, through the intensity of his will, the blisslessness of his desire, is not only separated from peace, which is higher than all reason, but he is also subject to torments which are greater than the torments of hell or the consequences of legal stigmatisation. "The fool's punishment is his folly."

And the immanent philosopher is supposed to spurn this savage, unhappy heart? How he would have to despise himself if he did! He draws that heart to his own bosom and has for it only words of love and consolation.

24.

We turn now to *fate*.

As we know, it is the motion of the entire world which is continually created out of the continual efficacy of all individuals of the universe. It is a power against which the individual's power cannot be asserted, since it contains within itself the efficacy of every particular individual along with that of all other individuals. Thus fate presents itself to us when considered from the highest standpoint. It is the fate common to all, the *fate of the universe*.

In contrast, from the standpoint of a particular man the view changes. Here it is *individual fate* (individual life-course) and shows itself as a product of two *equally valuable* factors: of the *particular individual* (dæmon and mind) and of *chance* (sum of the efficacy of all individuals). Or, as we found in the Physics, the individual has only a half-autocracy because he compels and is compelled by chance, which is a *foreign* opposing power totally independent of him.

The individual's constrained *half-independence* is a fact which cannot be overturned. Even from the highest standpoint, which we are now assuming, we see the individual just as we saw him in the Physics. In the world, let us search wherever and however we want, we shall only ever find individual and, specifically, half autonomous wills.

However, it is also a consequence of this view that all doctrines which shift the individual from this *middle* position between the two poles of complete autocracy and total dependence, but especially those doctrines which place the individual at one of these two poles, are false.

We thus see ourselves led once again before pantheism and exoteric Buddhism.

According to pantheism, the individual is a nothing, a poor marionette, a mere tool in the hand of a simple unity hidden *in* the world. The result of this is that no deed of an individual is *his* deed but is a divine deed which has been effected within him, and that he bears not a shadow of responsibility for his deeds.

Pantheism is a magnificent doctrine in which the truth lies half unveiled. There *is* a power *not* ruled by the individual, in whose hand the individual lies; but this power, *chance*, has been constrained by the individual himself, it is a half-power.

On the other hand, according to the Buddha's great doctrine of karma, a doctrine which in the Occident is unfortunately as good as unheard of (one usually clings to the frippery, the by-products of lush oriental fancy and overlooks the precious core), the individual is *everything*. Individual fate is *exclusively* the work of the individual. *Karma alone controls destiny*.

What a man does *and* what befalls him, be it fortune or misfortune, *everything* flows from his being, from his merits and demerits.

According to the Buddha's doctrine, man's innermost essence shapes what we call chance from within itself. If I go down the street and am struck by a bullet which was intended for another, then *my almighty* essence led the bullet into my heart. If all avenues of escape close up before me such that I, despairing, must go to my death, then no strange power but *I myself* have shifted and set the scene in such a way that I cannot remain in life. If an illness casts me for years onto a bed of suffering, then everything the illness had to bring about was made effective in this particular way by *me*, through my complete, individual autocracy. In short, everything, even that which we rightly ascribe to a strange power, to chance, is my exclusive work, is an emanation of my almighty essence which is subject only to the compulsion of its particular nature, i.e., of all its good and bad deeds in earlier life-courses. And what the individual *does* in his current life, in conjunction with the rest of those deeds from earlier modes of existence which have gone unrewarded or unatoned for, forms the particular essence for a new life-course, which in turn compiles, organises, and renders effective from within itself what we would call chance.

The doctrine of karma is a magnificent, profound doctrine, like pantheism, and in it, as in pantheism, the truth lies half unveiled. The individual *has* a real power which is *not* ruled by chance; but this power is constrained by chance, is a half-power.

Over man's thinking Buddhism casts a disproportionately greater spell than pantheism, although no more or less than pantheism it offends experience and distorts the truth; for whereas an omnipotent unity concealed within the world will always leave our hearts cold and remain strange to it, Buddhism stands solely on the individuality, on that which is genuinely real, on that which alone is certain for, immediately given to, and intimately known by us.

It is often downright confusing to the senses when one sees in some significant occurrence or other how the *external* world arranges itself, how the scenery suddenly closes or opens, when one's *inner* life has reached a decisive juncture. In such moments one becomes a devotee of the glorious, ingenious prince and cries out: Yes, he is right, the individual alone makes his fate.

But I repeat: *Half-autonomy* is a matter of fact in the immanent domain and cannot be overthrown.

However, it can be *supplemented* to become the individual's *complete self-mastery* if the passed transcendent domain is drawn up alongside the real immanent one.

25.

Everything which now *is*, once *was* in the simple premundane unity. Therefore, everything which *is*, figuratively speaking, took part in God's resolution not to be, resolved *in him* to pass over into non-being. The retarding element, the essence of God, made the instant carrying-out of this resolution impossible. The world, the process in which this retarding element is *gradually eliminated*, had to arise. This process, the general fate of the universe, was determined by the divine wisdom (we speak always figuratively), and *in this divine wisdom* everything which *is* determined its own *individual life-course*.

Now Buddha is correct: Everything that affects me, all the blows and blessings of chance, are *my work—I willed* them. But I do not bring them about with gradual, uncognisable force *in* the world; rather, *prior to* the world, *in* the simple unity, I determined that they should affect me.

Now pantheism too is correct: The *fate of the world* is a unitary one, is the motion of the entire world towards *one* goal; but no simple unity *in* the world carries out this motion, having an effect in *apparent* individuals now in this, now in that direction; rather, a simple unity *prior to* the world determined the entire process, and *in* the world *only real individuals* carry out this process.

And now Plato too is correct, who (*Republic*, 617d) lets each man, before he enters life, choose for himself his own fate, but he does not choose it *immediately prior to birth*; rather, *prior to* the world as such, in the transcendent domain, when the immanent domain still was not, each man himself determined his own lot.

Finally, *freedom* is now united with *necessity*. The world is the *free* act of a *pre*mundane unity; *in* the world, however, there reigns only necessity, because otherwise the goal could *never* be reached. Everything is interlinked of necessity; everything conspires towards a single goal.

And every action of the individual (not only of man, but of *all* ideas in the world) is at once *free* and *necessary*: free, because it was resolved upon *prior to* the world *in* a free unity; necessary, because the resolution is materialising, is becoming a deed *in* the world.

26.

A principle from which the solution to the greatest philosophical problems results so clearly, effortlessly, and unforced—problems which the most ingenious men who ever lived hopelessly abandoned after they had exhausted their powers of thought on them—*must* be correct. When Kant believed he had apprehended the co-existence of freedom and necessity by means of his distinction between an intelligible and an empirical character, he could not avoid remarking:

> It may be said that the solution here proposed involves great difficulty in itself, and is scarcely susceptible of a *lucid* exposition. *But is any other solution that has been attempted, or that may be attempted, easier and more intelligible?*

They all had to err, because they did not know how to create a pure immanent and a pure transcendent domain. The pantheists had to err, because they traced the actually present, unitary world motion back to a unity *in* the world; Buddha had to err, because he falsely inferred the complete autocracy of the individual *in* the world from the individual's actual feeling of complete responsibility for all his deeds; Kant had to err, because he wanted to grasp freedom and necessity in the immanent domain with one hand.

We, in contrast, laid the simple unity of the pantheists in the passed, transcendent domain and explained the unitary world-motion from the deed of this *pre*mundane simple unity; we unified the individual's half-autonomy and the power of chance in the world, a power which is totally independent of the individual, in the transcendent domain, in God's unitary resolution to pass over into non-being, and in the unitary choice of the means to carry this resolution out. Finally, we unified freedom and necessity not in the world, where there is no room for freedom, but in the midst of that gulf separating the perished, transcendent domain, which we have reconstructed with our faculty of reason, from the immanent domain.

We have not, by the use of sophisms, surreptitiously obtained the perished, transcendent domain. That it was and is no more we have already *proved* with logical rigour in the Analytics.

And now let us contemplate the consolation, the unshakeable confidence, the blissful reliance that must flow from the metaphysically justified, complete autonomy of the individual. Everything that affects man: want, misery, sorrow, cares, illness, ignominy, disdain, despair—in short, all the austerity of life—is not inflicted on him by some unfathomable providence which in some inscrutable way intends the best for him; rather, he suffers all of this because he *himself, prior to* the world, *chose* everything *as the best means to that end*. All the blows of fate which strike him he has chosen, because only through them can he be *redeemed*. His essence (dæmon and mind) and chance lead him *loyally* through pain and pleasure, joy and sorrow, fortune and misfortune, life and death to the redemption which he wants, which he wills.

Love of one's enemy is now possible for him, as for the pantheist, the Buddhist, and the Christian; for the person vanishes before his deed, which was only able to appear as a phenomenon by chance because the sufferer *willed* it prior to the world.

Thus metaphysics bestows on my ethics the final and highest blessing.

27.

Man has the natural tendency to personify fate and to apprehend absolute nothingness, which stares at him from every grave, as a place of eternal peace, as a *city of peace*, *Nirvana*—as a new Jerusalem:

And God shall wipe away all tears from their eyes; and there shall be no more death, neither sorrow, nor crying, neither shall there be any more pain: for the former things are passed away. (Rev 21: 4)

It cannot be denied that the notion of a personal, loving Father-God takes deeper hold of the human heart, "the defiant and despondent thing", than the abstract concept of fate, and that the notion of a kingdom of heaven where beatified individuals without wants rest blissful in eternal contemplation awakens a more powerful yearning than absolute nothingness. Here, too, immanent philosophy is also mild and benevolent. The principal concern remains that man has overcome the world through *knowledge*. Whether he leaves the recognised fate as it is or whether he gives it once again the lineaments of a loyal father; whether he leaves the recognised objective of the world standing as absolute nothingness or whether he transforms it into a garden of eternal peace bathed in light—this is completely beside the point. Who would want to interrupt this innocent, harmless game of the fancy?

> A fiction that gladdens me,
> Is worth a truth that saddens me.
>
> **Wieland**

The wise man, however, looks *absolute nothingness* firmly and joyfully in the eye.

www.ingramcontent.com/pod-product-compliance
Lightning Source LLC
Chambersburg PA
CBHW022036290426
44109CB00014B/879